The Cartoon Century

The Cartoon Century

Modern Britain Through the Eyes of Its Cartoonists

Timothy S Benson

rh
BOOKS

Published by Random House Books 2007

2 4 6 8 10 9 7 5 3 1

First published in Great Britain in 2007 by Random House Books
Random House, 20 Vauxhall Bridge Road, London SW1V 2SA
www.rbooks.co.uk

Addresses for companies within The Random House Group Limited can be found at:
www.randomhouse.co.uk/offices.htm

The Random House Group Limited Reg. No. 954009

A CIP catalogue record for this book is available from the British Library

ISBN 9781905211593

The Random House Group Limited makes every effort to ensure that the papers used
in its books are made from trees that have been legally sourced from well-managed
and credibly certified forests. Our paper procurement policy can be found at:
www.randomhouse.co.uk/paper.htm

Printed and bound in China by C&C Offset printing Co. Ltd

PUBLISHING DIRECTOR Nigel Wilcockson
EDITORIAL Emily Rhodes, Lydia Darbyshire, Rosalind Fergusson
DESIGN Richard Marston
COVER Jason Smith
PRODUCTION Neil Bradford, Simon Rhodes

Contents

Preface

My aim in this book is twofold: to give an idea of the sheer range and richness of the work of some of our best cartoonists, and to create a kind of pictorial history of the past 100 years. Some of the cartoons reproduced here will be immediately familiar – I have, for example, included perhaps the most famous cartoon of the 20th century, David Low's *Rendezvous* from 1939 – but the majority will be unfamiliar, and I have chosen them for the very reason that they have not appeared in other anthologies and, in a handful of cases, have never been published before. By the very nature of their job, cartoonists tend to be prolific, generally drawing three to six cartoons a week and perhaps thousands over the course of a successful career. It seemed right to me to try to give a sense of the sheer range of work that has been produced and also to include cartoons by artists who may be largely forgotten today but who nevertheless produced interesting work.

I have sought to cover most of the key political events of the past century, sprinkling in a few cartoons on social or cultural topics along the way – the arrival of television, mods and rockers, yuppies. Just occasionally, I have included cartoons from abroad that give a different perspective on events. Inevitably, I have not been able to find a suitable cartoon for every event I wanted to cover, and, for copyright reasons, I have not been able to include works by every cartoonist I would like to have represented, but I hope that my selection overall gives a reasonably full picture of a remarkable century and an astonishingly talented group of artists.

I would like to thank my publisher Nigel Wilcockson, without whose encouragement, input and enthusiasm this book would not be what it is, and also Emily Rhodes at Random House. I am very grateful to Rowan Lowe, who spent a considerable amount of time meticulously cleaning up many of the images that appear in this book. Alan Mumford was kind enough to give me access to his extensive collection of cartoon cuttings, especially the material he has on the First World War, which proved invaluable. I am also grateful to the following: Colin Dodds, John Gosling, David Low's great granddaughter Daisy Watts, Roy Douglas, Nick Hiley, Anita O'Brien, Andy Davey, Ken Layson, Colin Scott and Rebecca Barnard. Finally, I would like to thank the many cartoonists, their representatives and the newspapers in whose pages their work appeared, all of whom have been immensely kind and helpful. Detailed acknowledgements appear at the back of the book.

Sticky Wicket!

'Well – *you* tell the editor to think of something funny and topical.' The cartoonist's perennial challenge. [WILLIAM JONES 'Jon' *Sunday Graphic* 2 July 1950]

Introduction

People have been commenting on events and on each other in pictorial form ever since primitive man raised himself off all fours and started scribbling on cave walls, but the cartoon as we generally understand it today is quite a late development. It came into its own in the 18th century with the social and political satirical prints of Hogarth, Gillray and Rowlandson, started to find its way into periodicals and newspapers in the 19th century – Sir John Tenniel's political cartoons for *Punch* being the most famous examples – and finally spread its way through national newspapers in the course of the 20th century. In April 1980, by which time most papers were running regular cartoons, Margaret Thatcher gave the artform a prime ministerial seal of approval. The cartoon, she said, was 'the most concentrated and cogent form of comment and just about the most skilled and the most memorable, giving the picture of events that remained most in the mind'.

What is a political cartoon? Essentially, it is a visual essay that sums up complicated events or situations in a few, simple, sketched black lines. A newspaper article will probably take several minutes to read; the cartoon delivers its message in a couple of seconds. That is what makes it so powerful. It may be true that cartoons are reactive – cartoonists tend to get their idea for the next day's cartoon from that day's headlines – but, as Steve Bell puts it, they are also 'art with attitude'. They do not simply represent; they comment as well.

The best cartoons are generally against something. Hungarian-born cartoonist Vicky argued: 'It is difficult to do a cartoon praising anyone. I am more likely to emphasise the weakness of my subject rather than his strength.' Similarly *The Times* cartoonist Peter Brookes believes: 'It simply doesn't make sense to go out of your way to praise a politician; you're got to see the reality behind what politicians are saying and that always makes you indignant.' He sees himself as a sort of permanent opposition:

> It sounds pompous to say that you're looking for the truth behind appearances, but that's what it's actually about. You are trying to make sure that a particular point of view gets across, and even though you are not always spitting venom, you need at least to be as acerbic as you can.

Certainly it seems to be the case that cartoons that seek to praise rather than to bury generally do not work. Osbert Lancaster, for example, while admiring of David Low's attacks on Hitler, Mussolini and the Conservatives, felt he was much less successful when he was doing idealistic pictures of 'happy young workers marching into the dawn'. 'Like a soap ad,' he commented. Similarly, when tragic events take place, and humour and satire feel inappropriate, cartoonists all too quickly lose their way. Mawkishness or cliché become apparent, as you will see on occasion in the course of this book.

A certain lack of objectivity and sympathy, then, seems to be an important quality among cartoonists. The successful ones are not afraid to reveal their own views, prejudices and beliefs. Some have had their own fairly clearly defined political agenda – Michael Cummings, David Low, Vicky and Leslie Illingworth come to mind. Others, particularly the current generation, cannot be pigeonholed so easily. Steve Bell, for example, has stated that he dislikes all politicians, and in this he seems to share a widespread contemporary cynicism. One could possibly argue that all-critical cartoonists run the risk of losing impact over time because they attack everything. Equally, though, one could argue that people with particular political agendas can eventually seem repetitive and dull. It all comes down to the skill of the individual cartoonist and the inspiration of the moment.

One question that is endlessly rehearsed is 'Does a political cartoon need to be funny?' My own view is that if it is drawn to make a serious point, it does not have to amuse as well. Its aim should be to inform and to stimulate thought. Ralph Steadman similarly feels that humour is a secondary consideration:

> A cartoonist's purpose is not just to be funny. It is a sad fact, but oppression, deceit and injustice are the mothers of satire, the cartoonist's best weapon. A satirist without a cause is a frustrated person.

As to whether cartoons actually influence readers – even change their minds – I suspect that the answer is that, generally speaking, they do not, and I would go along with former *Punch* editor Alan Coren when he says: 'The political cartoon never stopped, never changed anything – it doesn't now.' It is probably truer to say that cartoons have a tendency to confirm our existing prejudices and opinions. After all, cartoonists, as a general rule, work for newspapers with which they feel politically sympathetic – although there are notable exceptions, such as David Low and Vicky at the *Evening Standard* – while we, for our part, usually buy the newspaper that accords with our own view of the world. In other words, the cartoons we look at have a tendency to encapsulate our existing mood, rather than present us with an alternative view.

As I have said, David Low is one of the great exceptions to this rule. Until his arrival at the *Evening Standard* in 1927 cartoonists were expected to support the editorial line of the paper they worked for, and they would have to produce several ideas or sketches for the next day's cartoon that would then be discussed with the editor. However, Low's contract with the *Evening Standard*'s proprietor Lord Beaverbrook gave him complete freedom in the selection and treatment of his subject matter, and although the paper reserved the right not to publish any of his cartoons it strongly objected to, many were nevertheless allowed to appear that the paper's readers thoroughly disliked – which is scarcely surprising given Low's left-wing sympathies. Readers wrote to complain of the mocking way he portrayed the Conservatives, and one wrote to say that the cartoonist was so 'Low' that he would go to hell in a balloon. Lord Beaverbrook, though, as a good newspaper man, knew that controversy made for sales, and he admired Low even when he disagreed with him. Low finally left the *Evening Standard* in 1950 to join the *Daily Herald*, which was more in sympathy with his own political beliefs. However, he then discovered that because he was preaching to the converted his cartoons had less impact than formerly.

Low may have been allowed some political slack, but there were many things he could not show in his cartoons that today's leading cartoonists, such as Steve Bell, Nick Garland and Peter Brookes, would not think twice about

Morning After

The managing director of the *Manchester Guardian* felt compelled to apologise publicly over the paper's decision to run a cartoon by David Low that was critical of the cost of Elizabeth II's coronation.
[DAVID LOW *Manchester Guardian* 3 June 1953]

caricaturing. Until the 1960s, for example, royalty had to be treated with cautious deference. When a monarch died, either no cartoon appeared at all (as in the case of George V) or only a solemn one (as for the deaths of Queen Victoria, Edward VII and George VI). Any suggestion of levity was frowned upon. In the early 1930s Low was accused of being a Bolshevik for drawing a rather benign caricature of the future Edward VIII, and during the abdication crisis a cartoon he drew entitled the 'Wallace Collection', featuring framed portraits of Wallace Simpson's two former husbands and one of Edward VIII, was resolutely refused publication. He got into hot water again when the *Manchester Guardian* published his cartoon criticising the cost of Queen Elizabeth II's coronation in 1953. Such a storm of complaints ensued that the newspaper's managing director felt it necessary to make a public apology.

Disability was another taboo. From the time he became US President in 1932 right up until his death in 1945 Franklin Roosevelt was never depicted in a wheelchair but as if he was entirely able-bodied. Attention was never drawn to Lord Halifax's missing left hand or to R A B Butler's crippled right arm. It was not possible to refer even to minor embarrassments on the part of individual politicians if they were personal rather than political. A Low cartoon inspired by news that Churchill had fallen into the pond at Chartwell was, for example, considered too 'below the belt'.

Things have changed, of course. Since the 1960s the monarchy has become as much a target for ridicule as politicians – as evidenced by the cartoons that accompanied the Princess Diana and Prince Charles separation saga. Physical incapacity is now shown – the former Home Secretary David Blunkett, for example, has always been portrayed as blind. Libel remains an ever-present danger, but otherwise everything goes – profanities, bare bottoms and phallic symbols among them. Whereas in 1937 the word 'nitwit' was removed from a cartoon for being too offensive, Steve Bell can get away with cartoons showing President George W Bush in a compromising position with a camel (a metaphor for what he believes the Americans are doing to Iraq). Some have gone even further. Gerald Scarfe and Ralph Steadman, for example, have carried out forms of visual mutilation, producing grotesquely accentuated images.

Yet while newspaper cartoons have been allowed to become more extreme in many ways, they probably have less impact than they once did, and that is because newspapers themselves are no longer the primary source of information that they were until the 1950s, when television started to make a serious bid for people's time. The importance of cartoonists in the inter-war years is apparent from the salaries they could command. In 1931, for example, the *Daily Express* doubled the salary of its cartoonist Sidney Strube to £10,000 in order to retain his services. This was a vast sum at the time and made him easily the highest paid employee in Fleet Street. Cartoonists were considered major celebrities and were often household names. Before the Second World War news-stands would regularly display billboards promoting a particular newspaper's cartoonist. Until 1940 Madame Tussaud's displayed waxworks of Low, 'Poy' and Strube. No cartoonist today enjoys quite that degree of public recognition, and the newspapers they work for have to compete for attention with 24-hour, wall-to-wall radio and television news coverage and the Internet.

What about the victims of the cartoonist's art? Some public figures, it seems, have enjoyed being caricatured, no matter how unsympathetically. Both Stanley Baldwin and Lloyd George, for instance, liked appearing in Sidney Strube's cartoons in the *Daily Express*. In 1934 Baldwin wrote to Strube, 'I love your work, both its draughtsmanship and its spirit', while, the previous year, when Lloyd George was asked how he had managed to keep so cheerful when suffering the stresses of being Prime Minister, he replied:

The first thing I did, even before I got out of bed, was to take up the *Daily Express*, a paper with whose policy I often profoundly disagreed, and looked at Strube's cartoon. That put me in good humour for the rest of the day. Strube taught me how to laugh at myself and that, believe me, is a virtue which many eminent men would do well to acquire.

For many, to appear in a cartoon was proof of public significance. Far more worrying was when the caricatures stopped. So while Churchill's daughter, Mary Soames, could not understand how her father not only collected often cruel and unflattering cartoons of himself, framing and hanging them at Chartwell, the Churchill's family home, Churchill for his part noted:

> Just as eels are supposed to get used to skinning, so politicians get used to being caricatured. In fact, by a strange trait in human nature they even get to like it. If we must confess it, they are quite offended and downcast when the cartoons stop. They wonder what has gone wrong; they wonder what they have done amiss. They fear old age and obsolescence are creeping upon them. They murmur: 'We are not mauled and maltreated as we used to be.' The great days are ended.

Or, as Labour peer Lord (Manny) Shinwell once put it to Michael Cummings: 'My boy, however angry politicians may get by the way you draw them in your cartoons, they'll be more angry if you leave them out!'

Some politicians have even gone so far as to make themselves easier to caricature, adopting what is known in the trade as 'tags of identity'. David Low summed up this strategy as follows:

> Statesmen must advertise. Indeed it is vital to the working of our modern democracy that the persons of political leaders be readily identifiable. Cartoonists and caricaturists have their use in creating or embellishing tags of identity, a fact which is not lost on astute politicians.

Stanley Baldwin felt it vital to be seen smoking his pipe, which he believed gave him a 'man of the people' appearance (in fact, he preferred cigarettes). Harold Wilson also made sure he was depicted with a pipe (he actually preferred cigars). Austen Chamberlain, Foreign Secretary in the 1920s, in a desperate attempt to emulate his more famous father Joseph went so far as to wear a monocle, even though he was dreadfully short-sighted (he confessed as much on one occasion while sitting for David Low: 'Must I wear my monocle? I cannot see to read with it very well …'). Winston Churchill, for his part, adopted the cigar and the V sign. In some cases, a politician's accessory came to represent not just the individual but a whole policy or approach. Neville Chamberlain's umbrella became a symbol of appeasement. Margaret Thatcher's handbag came to personify her combative style.

Of course, not everyone has enjoyed the cartoonist's attentions. Tory peer Lord Birkenhead loathed the way he was portrayed by David Low and even sent the cartoonist a photograph of himself to show what he really looked like. He let out his frustration in a letter to the *Evening Standard*'s proprietor Lord Beaverbrook.

> Your cartoonist over a long period of time published filthy and disgusting cartoons of me which were intended and calculated to do me great injury. He did not even spare my family after one of the most pleasant weekends which I have ever spent with you as your guest. As to your filthy cartoonist I care nothing about him now. But I know about modern caricature and I never had cause for grievance until you, a friend, allowed a filthy little Socialist to present me daily as a crapulous and corpulent buffoon.

Three Conservative Prime Ministers, Stanley Baldwin, Anthony Eden and John Major, were also rattled by the way cartoonists viewed them on occasion. Baldwin once referred to Low as 'evil and malicious'; Eden frequently complained to his Chief Whip Edward Heath about the punishment meted out to him by cartoonists during the

John Major
Steve Bell's iconic image of the Conservative leader, complete with Y-fronts over his trousers.

after the famous ZEC cartoon

The Price of Sovereignty Has Increased – Official

Les Gibbard's Falklands War cartoon created almost as much fuss as the Second World War cartoon by Zec on which it was based. [LES GIBBARD *Guardian* 6 May 1982]

1956 Suez crisis; and Major, reportedly, was hurt by Steve Bell's portrayal of him as a 'naff' superman sporting Y-fronts outside his trousers. At the other end of the political spectrum, Labour leader Hugh Gaitskell bemoaned the way he was caricatured by Vicky, even asking Vicky's colleague at the *Evening Standard*, Milton Shulman, to speak to the cartoonist about the way he incorrectly drew his nose. 'He makes it look like a ski run,' Gaitskell told Shulman, running his finger down his nose. 'It's not sharp at all. Can't he be more accurate?'

There is one case, though, where a cartoonist's attempt to ridicule his prey actually backfired. Vicky had created the character of 'Supermac' to send up Prime Minister Harold Macmillan. However, things did not quite turn out the way he had hoped. According to Michael Cummings, 'Vicky as a leftwing cartoonist had meant it to be an ironic joke, but it all went wrong. By turning Macmillan into a figure that could handle any crisis, Vicky did wonders for the Tories in the 1959 General Election.'

Vicky's experience shows that, as with all visual media, cartoons can occasionally be misinterpreted. Perhaps the most famous example of this is Philip Zec's *Daily Mirror* cartoon of March 1942, with the caption 'The Price of Petrol has been Increased by One Penny', showing a torpedoed merchant seaman hanging on to a life-raft.

What Zec was actually trying to say was that the public should use fuel sparingly as it was costing lives to bring it across the North Atlantic. However, the Home Secretary, Herbert Morrison, assumed that it was a veiled attack on 'profit-seeking' oil companies. 'Very artistically drawn,' he sneered, 'witty – Goebbels at his best. It is plainly meant to tell seamen not to go to sea to put money in the pockets of the petrol owners.' Churchill also misread it and almost had the paper shut down. Forty years later, the *Guardian*'s Les Gibbard redrew the image of the Zec cartoon to comment on the sinking of the *General Belgrano* during the Falklands War of 1982. He was accused of being a traitor on the front page of the *Sun*.

Producing cartoons day after day is gruelling work. Both Strube and Low admitted to bouts of depression, while Peter Brookes talks of the almost unbearable pressure of having to come up with the goods without letting standards slip. This is particularly tough for those cartoonists who are expected to draw six cartoons a week, though *Daily Telegraph* cartoonist Nick Garland believes that the discipline of having to draw regularly gets the cartoonist into a sort of rhythm. But no matter what the problems and challenges, the ingenuity, imagination and quality of political cartoons have been and continue to be astonishingly high – as I hope this book demonstrates.

At the beginning of the 20th century, political cartoons were carried by only a few of Britain's national newspapers – the *Daily Graphic*, *Reynolds's News*, and the Sundays in the form of the *People* and the *News of the World*. Broadsheets such as the *Morning Post*, *The Times* and the *Daily Telegraph* considered them far too frivolous, and did not start running them until the 1960s. The best-selling 'popular' papers – for example, the *Daily Mail* and *Daily Express* – did include some, but had yet to maximise their full potential as a means not only to break up the otherwise visually monotonous, text-heavy format of newspapers, but to inform, educate and amuse the reader. At this time, photographic reproduction was technically so primitive that leading articles tended to be illustrated by sketches, and the only other visual images to be found were illustrated adverts or fashion designs for the fashion page – though, strangely, the *Daily Mail* occasionally included a section of cartoons from around the world on a particular newsworthy subject or simply took ones from *Punch*. By contrast, some provincial newspapers regularly carried political cartoons. The *Manchester Evening Chronicle*, for example, ran cartoons by 'Poy', while the *Western Mail*, the best-selling daily in Wales, used Joseph Staniforth, whose work also appeared every Sunday in the *News of the World*.

The most prominent political cartoonist of the era was Francis Carruthers Gould, who in 1887 had become the first ever cartoonist to be employed full-time by a daily newspaper, the *Pall Mall Gazette*. By 1900, Gould had been working for a London evening newspaper, the *Westminster Gazette*, for seven years. He and his fellow cartoonists were expected to be in total sympathy with the politics of their newspaper and prepared to support its editorial line. Each morning they would produce several ideas, in the form of sketches, which would then be discussed with,

and explained to, their editor. Recalling a slightly later period, Carl Giles described how the cartoonist would 'nervously approach the editor's office with a number of rough ideas and hope that at least one might meet with approval'. If the editor was unhappy with the cartoonist's initial efforts, he would instruct him to come up with something more in line with his own ideas.

If newspapers were reticent when it came to including cartoons, then plenty could always be found in the satirical magazines of the day, notably *Punch* (which had been running fortnightly since 1841) and its two lesser-known competitors, *Judy* and *Fun*. By 1910, *Judy* and *Fun* had folded, leaving *Punch* to reign supreme for a further 50 years until *Private Eye* came along to overshadow it in 1961.

The issues and events that dominated the minds of political cartoonists from 1900 until the outbreak of the First World War may have been few in number but all were long-running. The first was the Boer War, culminating in the apparent victory over the Boers in 1901 and the calling of a snap 'Khaki' General Election in 1900. This the Conservatives easily won, but the Boers' continued resistance to British rule and scandals in South Africa over Chinese slavery and British concentration camps did much to damage the Government's reputation over the next few years. Another major and divisive issue was that of Protection. Coming at a time when Britain's industrial supremacy was under threat from foreign competition, it pitched the Liberal opposition, who had long believed in free trade, against the Government, and particularly against the Colonial Secretary Joseph Chamberlain, a powerful advocate of placing tariffs on goods from countries that were not part of the British Empire. Chamberlain's dominating presence in British politics made him the most

1900–14

Dropping the First Pilot

Sir John Tenniel, illustrator of the *Alice* books and contributor to *Punch*, was perhaps the most famous of all Victorian cartoonists, and this is a tribute to his most famous cartoon, which appeared in 1890 and which depicted a humiliated Otto von Bismarck being forced from office by the new ruler of Germany, Kaiser Wilhelm II. Tenniel retired from *Punch* in 1901 and is shown here leaving for the last time, watched by Mr Punch himself.
[FRANCIS CARRUTHERS GOULD *Fun* 19 January 1901]

popular of figures for cartoonists until 1906 when a heart attack ended his political career. After that they turned to Prime Minister Herbert Asquith, Chancellor of the Exchequer David Lloyd George and the intransigent Ulster Unionist leader, Lord Carson.

In 1906 the Liberals scored a landslide victory, and cartoonists proceeded to focus on the key elements of their political agenda: a radical programme of social reform that precipitated a showdown with the hereditary House of Lords, the thorny issue of Home Rule for Ireland and women's suffrage. So obsessed were cartoonists by these domestic issues that when the heir to the Austro-Hungarian throne, Franz Ferdinand, was assassinated in July 1914 they initially failed to see its significance. Whereas the lead-up to the Second World War was to be minutely chronicled, the outbreak of the First World War came suddenly and caught cartoonists unawares.

One striking feature of these early 20th-century cartoons is the continued use of various national stereo-types (many of which had been around for decades). Russia was represented by a bear. Britain was epitomised either by the portly and eminently sensible John Bull or the imperial might of the king of the jungle, the lion. In times of tragedy, though, the feminine qualities of Britannia tended to be called on. America was personified by the gangly and goatee-bearded figure of Uncle Sam, commonly known as Brother Jonathan, who had been around since the War of Independence in the 18th century. Other countries, such as Germany, France, Japan and Italy, were summed up not in one specific figure but as compos-ites of what cartoonists believed their respective average citizen looked like. German men, for example, tended to be portrayed as portly, moustached, shaven-headed and wearing *lederhosen*.

Calm before the Storm

1900

The Unionist Lion

Drawn during the 1900 General Election campaign, this cartoon, showing pride in the power of the British 'lion', was intended to reinforce the patriotic link between the Conservatives and the British Empire. [HARRY FURNISS *People* 30 September]

La Perfide Albion

'Après moi, s'il en reste' ('After me, if there's anything left'). The French view of the British Empire was rather less flattering. [*Le Charivari* (France) 3 January]

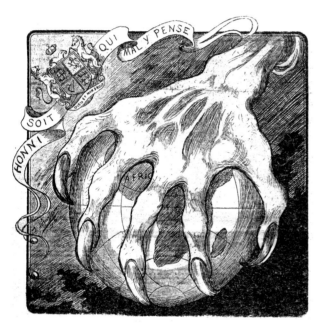

The Leaguer of Ladysmith

The war between the British and the Boers in South Africa had started in 1899 and was fought with great bitterness on both sides. This British cartoon takes a characteristically callous view of the Boer civilians. [CAPTAIN CLIVE DIXON]

At Last

Ladysmith (in northern Natal) had been subjected to a four-month siege during the Boer War. On 2 March it was reported in the British press, to much national rejoicing and remarkable scenes of celebration in London, that the town had been relieved. Here, 'John Bull', the emblematic Englishman, joins the festivities. Lieutenant General George White, in command of the British forces in Ladysmith, reportedly greeted the relief column with the words 'Thank God we kept the flag flying'. [J M STANIFORTH News of the World 4 March]

The Boxers

In China the Boxer rebels began a violent nationalist uprising in Peking (Beijing) against all foreigners, many of whom took refuge in the part of the city where their legations were located and were then besieged by the rebels. By mid-August a relief expedition, consisting of British, French, Japanese, Russian, German and American troops (represented here by national stereotypes), had relieved the besieged quarter and occupied Peking. [N STRETCH Fun 19 June]

Political Thinness

'Lord S: "Get under cover – don't expose yourselves!"' Prime Minister Lord Salisbury called a General Election, known as the 'Khaki election', two years earlier than he needed to do in order to capitalise electorally on British successes in the Boer War. The Conservatives exploited patriotic sentiment, as Carruthers Gould suggests here, and labelled the Liberal opposition pro-Boer and anti-British. The Conservatives duly secured a large majority, despite securing only slightly more votes than Henry Campbell-Bannerman's Liberals. The Boer War was to last two more humiliating years and contributed to the Conservatives' spectacular defeat in 1906. In the cartoon the Prime Minister, Lord Salisbury, and his cabinet are seen hiding behind Lord Roberts, Commander in Chief of British Forces in South Africa. [FRANCIS CARRUTHERS GOULD Westminster Gazette 18 September]

1901

The Mourner

Queen Victoria died on 22 January 1901 after a reign lasting 63 years and seven months, longer than that of any other British monarch. The deeply respectful treatment here, showing a mourning British lion, remained typical of the way in which cartoonists dealt with such moments for most of the century.
[FRANCIS CARRUTHERS GOULD *Fun* 2 February]

His First Service

Edward VII's reign began auspiciously with a Privy Council at St James's Palace at which the king announced his intention to follow in his predecessor's footsteps and to govern as a constitutional sovereign. He then received the oaths of allegiance. On 14 February the king took part in his first state opening of Parliament. Here John Bull congratulates the 'New Man' on opening his 'bag'.
[J M STANIFORTH *News of the World* 17 February]

Our Veterans Begin the Season Well

W G Grace, in a career already spanning 37 years, was still playing first-class cricket at the age of 53, while at the age of 71 Lord Salisbury was just entering his third term of office, having already served as leader of the Conservatives since 1881.
[HARRY FURNISS *People* 19 May]

Different Points of the Compass

The Colonial Secretary, Joseph Chamberlain (appointed to this office in 1895), was a man with a passionate commitment to strengthening the commercial and political ties between the increasingly self-governing colonies. His tenure of office as minister for the colonies transformed his originally nationalistic ideals to ones of imperial proportions. Others, including many Conservatives, saw Britain's future lying with Europe. [J M STANIFORTH *News of the World* 7 July]

A Record Catch

With most in Britain considering that the war against the Boers had already been won, Lord Kitchener, the British commander, implemented a scorched-earth policy: Boer farms were destroyed and Boer civilians were herded into disease-ridden camps. More than 20,000 men, women and children died as a result, causing international outrage. The 'Ratcatcher' here is saying, 'Eight hundred and twenty-nine! That's the best week's work I've done yet!' [J M STANIFORTH *News of the World* 18 August]

The Two Artists

Kitchener's ruthless treatment of the Boers brought condemnation from a number of opposition MPs in Parliament. Henry Campbell-Bannerman, leader of the Liberals, shown here painting the picture of 'The Barbarian', declared: 'When is a war not a war? When it is waged in South Africa by methods of barbarism.' Joseph Chamberlain as Colonial Secretary (shown on the right) was primarily responsible for British policy during the Boer War and defended Kitchener in the House against his critics. [J M STANIFORTH *News of the World* 3 November]

1902

A Way They Have in the Army

Despite the fact that flogging had theoretically been stopped in the British army in 1881, it still occasionally took place as a form of punishment. Here John Bull laments, 'I thought my army officers were all gentlemen; but if this picture is true, some of 'em are blackguards.' [J M STANIFORTH *News of the World* 15 February]

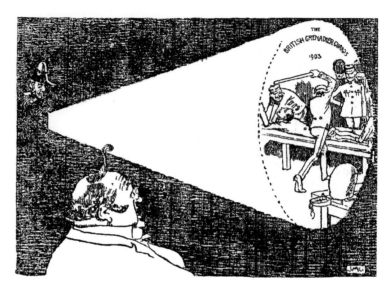

A Protest

The Irish Nationalists boycotted the coronation of Edward VII in protest at the Government's refusal to introduce Home Rule in Ireland. [J M STANI-FORTH *News of the World* 22 June]

The Shadow of a Great City

A reflection of worries about the 'epidemic of crimes of violence' that swept London in the early Edwardian period. [HARRY FURNISS *People* 7 September]

An Alliance which will Make the Greedy Powers Hesitate

The Anglo-Japanese alliance, signed on 30 January 1902, ended the 'splendid isolation' of Britain, which had previously fought shy of 'entangling' alliances, and it also recognised Japan's interests in Korea. This American cartoonist was less than impressed. [*Utica* (USA) 1 March]

A Cecil, Ho!

In July 1902 Lord Salisbury resigned as Prime Minister on the grounds of ill-health and was succeeded by his nephew, Arthur Balfour. Not surprisingly, accusations of nepotism were widely made. [PERCY FEARON 'Poy' *Judy* 30 July]

Peace

'The "Boar" comes under the folds of the old flag at last.' The Boer War finally came to an end when the Boers accepted defeat by the British at the Peace of Vereeniging, signed in May 1902. [PERCY FEARON 'Poy' *Judy* 4 June]

1903

A Fable without Words

The slave trade may have been abolished by the British nearly 100 years earlier, but this cartoonist was disgusted by 'John Bull's' treatment of the 'kaffir' (a derogatory term for black southern Africans). [C J HORRABIN *Reynolds's Newspaper* 12 April]

In Search of a Leaf: Caterpillars of the Liberal Party

Former Liberal Prime Minister Lord Rosebery described his party in a speech as a 'caterpillar in search of a leaf' – in other words, searching for a policy that would attract public support. Options included Home Rule for Ireland and the 'Newcastle Programme', which consisted of various social and political reforms. Following behind is the Liberal leader Sir Henry Campbell-Bannerman and his colleague Sir Edward Grey. [*Daily Graphic* 7 March]

How it is Managed on the Other Side ➤

American social habits had fascinated the British since Victorian times. Hutton Mitchell depicts a 'quick lunch' at a New York restaurant and the arrival of the concept of 'fast food'. [HUTTON MITCHELL *Daily Graphic* 7 March]

Illustrations on the Platform …

Colonial Secretary Joseph Chamberlain campaigned vigorously against free trade (which had been introduced in Victorian times) and in favour of the introduction of tariffs on goods imported from countries not in the British Empire. A hugely divisive issue before the 1906 General Election, it pitched Liberal cries of 'no taxes on food' against Conservative fears that Britain was losing out to increasingly powerful foreign competitors. This cartoon is clearly sympathetic to Chamberlain's views, but, in general, the Liberal 'big loaf' set beside the Tory 'little loaf' became the more popular view of things, and a potent electoral symbol. [E T REED *Punch* 11 November]

Crowded out

'Stage-struck costermonger to his donkey: "Othello, Othello, *your* occupation'll soon be gone!"' Motor vehicles had started appearing on British roads some years before, but it was only in the early 1900s that they started to make a real impact and replace more traditional methods of transport. Accidents reached alarming levels, and the Motor-Car Act of 1903 introduced compulsory registration and number plates. [TOM BROWNE *Punch* 23 November]

The International Menagerie is Disturbed

The Boxer rebellion of 1900 had been a reaction against foreign involvement in China. Following its defeat, Russia's ambitions in the Far East grew, threatening the 'Open Door' policy that had promised all foreign powers equal access to lucrative Chinese trade. Increasing Russian involvement in Manchuria proved particularly contentious and helped spark war with Japan the following year. [*Utica* (USA) 2 May]

1904

Do We Believe?

This cartoon was a response to an observation by the Bishop of London that only 18 out of 100 people in the city attended church or chapel. Worries about falling church attendance had started to be voiced in the 1850s. [J M STANIFORTH *News of the World* 4 December]

The Alien's Champion

'Bravo, Sir Charles! Am I not a man and a brother?' Britain traditionally had no immigration controls, but as large numbers of Jewish refugees, fleeing pogroms in eastern Europe, started to settle in the East End of London pressure grew for an Aliens Act to be passed to limit further arrivals. Media hysteria in support of restrictions was very similar to today's tabloid outcries: the *Manchester Evening Chronicle* supported the proposed law on the grounds that it would exclude 'the dirty, destitute, diseased, verminous and criminal foreigner'. Sir Charles Dilke (portrayed here), the Liberal MP for the Forest of Dean, had publicly opposed the Aliens Act and, ironically, had written a book presenting the British as a benevolent master race. [HARRY FURNISS *People* 1 May]

At Bay

In February 1904, in the wake of growing friction between Japan and Russia, the Japanese navy launched a surprise attack on the Russian fleet at Port Arthur. The Russian navy tried to relieve the port but was defeated at Liaoyang and Shaho and forced to withdraw. The Russian government came in for considerable criticism at home, and the debacle helped precipitate the revolution of the following year. [LINLEY SAMBOURNE *Punch* 7 September]

The Pipe of Peace

On 8 April the Entente Cordiale between France and Great Britain was signed, marking an end to centuries-long disputes between the two powers, and coming only six years after the Fashoda Incident, when the two powers had gone to the brink of war over rival interests in Africa. It was partly intended to encourage cooperation against the perceived threat of Germany. Standing in the background in this cartoon are Edward VII (who did much to foster the entente) and the president of the French Republic, Emile François Loubet. [J M STANIFORTH *News of the World* 10 April]

Well, I Never!

After the conclusion of the Boer War the shortage of native labour in the Transvaal goldmines led, in February 1904, to the importation of Chinese 'coolie' labourers, who were kept in camps under appalling conditions. To Liberals, many of whom had opposed what they termed the 'methods of barbarism' deployed against the Boer civilians in the recent war, this was an affront to civilised behaviour. Here John Bull, the archetypal Englishman, ignores the attempts of Henry Campbell-Bannerman, the Liberal leader, to alarm him over what is happening, but in fact the issue of Chinese slavery did attract attention and contributed to the Liberal landslide victory of 1906. [J M STANIFORTH *News of the World* 27 March]

Kindred Spirits of the 'Strenuous Life'

A cartoon about a cartoon. Two weeks before, *Punch* had run a caricature (shown here on the wall) of Kaiser Wilhelm of Germany and the US President Theodore Roosevelt, comparing their physical appearance. The Berlin police had taken grave exception to the caricature and had confiscated the offending page from copies of *Punch* distributed locally. [E T REED *Punch* 30 November]

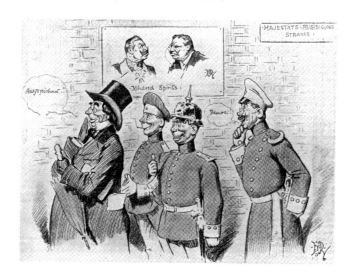

1905

The Tsar of All the Russias

On 22 January a peaceful march of striking workers was fired upon by troops outside the Winter Palace in St Petersburg. Over 1,000 marchers were killed or wounded. The incident, known as Bloody Sunday, signalled the start of the 1905 revolution. [LINLEY SAMBOURNE *Punch* 1 February]

How We Encourage Recruiting for the Navy

For many years the Royal Navy relied on the cane and birch to discipline its boy recruits, with both ratings and officer cadets being subjected to corporal punishment. In the words of one vice admiral: 'The best, and to my mind the most suitable, punishment for a boy is to cane him. It is quickly over, it does not stop his recreation, and if it hurts him sufficiently at the time, he does not want to have it again.' The caning of boys in naval training establishments continued into the 1960s. [*Morning Leader* 20 August]

The Peacemaker

After the Japanese destroyed the Russian fleet at the Battle of Tsushima on 27–8 May 1905, the tsar accepted an offer by US President Theodore Roosevelt to act as a mediator with the Japanese (he later earned a Nobel Peace Prize for his efforts). The Japanese were also keen to find a settlement as, despite their military successes, they were experiencing severe financial difficulties. The British acted as peacekeepers while negotiations took place. [J M STANIFORTH *News of the World* 18 June]

The German Eagle and the Dove of Peace

Britain was becoming increasingly alarmed at Germany's determination, boosted by Kaiser Wilhelm's deep-rooted envy of the Royal Navy, to step up its own armaments production. The arms race that resulted greatly increased international tensions. [*London Opinion* 2 September]

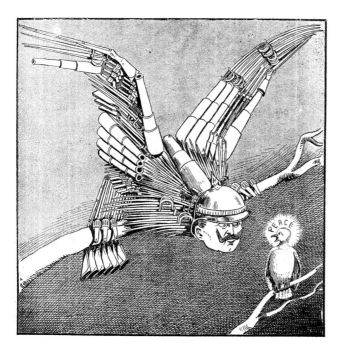

This is the House that Man Built

A popular postcard showing a suffragette being taken to Holloway prison.

United Effort

The growing unpopularity of the Conservative government, coupled with internal divisions, led Prime Minister Balfour to resign on 4 December 1905. The Liberals took over the reins of power, with Sir Henry Campbell-Bannerman as Prime Minister. Here Campbell-Bannerman and Lord Rosebery, now leader of the Liberal Imperialist division of the party, look forward to snuffing out the Conservatives at the next election, which was about to be set for early January 1906. [PERCY FEARON 'Poy' *Manchester Evening Chronicle* 29 October]

27

1906

True till Death

On 19 May a delegation of women from both the Women's Social and Political Union and the National Union of Women's Suffrage Societies met with the Prime Minister, Henry Campbell-Bannerman, to discuss the issue of women's suffrage. Here he is depicted as Dickens's Mr Micawber, with his 'wife' saying, 'No, Mr Micawber, I will never leave you!' [J M STANIFORTH *News of the World* 27 May]

A Surprise Shot 🎖

Tsar Nicholas II agreed to call the Duma, Russia's first democratic ruling council chamber, in the wake of the 1905 revolution, but then, deeming it too radical, he dissolved it and re-introduced martial law in its place. On hearing the news, the Prime Minister, Henry Campbell-Bannerman, in a speech to the House of Lords on 23 July 1906, stated: 'New institutions have often a disturbed, if not a stormy youth. The Duma will revive in one form or another. We can say with all sincerity, "The Duma is dead, long live the Duma."' [J M STANIFORTH *News of the World* 29 July]

Stepping Stones to Office

In the General Election of January 1906 the Liberals won a landslide victory, which gave them an effective working majority of over 100. As this cartoon suggests, the result can be viewed as much as a negative reaction to Conservatism as an endorsement of Liberalism. The personified issues shown helping the Liberals into power are, from the top, the demand for Irish Home Rule, the downturn in the economy (in the guise of an undertaker), trade union unrest and the use of forced Chinese labour in South African goldmines. [J H ROBERTSON *London Opinion* 16 February]

Next, Please

The new Liberal government's radical political programme soon came under fire from the House of Lords. Lloyd George, President of the Board of Trade, was responsible for various pieces of legislation aimed at improving the working conditions of the poor. Behind him stand Irish parliamentary leader John Redmond and Labour leader Keir Hardie. Lloyd George famously referred to the House of Lords as 'a body of five hundred men chosen at random from amongst the unemployed'. [J M STANIFORTH *News of the World* 14 October]

The Better Part of Valour

Leader of the opposition in the House of Lords, Lord Lansdowne was instrumental in attempting to obstruct, albeit unsuccessfully, the Trades Disputes Act, which removed trade union liability for damages caused by strike action. However, the Lords were able to kill off an Education Bill designed to conciliate religious nonconformists. [LINLEY SAMBOURNE *Punch* 12 December]

The Power of Imagination

'Biologists of the future discovered unearthing the long extinct "Liberosaurus" and "Torydactyl".' At the 1906 General Election the Labour party gained its first foothold in Parliament, winning 29 seats, largely thanks to a pre-election pact with the Liberals. This cartoon by 'Poy' came in the wake of a speech by Labour founding father Keir Hardie in which he claimed that the only two parties in the future would be socialists and anti-socialists. [PERCY FEARON 'Poy' *Manchester Evening Chronicle* 18 September]

1907

Good Gracious!

The Prime Minister, Sir Henry Campbell-Bannerman, found himself under pressure from Irish parliamentary party leader John Redmond, who was frustrated over the Government's lack of urgency in introducing Home Rule for Ireland. [PERCY FEARON 'Poy' *Daily Dispatch* 20 March]

The Bogey Man

'Isn't it dreadful, sir! Don't you feel alarmed?' Scare stories in the British press about the dangers of a German invasion of Britain were rife in the early 1900s. In this cartoon, though, John Bull shows himself unconcerned. [J M STANIFORTH *News of the World* 5 May]

Joint Authorship

Some months after 'The Bogey Man' cartoon appeared the Kaiser made a state visit to Britain to see his uncle, King Edward VII. Both men reaffirmed their friendship and pledged to work for lasting good relations between their countries. [J M STANIFORTH *News of the World* 17 November]

To the Rescue

The Conservative-dominated House of Lords rejected most of the legislation presented by the new Liberal government. In response, Campbell-Bannerman, shown here as a fireman trying to rescue various government Bills from the flames, suggested that, as and when the Lords rejected a Bill, a small group of peers and MPs should meet to see if a compromise could be reached. If this failed the legislation should pass through the Commons again and then be sent back to the Lords, and if this failed, the Bill in its latest form should automatically become law six months later. His proposal was carried in the House of Commons, but, predictably, the House of Lords ignored it. [J M STANIFORTH *News of the World* 9 June]

What are You Shouting about …

A capitalist justifies what Ronald Reagan would later call 'trickle-down' economics. [*Judy* 2 October]

This Land to be Let for Building

The Edwardian era saw a housing boom, especially in city suburbs. [W G ASTON *Judy* 18 September]

1908

Still Rising

On 10 June the Chancellor of the Exchequer, David Lloyd George, introduced old age pensions, offering security to the elderly for the first time, though excluding those who had failed to find work, prisoners, the insane and paupers. Staniforth contrasts the old man's observation that it's 'grand weather' for old people with Lloyd George's concern about the likely cost of the scheme. [J M STANIFORTH *News of the World* 5 July]

Adieu to the Old Captain

Sir Henry Campbell-Bannerman achieved the honour of becoming the only serving British Prime Minister to become Father of the House (i.e. the longest continuously serving member). On 3 April he was forced to resign as Prime Minister because of declining health and was succeeded by the Chancellor of the Exchequer, Herbert Asquith. Campbell-Bannerman remained in residence at 10 Downing Street in the immediate aftermath of his resignation and became the only Prime Minister to die there – on 22 April 1908. [J M STANIFORTH *News of the World* 12 April]

No Regard for Their Reputation

Prime Minister Herbert Asquith is seen here dressed as John Bull, handing out benefits to the poor while endorsing the Liberal policy of free trade. The two 'doctors', Henry Chaplin (Conservative MP for Wimbledon) and Joseph Chamberlain (leading opponent of free trade), feel that Asquith has not paid sufficient respect to the alternative treatment they propose. [FRANCIS CARRUTHERS GOULD *Westminster Gazette* 11 May]

The Modern Gulliver: How Soon will He Break His Bonds?

By the end of 1908 the constant vetoing of government legislation by the House of Lords was causing a political crisis. This cartoon, deeply critical of the peers, shows a representation of the common man being force-fed humble pie. Conservative leader Arthur Balfour, standing by the pie, appears to be instructing the peers. [*Reynolds's Newspaper* 6 December]

A Block on the Line

Asquith, seen here with Lloyd George and other members of the Liberal frontbench, now felt the time had come to deal with the House of Lords. [J M STANIFORTH *News of the World* 20 December]

33

1909

When Constabulary Duty's to be Done

At the annual meeting of the British Medical Association delegates singled out smoking among Britain's children as a matter for particular concern, referring to offenders as 'cigarette fiends'. It was suggested that every boy and girl should be encouraged to sign a pledge never to take up the habit. [J M STANIFORTH *News of the World* 11 April]

Paying through the Nose

Lloyd George's radical 1909 'People's Budget', which, among other things, sought to introduce unprecedented taxes on the rich, caused a storm of opposition. Former Prime Minister Arthur Balfour led one of the fiercest attacks, suggesting that the Chancellor of the Exchequer sought to equate robbery with democracy. Here Lloyd George is pumping money out of the taxpayer with the words, 'My dear old friend, it is delightful to meet you again. Permit me to shake you by the hand.' [PERCY FEARON 'Poy' *Daily Dispatch* 10 May]

A Bad Shot

A fairly typical anti-Lloyd George cartoon, arguing that by seeking to tax the rich he is in fact threatening national prosperity. [Conservative party poster]

The Threat

After seven months of intense struggle the House of Lords threw out the 'People's Budget'. This was the final straw for Asquith, who declared that the Lords' opposition to the budget was unconstitutional. He also hinted that he might be prepared to abolish the Upper House. [J M STANIFORTH *News of the World* 5 December]

A Peep into the Near Future

'Well, 'Arriet, me dear, where shall we go Bank 'Oliday? Wot d'yer si to poppin' over to Gee-pan?' A cartoon inspired by the first cross-Channel flight made by Frenchman Louis Bleriot in his mono-plane in just 43 minutes on 25 July 1909. The flight had a potent political effect in Britain, with Lloyd George observing: 'Flying machines are no longer toys and dreams, they are established fact. The possibilities of this new system of locomotion are infinite. I feel, as a Britisher, rather ashamed that we are so completely out of it.' [J M STANIFORTH *News of the World* 1 August]

A Drama in Three Acts

By 1909 the suffragettes' campaign to win the vote had become more radical, with many going on hunger strike in prison. The official response was to force-feed them, an appalling process that involved shoving a steel tube down the woman's throat or nose. Once the press found out, there was a public outcry, though this particular cartoonist clearly felt unsympathetic to the women's plight. The thin suffragette of 'Act I' (left-hand side) who, in the accompanying caption, declares, 'I'll be a living skeleton when I come out', looks distinctly plump by 'Act III' (right-hand side). [J M STANIFORTH *News of the World* 3 October]

1910

The Second Chamber (of Horrors)

A Liberal view of the House of Lords. [FRANK HOLLAND *Reynolds's Newspaper* 10 April]

The Course of Treatment

Having narrowly won a General Election in January on the issue of ending the House of Lords' veto, the Government introduced a Bill to do so. In this cartoon 'Dr' Asquith is saying to Lloyd George, his Chancellor of the Exchequer, 'We will try him with the pills first, and if he rejects them we must resort to the draught.' [J M STANIFORTH *News of the World* 6 March]

No Luck

'Noble Lord: "H'm! It's heads he wins; tails I lose!"' Another General Election was called for 19 December in the hope of breaking the parliamentary deadlock produced in the January General Election. This time the Liberals and the Tories captured 272 seats each. Despite the fierce controversies over both the 1909 budget and House of Lords reform, the two General Elections of 1910 came up with basically the same result. [J M STANIFORTH *News of the World* 11 December]

Fettered!

The 1909 legal ruling known as the Osborne Judgment stated that trade unions could not raise funds for political purposes. This was especially bad news for the Labour party as its supporters were generally poorer than those of other political parties and its MPs were dependent on sponsorship by the trade unions. [FRANK HOLLAND *Reynolds's Newspaper* 28 August]

FETTERED!

(Trade Unionists everywhere are up in arms against the Osborne judgment which has shackled the movement to the point of making progress impossible.)

An Unendurable Handicap.

The Peacemaker

Britannia mourns Edward VII, who died at Buckingham Palace on 6 May 1910. His reputation as a peacemaker stemmed largely from his desire to promote better Anglo-French relations. [J M STANIFORTH *News of the World* 8 May]

John Bull Concerned

The industrial supremacy that Britain had enjoyed for decades was being increasingly challenged by the Edwardian era. [ARTHUR MORELAND postcard]

1911

A Family Group

On 4 May Lloyd George unveiled the Liberal government's Insurance Bill to deal with sickness and unemployment. The accompanying caption to this cartoon rightly sees the Bill as forming part of a wider programme: 'They are all items in one vast policy – to give freedom, health, and opportunity to the whole of the People.' [FRANK HOLLAND *Reynolds's Newspaper* 21 May]

Pensions and Pauperism

'Aged Inmate (to Workhouse Porter): "Well, ta ta, James, you may expect me back by tomorrow morning at the latest."' Contrary to what this cartoon suggests, the newly introduced pensions (see 1908) were not over-generous – apart from anything else, only people over 70 were eligible to claim. [JACK WALKER *Daily Graphic* 17 January]

Little Johnnie Redmond Gets More Than He Bargained for

After a meeting of 50,000 Ulster Unionists their leader, Sir Edward Carson MP, rejected the Liberal government's Irish Home Rule Bill. Carson also formed a secret committee to buy weapons and form an army to resist Home Rule, should it ever come. At the same time, the Irish parliamentary party leader, John Redmond, reasserted his desire to end Westminster's dominance in Ireland. [SIDNEY STRUBE *Conservative and Unionist* November]

Balfour's Shoes

Ill-health forced Balfour to resign as leader of the Tories. The day after this cartoon was published Andrew Bonar Law became Tory leader, but only as a compromise choice after neither Austen Chamberlain nor Walter Long could muster majority support. In the cartoon Bonar Law, Long and Chamberlain are considering whether to run for the leadership. F E Smith, at the time a prominent member of the Unionist wing of the Conservative party, is shown being encouraged to throw his hat into the ring. [FRANK HOLLAND *Reynolds's Newspaper* 12 November]

Wanted – Clean Slates!

The Agadir crisis of July 1911, when the Germans sent a gunboat into the Moroccan port of Agadir, provoked a major war scare in Britain. This, combined with the long-standing naval rivalry, led to the worsening of Anglo-German relations. German Chancellor Theobald von Bethmann Hollweg and Sir Edward Grey, the Foreign Secretary, are shown here as two schoolboys. [FRANK HOLLAND *Reynolds's Newspaper* 10 December]

Victory at Last

After two years' struggle, during which the House of Lords had blocked government legislation at every turn, the peers reluctantly accepted the Government's Parliament Bill, asserting the supremacy of the Commons, on 10 August. Only King George V's promise to side with the Government if it came to an ultimate showdown had persuaded the peers to climb down. Here a triumphant Prime Minister Asquith stands on the defeated 'monster'. [FRANK HOLLAND *Reynolds's Newspaper* 13 August]

1912

Nearing the Precipice

The first coal dispute to affect the nation as a whole started when 2,000 Derbyshire coalminers went on strike over the principle of a minimum wage. By 1 March over 1 million miners were on strike. The dispute lasted six weeks, but was called off when the Liberal government promised to introduce protective legislation on pay.
[J M STANIFORTH *News of the World* 25 February]

The Tragedy of the Titanic

'Fifty-eight "men" of the first-class were saved; one hundred and thirty-four steerage women and children were lost.' The plutocrat sitting astride a coffin offers a stark commentary on the sinking of the 'unsinkable' SS *Titanic*, which hit an iceberg in the North Atlantic while on its maiden voyage to New York. Of its 2,340 passengers more than 1,500 drowned, and, as the cartoon intimates, a higher proportion of first-class men survived than of second-class women or children. [*Daily Herald* 29 April]

Yesterday's Eclipse

On 11 April Herbert Asquith introduced the third Irish Home Rule Bill, offering a greater degree of autonomy to Ireland than the two previous Bills. It was passed by the Commons by ten votes, but the House of Lords rejected it by 326 votes to 69. This cartoon, showing Asquith eclipsed by the Irish leader John Redmond, appeared a day after London had witnessed a total eclipse of the sun.
[JACK WALKER *Daily Graphic* 18 April]

Wilful Willie

'Nurse Reichstag: "But, Master Willie, you haven't enough money to buy every Dreadnought. Do come and look at the next window."' The 1900s witnessed an arms race, with Kaiser Wilhelm II of Germany determined to build a High Seas Fleet that could challenge the Royal Navy and Britain responding by building six and then eight Dreadnought class ships. By 1912 the German High Seas Fleet was still only two-thirds the size of the Royal Navy and had a far more limited area of operation. Here Winston Churchill (in the background), now First Lord of the Admiralty, is clearly suspicious of the Kaiser's intentions. [ROBERT BROWY *News of the World* 19 May]

The European Situation

At a time of growing European tension, Serbia, Montenegro, Bulgaria and Greece formed an alliance, known as the Balkan League, in order to eject the Turks from Europe and divide its European empire among themselves. Four days after this cartoon was drawn, Greece, Bulgaria and Serbia launched an attack on Turkey. [WILL DYSON *Daily Herald* 4 October]

A Risky Performance

By December, after only a month of the First Balkan War, Turkey was close to defeat. Staniforth's cartoon comments on the fears held by many that Greece, Bulgaria and Serbia would ignore Turkish calls for a ceasefire and that this in turn would cause intervention by other European countries that did not wish to see the Turks humiliated. [J M STANIFORTH *News of the World* 1 December]

1913

England's Eleven in 1917 – A Forecast

'Professional clubs all over the country have taken to signing-on foreign players to the detriment of the home-grown product,' laments this cartoon. [CHAS GRAVE *Daily Express* 6 December]

Turkish Delight

'Miss Peace: "Oh! Do be good boys. I once thought you were my friends."' The Treaty of Bucharest was signed by all combatants, bringing an end to the Second Balkan War. Turkey had been obliged to submit to such terms as her victorious enemies had chosen to impose upon her. The First Balkan War had ended in May 1913. Only a month later, the Second Balkan War broke out following quarrels among the victors. [J M STANIFORTH *News of the World* 3 August]

Britannia Mourns Her Heroes Now at Rest

Naval officer and explorer Robert Falcon Scott, better known as Scott of the Antarctic, had attempted to be the first to reach the South Pole, but when his expedition reached it on 17 January 1912 they discovered that a Norwegian party led by Roald Amundsen had got there first. Scott and his companions perished on the return journey, and eight months later a search party found their tent, their bodies and Scott's diary. [J M STANIFORTH *News of the World* 16 February]

Rural Labourers!

When the Government decided on a land reform programme in the autumn of 1913, in order to arrest the decline of British agriculture and the attendant threats to rural society, Lloyd George became its leading protagonist. He promised to improve conditions in farming by introducing a minimum wage for farm labourers and better housing for agricultural workers, along with 'fair' rents and security of tenure. [EDWARD HUSKINSON *People* 12 October]

The Suffragette Silenced

A characteristically critical view of the suffragettes. 1913 was a year of considerable suffragette activity, culminating in the death of Emily Wilding Davison, who threw herself under the king's horse during the Derby. [postcard]

The Devil's Brew

As this cartoon suggests, the Conservative opposition was swift to blame widespread labour and union unrest on the speeches and actions of the Chancellor of the Exchequer, Lloyd George, and the two Labour stalwarts Keir Hardie and Ramsay MacDonald. The word 'Slimehouse' written on Lloyd George's spoon is a reference to his best-known speech, given at a public house in Limehouse, East London, in 1909, when he attacked the reactionary opposition of the hereditary House of Lords. [EDWARD HUSKINSON *People* 7 September]

1914

Pulling the Wrong Lever

'John Bull to Signalman Asquith: "Here, my man, you're going to bring about a shocking disaster".' Until August 1914 the growing threat of civil war in Ireland between the Catholic South and the predominantly Protestant North dominated the front pages of the British press. Asquith's government, reliant on Irish Nationalist votes to stay in office, attempted to pass a Home Rule Bill for the whole of Ireland. This was bitterly opposed by the Conservative opposition and by the Ulster Protestants. [EDWARD HUSKINSON *People* 21 June]

The Primary Cause

'John Bull (pointing to Home Rule Bill): "If you want to find the real culprit you must look nearer home."' A critical view of Irish Home Rule. One day later the Government agreed to shelve the Home Rule Bill in the face of the growing crisis in Europe. [JACK WALKER *Daily Graphic* 29 July]

A Dangerous Game

On 28 June 1914 the heir to the Austro-Hungarian throne, Archduke Franz Ferdinand, and his wife were assassinated by a Serbian nationalist. Initially, there was much international sympathy for Austria. However, the Austrian government saw this as an ideal opportunity to deal with Serbia once and for all and, with German backing, issued a formal series of demands which became known as the July Ultimatum. With Austro-Hungary threatening war if Serbia did not accept all of its demands within 48 hours, and Serbia calling on Russia for help, a general European war started to look unavoidable between the 'Dual Alliance' of Austro-Hungary and Germany and the 'Triple Entente' of Britain, France and Russia. [J M STANIFORTH *Daily News* 1 August]

The Holiday Season AD 1914

On 3 August Germany declared war on France. When, a day later, Britain declared war on Germany, Francis Carruthers Gould produced a prophetic doom-laden cartoon that was to be the only cartoon he ever drew that was refused publication. The editor of the *Westminster Gazette*, John Spender, objected to it as being contrary to public sentiment and, in his words, 'likely to offend'. [FRANCIS CARRUTHERS GOULD *Westminster Gazette* August (unpublished)]

Unleashed

This cartoon was obviously what was expected from a British cartoonist. It reflects perfectly the jingoistic fervour in Britain that greeted the declaration of war on Germany. [ROBERT BROWY *News of the World* 9 August]

Regrouping

An Austrian view of the outbreak of war. Russia, Britain, France and Italy (who joined the Allies a few months after war was declared) are shown in full retreat.

45

The jingoistic fervour that followed Britain's declaration of war on Germany in August 1914 was picked up not only on the editorial pages of newspapers but in their cartoons as well. Critical or sombre viewpoints were not represented; anti-German feeling was rife. Much was made, for example, of the atrocities against women and children that the invading German army in Belgium was believed to have perpetrated, and German barbarism, or 'Kultur' as it mockingly became known, was a common cartoonists' theme. These atrocities were, in reality, often invented or exaggerated by the British War Propaganda Bureau, and they became a recurrent feature in the work of, among others, the Dutch cartoonist Louis Raemaekers, although Raemaekers did not once visit Belgium to witness events for himself. It is said that Kaiser Wilhelm became so upset by Raemaekers's vivid depictions of German atrocities that he took a contract out on him.

Not surprisingly, Kaiser Wilhelm became the number one target for cartoonists. In October 1914, for example, William Haselden created a cartoon strip in the *Daily Mirror* entitled 'The Sad Experiences of Big and Little Willie', mocking the Kaiser and his son. It proved such a huge hit with readers that it ran throughout the war. In contrast, the Kaiser's main ally, the Austro-Hungarian Emperor, Franz Joseph, rarely appeared as a subject in Allied cartoons, and when he did so he was treated with far less venom. The Russian tsar was not used in cartoons to represent his country. Although Russia was Britain's ally, cartoonists were very conscious of the autocratic nature of Tsar Nicholas's regime and preferred to use the Russian bear instead.

Given the strength of anti-German feeling, it is perhaps surprising that the *Daily Express* should have published cartoons, including strongly anti-British ones, from the leading German satirical weekly *Simplicissimus* and the Berlin comic journal *Lustige Blätter*. This continued until December 1916 when Lord Beaverbrook, the *Daily Express*'s new proprietor, put an abrupt stop to it.

British cartoons became important morale boosters. At first, when newspapers found themselves having to give ever more column inches to the daily lists of those killed on the Western Front and reports of unsuccessful military actions, some editors decided to drop cartoons, believing that they were too frivolous for such a serious situation. However, as the war ground on, some decided to bring them back, feeling that they could help raise the morale of their disheartened readers. The cartoons of Bruce Bairnsfather, a young army officer serving with the Royal Warwickshire Regiment, proved particularly popular. He depicted the stoicism and good humour the average British soldier displayed in the face of appalling and dangerous conditions in the trenches, and his drawings, which he initially drew on the wall of a bombed-out cottage at St Yvon, reached a wide audience when *Bystander* started to run them. His stocky, walrus-moustached 'Tommy', called 'Old Bill', became iconic, and his most famous work, 'If you know of a better 'ole, go to it' was frequently alluded to by other cartoonists.

As the war continued, a number of cartoonists packed up their pencils and joined the army. Among them was Kenneth Bird, who came up with the pseudonym Fougasse, the French for landmine, after he was blown up by one. H M Bateman, Bert Thomas and Sidney Strube all enlisted in the London Regiment in 1915, and all survived the war, although Bateman and Strube were eventually invalided out. Both Bateman and Strube sent cartoons

1914–18

home from the front for publication, Strube sometimes having to resort to mud from the trenches when he ran out of pencils and pens. In Australia David Low, who drew cartoons for the *Sydney Bulletin*, so upset the Australian Prime Minister, Billy Hughes, by ridiculing him in his cartoons that Hughes tried to silence him by getting him conscripted.

One striking aspect of British cartoons from the First World War is that very few cover the major battles on the Western Front. This was partly because the static nature of the war offered little in the way of inspiration for cartoonists, but it was also because news from the front was heavily censored. And when it came to Allied military setbacks, these were never covered by cartoons in British newspapers. For disasters such as the Dardanelles campaign and the humiliating surrender of the British at Kut in Mesopotamia we have to turn to American and Canadian cartoonists. What cartoonists in Britain were left to focus on was their continuing demonisation of the enemy and the evils of German U-boats, Zeppelins and poison gas. On the Home Front they showed little mercy either to those 'shirkers' or 'slackers' who had, in their eyes, not yet had the sense of honour to join up or those 'traitors' who, as pacifists and conscientious objectors, refused to.

The Minister for War, Lord Kitchener, who was immortalised in the 'Your Country Needs You' recruitment poster drawn by cartoonist Alfred Leete, became an avid follower of wartime cartoons. On one occasion he even wrote to the editor of the *Daily Express* to congratulate the paper's cartoonist Sidney Strube for his morale-boosting work. 'Your artist is a genius!' he stated. 'And in this time of stress and sorrow his sense of humour and power of conveying it are invaluable.'

The Point of View

'Well, if it don't get merrier than this by Christmas, it won't be up to much!' Bruce Bairnsfather produced many of the most iconic images of the Western Front during the First World War, featuring gallows humour and stoical British Tommies.
[BRUCE BAIRNSFATHER *Bystander* 24 November 1915]

The War to End All Wars

1914

AWKWARD FOR THE DACHSHUND.

There once was a dachshund of Prussia,
Who said, " Here's a poodle! I'll crush her!"
    Then he squealed out, " Oh dear,
    I'm attacked in the rear!"
And he found there the big Bear of Russia.

Awkward for the Dachshund

The direction of international relations in the early 1900s had led Germany to prepare for a war on two fronts. The plan originally drawn up in 1905 by the military strategist Alfred von Schlieffen aimed to defeat France quickly, and then move all German forces to the Russian front before Russia was fully able to mobilise its large army. The danger, of course, as suggested here, was that if the plan failed, Germany would end up having to fight a war on two fronts. [FRANK HOLLAND *Reynolds's Newspaper* 6 September]

The Wrong Timetable

The Schlieffen Plan failed largely because the Germans faced greater resistance from the Belgian army and the British Expeditionary Force than they had expected, giving the French more time to transfer troops. Consequently, as the Germans reached France, their attack started to lose momentum. The result was the First Battle of the Marne, a stalemate, trench warfare and a war on two fronts for Germany. Holland's cartoon recalls the speed and success of Prussia's attack on France in 1870. [FRANK HOLLAND *Reynolds's Newspaper* 25 October]

THE MOST CULTURED NATION ON EARTH

THE CULTURED ONES AT WAR

German 'Culture' in War

Lloyd George was given the task of setting up a British War Propaganda Bureau and appointed the successful writer and fellow Liberal MP Charles Masterman as head of the organisation. One of the first things the BWPB did was to give credence to the idea that the German army was systematically carrying out atrocities and torturing Belgian civilians. [W K HASELDEN *Daily Mirror* 16 September]

The War Lord

A characteristic view of the 'Hun'. [*Truth* 25 December]

A Blot on Europe

'Magnifique! Mon cher Atkeens, we will get her clean again at last, ma Belle France.' England and France are shown working together to expel the invading German army. In reality, relations between the two allies were not always that smooth. (The 'Atkeens' or, rather, 'Tommy Atkins' of the caption was the personification of the British soldier.) [BYAM SHAW *Daily Express* 23 October]

1915

Hun Civilisation

The Germans first used chlorine gas against the British in April at the Second Battle of Ypres. Chlorine gas destroyed the respiratory organs of its victims, and this led to a slow death by asphyxiation. The British responded in September with a gas attack on German positions at Loos. Here the cartoonist takes the high moral ground. [CHAS GROMBI *Passing Show* 22 May]

Gee, but This is a Tough Old Bird

In February 1915 the British embarked on the Dardanelles campaign, intended to knock Germany's ally Turkey out of the war. However, when landings on the Gallipoli peninsula failed to progress beyond the beaches, the campaign became, like that on the Western Front, a battle of attrition fought from deeply incised trenches. By the time this American cartoon was published, plans were being drawn up to evacuate all Allied troops. Not surprisingly, there were no similar cartoons in the British press on the failure of the Dardanelles campaign. [*St Joseph News Press* (USA) 17 November]

Too Much to Swallow

'Kaiser Wilhelm: "Every time that I bite in it … I break my teeth".' An Italian view of the war. Italy agreed to join the Allies in April. [*L'Asino* (Italy) November]

The Fight for Hill 13

'Who holds the hill?' The blowing up of mines below enemy frontline positions became a regular activity on the Western Front. In some areas both sides mined and counter-mined intensively. For the infantry above ground, the wait for underground explosions was a nerve-racking experience. For the men underground – often former coalminers – it was a hard and dangerous task. [*Budget* 25 November]

Which Does the Slacker Prefer?

By the end of 1915 the pace of volunteering was not enough to meet the needs of the army. Public hostility to so-called 'slackers' was pressing the British government to consider conscripting young bachelors. [W K HASELDEN *Daily Mirror* 23 October]

After the Zeppelin Raid

'Policeman to reporter: "Make a note! No material damage. Three children killed!"' Although aircraft technology was in its infancy, Germany had a major advantage in its airships. By 1915 the Zeppelins were carrying out raids on targets in eastern England and east and south London. On 13 October a Zeppelin raid on south London killed 59 civilians and injured 114. This German cartoon tries to imply that the Zeppelins were doing far more damage than the British authorities would admit. [*Simplicissmus* (Germany) 16 October]

1916

The Murder of a Nation: Grim Cartoon

Full-scale massacres and deportations of Armenians by an invading Turkish army occurred in 1915 and 1916 and continued, albeit with less intensity, until 1923. Almost 2,000 towns and villages were emptied of their native Armenian inhabitants in what many believe was the first genocide of the 20th century. [MORRIS *Harper's Weekly* (USA) 4 January]

German Kultur – 1915

Nurse Edith Cavell was arrested in Belgium by the Germans and charged with having helped about 200 Allied soldiers to escape to neutral Holland. Her execution by firing squad on 12 October 1915 led to an upsurge in anti-German feeling in Britain and the US, exacerbated by the wide circulation of a false story that she had fainted on her way to the execution post and had been shot while lying on the ground by the officer in charge of the firing squad. Here Raemaekers helps perpetuate the myth. [LOUIS RAEMAEKERS *Weekly Dispatch* 2 January]

An Unkind Kut

'The Bear: "He told me he was the king of the beasts!"' The British campaign against the Turks in Mesopotamia reached its lowest ebb when General Townshend was forced to surrender Kut al-Amara on 29 April 1916. Following only four months after the end of the disastrous Gallipoli campaign, and with 8,000 British soldiers now in Turkish hands, it was a humiliating defeat. No British newspaper ever ran a cartoon on the surrender at Kut. This one comes from the US. [*Columbus Dispatch* (USA) 28 May]

Too Late! Too Late! is Still the Cry

In May 1915, after the failure of the Dardanelles campaign Prime Minister Herbert Asquith had had to bring in the Conservatives to shore up the Government. The Conservatives were not impressed with the positions they were offered, and Bonar Law soon became dissatisfied with Asquith's running of the war. In the cartoon John Bull is seen riding Asquith. [EDWARD HUSKINSON *People* 16 January]

The Crisis

'Lloyd George: "A more vigorous war policy, or your job!"' The coalition government was impressed with Lloyd George's abilities as Minister of War and began to question Asquith's leadership of the country in a year when few military successes were achieved. In December 1916 Lloyd George agreed to collaborate with the Conservatives in the cabinet to take over from Asquith as Prime Minister. [BERT THOMAS *London Opinion* 16 December]

Non-stop to Berlin

The tank made its battlefield debut on 15 September 1916 when 50 were used on the Western Front at the Battle of the Somme. While they gave the British the advantage of surprise, these early tanks were unwieldy and unreliable, and in their first action, mechanical failures swiftly reduced their numbers to 24. Much, though, was made of them in propaganda terms. [FRANK HOLLAND *Western Mail* 26 October]

1917

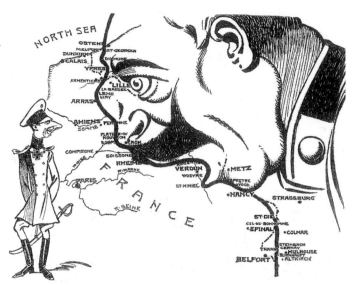

Changing His Map

On 9 April 1917 the Battle of Arras began and British and Canadian soldiers made the deepest advance of the war so far into German lines, using a series of unique tunnels and ground-breaking artillery tactics. Here William, Crown Prince of Prussia, is saying to the Kaiser, 'Oh, papa! They've put your nose out of joint.' [J M STANIFORTH *News of the World* 15 April]

The Gambler's Last Stake

In February 1917 the Germans declared a policy of unrestricted submarine warfare, the Kaiser stating, 'We will frighten the British flag off the face of the waters and starve the British people until they, who have refused peace, will kneel and plead for it.' The 'gamble' ultimately did not pay off. [LEO CHENEY *Passing Show* 17 February]

THE GAMBLER'S LAST STAKE.

Adam and Eve

Germany's unrestricted submarine campaign led American President Woodrow Wilson to break off diplomatic relations, hoping that he could force Germany to backtrack. This did not happen, and relations between the two countries became even more strained when British intelligence intercepted a telegram from German foreign minister Arthur Zimmermann promoting a major conflict between Mexico and the United States. By 21 March seven American merchant ships had been sunk by the Germans. Wilson summoned Congress, and on 6 April America entered the war. *Bull* was an American journal, anti-British in tone and dedicated to keeping America out of the war. [ART ADAMS *Bull* (USA) March/April]

Jee-rusalem!!

Under General Allenby British fortunes in the Near East improved, and the army entered Palestine after defeating the Turks at Gaza. By December the British would be in Jerusalem. [G E STUDDY *Passing Show* 12 May]

The Only Way

During the First World War pacifists became known as conscientious objectors and were vigorously pursued by the authorities. By the end of the war 8,608 had appeared before military tribunals, of whom 528 were severely punished (including 17 who were sentenced to death). There was very little public sympathy for their stance, conditions were made very hard for them, and 69 of them died in prison. [*People* 25 November]

Brought to a Standstill

'Russia (to the Allies): "Well, boys, I'm fixed! It's all up to you now!"' Russia's disastrous role in the First World War precipitated a revolution in March 1917 and the overthrow of the tsar. Eight months later the Bolsheviks ousted the Provisional Government in Petrograd, and Lenin set about extricating Russia from a highly unpopular war. Trotsky was instructed to start negotiating with the Germans. [FRANK HOLLAND *Reynolds's Newspaper* 4 November]

Let Me Sit Heavy on Thy Soul Tomorrow

Kaiser Wilhelm is haunted by those he has made to suffer, including nurse Edith Cavell (shot in 1915) and Captain Charles Fryatt (shot in 1916). [*Truth* 25 December]

1918

Mud Slinging

'John Bull: "No you don't, you little sniper; we've had too much of this lately."' The *People*'s response to criticisms made by the *Daily Mail* of Britain's leading generals, Sir John French and Sir Douglas Haig, for their failures at the Battle of the Somme and the Battle of Ypres despite huge British casualties. Lloyd George was also critical of the military top brass, but they had powerful defenders, including the king. [*People* 3 February]

A Gutter Artist

'All my own work.' Kaiser Wilhelm is held accountable for all German atrocities during the war, including the sinking of the Cunard liner *Lusitania* in 1915 and the execution of Charles Fryatt, captain of a railway steamer, in 1916 for attempting to ram a German submarine. [J M STANIFORTH *News of the World* 12 May]

Side by Side – Britannia

By 1918 American forces were starting to arrive in Europe in significant numbers. This American cartoon reflects the new spirit of cooperation. [JAMES MONTGOMERY FLAGG poster]

Then and Now

Faced with a drastic shortage of manpower, the army increased the age limit for joining to 48. Here the father writing to his soldier son himself becomes a soldier. [FRANK HOLLAND *Reynolds's Newspaper* 26 May]

Don't Worry – They Know the Character of Our Guest

The Germans, now facing defeat on the Western Front, appealed for an armistice on the basis of the Fourteen Points that President Wilson of the US had set out in a speech in January. Wilson's stance was idealistic and even-handed, but, as this cartoon makes clear, Britain and France had other ideas. Four days after this cartoon appeared, a general ceasefire came into effect. [J N DING *New York Tribune* (USA) 7 November]

The Road Mender

Taking advantage of the euphoria of the victory over Germany and her allies, Lloyd George called a snap General Election. Maintaining the wartime coalition with the Conservatives, he famously promised voters 'a land fit for heroes to live in'. [J M STANIFORTH *News of the World* 1 December]

There's No Question of a Better 'Ole

Kaiser Wilhelm II was forced to abdicate on 9 November, and he fled to neutral Holland with the rest of his family. The Allies demanded that the ex-Kaiser stand trial before a special tribunal composed of five judges from each of the victorious powers, but the Dutch refused to surrender their refugee. The cartoon is an allusion to Bruce Bairnsfather's most famous work. [BRAD WILSON *Passing Show* 28 December]

The return to civilian life after the carnage of the First World War proved difficult for a number of the cartoonists who had served in the trenches. Sidney Strube, for example, found the noise of the print machines at the *Daily Express* unnervingly reminiscent of German artillery fire and admitted he had temporarily lost the art of drawing. 'An elephant may be able to pick up a pin with his trunk,' he said, 'but how can a soldier draw cartoons with a pen, after wielding a three-hundredweight rifle for more than three years?'

There were, however, plenty of issues to occupy cartoonists' attention: the post-war settlement agreed at Versailles; civil war in Ireland, culminating in the establishment of the Irish Free State; the opening up of the franchise to women; and the first Labour government. Left- and right-wing agendas became apparent. The harsh peace terms forced on Germany at Versailles were decried by left-wingers such as the Australian Will Dyson and New Zealander David Low, but more conservative cartoonists, such as Frank Holland, were distinctly unmoved by Germany's plight. Similarly, the first Labour government, elected in 1924, was defended by David Low but roundly attacked by, for example, Percy Fearon ('Poy') in the *Daily Mail*. In the wake of the 1917 revolution in Russia Conservative cartoonists raised the spectre of international Bolshevism, while left-wing commentators dismissed this as scaremongering.

David Low's arrival in Britain in October 1919, fresh from Australia's *Sydney Bulletin*, marks a watershed in the history of cartoons. Invited to work for the radical London evening newspaper the *Star* by the Cadbury family, which had heard of his growing reputation in Australia, his unique and forceful draughtsmanship, with its uncomplicated, almost oriental style, was way ahead of its time. In a few brushstrokes Low could reproduce the features that would make a character or personality instantly recognisable. As *Daily Telegraph* cartoonist Nick Garland has said:

> Low's ability to catch a likeness is downright uncanny. If he gives us only a forehead and one eye peeping round a corner, we are able to identify the owner, even now, 50 or 60 years later. He could capture an expression with extraordinary subtlety, adding just a touch of apprehension to a scowl, or a glimmer of hope to a mask of defeat.

It was not long before Low was exerting an influence on such contemporaries as Strube, Wyndham Robinson and George Whitelaw. He was also a significant figure for the next generation of cartoonists – Vicky, Zec and Gabriel.

Low's prowess brought him in time to the attention of the Canadian-born peer and former Minister of Information Lord Beaverbrook, who had acquired a controlling stake in the *Daily Express* in 1916 and was later to add the London *Evening Standard* to his stable of papers. Beaverbrook was ahead of his time in championing the cause of editorial cartooning. He not only retained Strube's services after the war but gave him more newspaper space for each of his cartoons. And then in October 1927 he made newspaper history when, in order to secure David Low's services at the *Evening Standard*, he agreed that Low was to be given a half page for each of his cartoons – unprecedented then and unheard of today. Low also demanded – and got – the freedom to follow his own political line rather than that of the newspaper. His upbringing in the egalitarian and liberal environment of New Zealand and Australia gave him what in Europe appeared as a left-wing perspective on the world and also inspired in him a loathing of the snobbery and inequalities he found in Britain.

1919–29

As for Low's fellow cartoonist Sidney Strube, once he had recovered from his wartime experiences he returned to form and established his best-known creation, the put-upon, overburdened taxpayer known as the 'little man'. Strube believed that the character he had created was an accurate representation of the typical Briton:

> I feel that he represents the average man in the street, with his everyday grumbles and problems, trying to keep his ear to the ground, his nose to the grindstone, his eye to the future, and his chin up – all at the same time. So I try to show him facing what's coming to him with the sort of cheery philosophy which is so British.

Another representation of the 'average man' came from Percy Fearon, better known as 'Poy', whose work first appeared in the London *Evening News* and then in the newspaper that had the largest circulation in Fleet Street, Lord Rothermere's *Daily Mail*. 'John Citizen' was intended to personify the man in the street and, according to David Low, it was he rather than Bairnsfather's First World War creation Old Bill who became 'the first variant of the obsolete figure of John Bull to win general acceptance'. As international and domestic problems continually beset Britain in the 1920s both the little man and John Citizen had much to contend with.

Hello! Everybody
Strube's 'little man' sees the world return to normal after the turmoil of the 1926 general strike.
[SIDNEY STRUBE *Daily Express* 15 May 1926]

A Land Fit for Heroes?

1919

John Bull Triumphant

A Norwegian view of Britain at her moment of triumph at the end of the First World War.
[G LJUNGGREN *Exlex* (Norway) 14 May]

The Gaol Bird

'Madam you are free!' The resentment in Germany at the harsh terms of the Treaty of Versailles made a peaceful long-term settlement in Europe seem somewhat unrealistic. Here, Dyson features the architects of the treaty: French President Georges Clemenceau, American President Woodrow Wilson and British Prime Minister David Lloyd George.
[WILL DYSON *Daily Herald* 30 June]

The Bully's Threat

Having removed the Kaiser from power and established a democratic form of government, the Weimar Republic's first president, Friedrich Ebert, expected to be treated fairly by the Allies. Instead the terms offered were punitive, and invasion was threatened if his government failed to sign the Treaty of Versailles. Weimar Republic politicians came under huge pressure from right-wingers in Germany (as suggested by the threatening figure of the Prussian Junker here) and were accused of having 'stabbed Germany in the back'. [FRANK HOLLAND *Reynolds's Newspaper* 29 June]

Over!

On 28 November American-born Viscountess Nancy Astor became the first woman to sit as an MP. Here she is seen riding Low's first great allegorical creation, the two-headed donkey that characterised Lloyd George's coalition government between 1918 and 1922. The donkey, 'without pride of ancestry or hope of posterity', was an instant success for Low. Michael Foot, later Low's editor at the *Evening Standard*, believed that its constant appearance in the *Star* undermined Lloyd George's coalition possibly more than any other single factor. [DAVID LOW *Star* 29 November]

What We May Have Come To!

Between August 1918 and March 1919 Spanish influenza spread worldwide, claiming over 25 million lives – more than the number who perished in the fighting of the First World War. The virus killed 228,000 people in Britain, the highest mortality rate for any epidemic since the cholera outbreak of 1849. Desperate methods were used to prevent the spread of the disease: streets were sprayed with chemicals, and people started wearing anti-germ masks. However, despite valiant attempts, all treatments devised to cope with this new strain of influenza were completely ineffectual. [W K HASELDEN *Daily Mirror* 19 February]

The Pocket Telephone: When it will Ring!

'The latest modern horror in the way of inventions is supposed to be the pocket telephone. We can imagine the moments this instrument will choose for action!' An inspired bit of crystal-ball gazing. [W K HASELDEN *Daily Mirror* 5 March]

1920

Take That! And That!

David Low's cartoon neatly comments on two events: the aftermath of the previous year's Amritsar massacre, when British troops under the command of Brigadier General Dyer had fired on an unarmed crowd in the Punjab; and Lloyd George's use of ex-servicemen, known as the Black and Tans, to suppress (often very brutally) civil unrest in Ireland. The Hunter Report's findings on the Amritsar massacre concluded that Dyer had acted with unnecessary harshness, but many felt that this was too lenient a view, given that nearly 400 Indian civilians had been killed and more than 1,200 wounded. Here Lloyd George tells Dyer off with a feather – and then sends him to Ireland. [DAVID LOW *Star* 28 May]

It's Bound to Come!

In 1918 an Act had been passed giving the vote to over 8 million women and making it possible for women over 21 to become MPs. This cartoon by Strube was a response to a recent call for more women to serve in Parliament. [SIDNEY STRUBE *Daily Express* 13 February]

The Outcast

President Wilson had championed the setting up of an international community of nations, the League of Nations, at the end of the First World War, but, as this cartoon shows, he failed to persuade the United States Senate to ratify the Charter that established it or join the League. [J M STANIFORTH *News of the World* 28 March]

With Useless Endeavour

'Forever, forever is Sisyphus rolling his stone up the mountain.' At the San Remo peace conference of Allied powers, Britain was given the mandate to govern Palestine, Transjordan and Mesopotamia (the latter was renamed Iraq). The Government's call for an extra 20,000 reservists to meet its commitments in the Middle East was criticised in the press for the burden it was felt to place on the British taxpayer. [SIDNEY STRUBE *Daily Express* 28 June]

Not Enough to Go Round!

The British army had suffered the loss of approximately 800,000 men during the First World War, leading to a noticeable post-war gender imbalance. [PERCY FEARON 'Poy' *Daily Mail* 6 February]

A Disastrous Intrusion

As Lloyd George's government prepared to introduce a fourth Home Rule Bill, providing one parliament for Northern Ireland and another for Southern Ireland, the IRA fought an outright war of independence against British rule. In the cartoon Lloyd George is seen with the Conservative leader, Andrew Bonar Law, who as a member of the coalition had been given the title of Lord Privy Seal. [FRANK HOLLAND *Reynolds's News* 27 June]

Holding the Mirror up to Winston

According to a document obtained by the Labour party, Winston Churchill had, in May 1919, promised General Golovin, a White Russian emissary, every assistance against the Bolsheviks in the civil war that followed the 1917 revolution, even to the extent of making British taxpayers' money available. There was uproar in the House of Commons when, on being challenged over the Golovin revelations, Churchill refused to comment. It was alleged in the left-wing press that he had been gagged by the cabinet in order not to implicate his colleagues. [DAVID LOW *Star* 7 July]

1921

What's Going to Happen to the Show?

'Lloyd George: "There go the best hind legs in the world!"' On the day this cartoon was published Bonar Law resigned as leader of the Conservative party on the grounds of ill-health. Law had acted as deputy Prime Minister in Lloyd George's coalition government. He was replaced by Austen Chamberlain. [PERCY FEARON 'Poy' *Daily Mail* 21 March]

Rival Delegates

In January the Allies agreed that £6.6 billion should be paid by the German government over 42 years in reparations for the First World War. There was outrage in Germany, with Foreign Minister Walter Simons characterising the Allied demands as impossible to fulfil and economically enslaving the German people. Low prophetically suggests that the size of the reparations will lead to future conflict. Lloyd George and French prime minister Georges Clemenceau look on somewhat perplexed by it all. [DAVID LOW *Star* 1 March]

Those Elusive Marbles

When the Government removed wartime controls on coalmines, the mine owners immediately decided on wage cuts for their miners. The Miners Federation threatened a national strike, and the Government responded by declaring a state of emergency and dispatching troops to mining areas. On 15 April 1921 – Black Friday – the leaders of transport and rail unions announced a decision not to call for sympathetic strike action, and the miners were consequently forced to accept wage cuts. [FRANK HOLLAND *Reynolds's Newspaper* 1 May]

HIS OLD PRE-WAR FACE

A Chance for Beauty

Following a brief post-war boom, the Government's decision to deflate the economy in order to return sterling to the gold standard at its pre-war parity led to a severe economic recession. Frank Holland's cartoon was inspired by recent claims by 'beauty doctors' that they could change old faces into new ones. [FRANK HOLLAND *Reynolds's News* 19 June]

Charley Coalition

At the height of his fame, Charlie Chaplin visited London for the first time since he had left for America in 1912 and was mobbed by crowds wherever he went. Low depicts members of the coalition cabinet as Chaplin's 'Tramp'. From left to right, Lloyd George, Austen Chamberlain, Lord Haldane, Lord Curzon and Sir Alfred Mond. [DAVID LOW *Star* 8 September]

A Grave Dispute

After more than a year of civil war in Ireland, Lloyd George invited the president of Sinn Fein, Eamon de Valéra, to London to discuss a settlement. De Valéra did not come himself, but sent representatives who accepted terms that fell far short of the nationalist demand for a united Ireland, but did give dominion status to the 26 counties of Southern Ireland. The Anglo-Irish Treaty was ratified by the British Parliament in December 1921 but was repudiated by de Valéra, who argued that his envoys had agreed to terms beyond their brief. In this cartoon there is no agreement between Lloyd George and de Valéra as to where to bury the hatchet. [FRANK HOLLAND *Reynolds's News* 25 September]

1922

To Blow Brains out/
To Blow Brains in

A report from the Committee on National Expenditure, under the chairmanship of Sir Eric Geddes, advised the Government to cut £87 million from such public spending programmes as education. This became known as the Geddes Axe. [DAVID LOW *Star* 17 February]

Trapped by the Tide

'No wonder Fritz is getting tearful, for things are looking far from cheerful.' German war debts triggered massive currency inflation. The rate of exchange went from 2,850 marks to the pound on 1 August to between 30,000 and 40,000 by December. [FRANK HOLLAND *Reynolds's News* 27 August]

Wat-er Nuisance!

'The authorities have issued a warning against the waste of water owing to the shortage of supplies.' May had seen a heatwave in East Anglia and the southeast. [FRANK HOLLAND *Reynolds's News* 11 June]

Halted!

Turkish attempts to regain territory lost to Greece after the First World War culminated in the Chanak crisis, when Turkish troops advanced towards British positions at Chanak on the Asian side of the Dardanelles. Lloyd George's threat of war against Turkey was regarded as reckless by his Conservative coalition partners and precipitated a meeting at the Carlton Club at which it was agreed that the Conservatives would leave the coalition and fight the next election as a separate party.
[FRANK HOLLAND *Reynolds's News* 17 September]

Who Pushed the Taxpayer in?

At the 1922 General Election the Liberal party was split between the National Liberals led by Lloyd George and the Liberals led by Asquith. Low gave his active support to the latter by drawing a series of election posters for them. According to Low: '1922 was my first British General Election. I put other things aside and threw myself into it. The *Star* worked closely with Liberal headquarters and we arranged that I would make at least one poster per day. It was probably the last election poster campaign in Britain.' [DAVID LOW Liberal election poster]

Waste

The Liberals attacked Lloyd George's coalition government on its record of extravagant and wasteful expenditure. In the event the Conservatives won the General Election. Bonar Law became Prime Minister, but ill-health drove him to resign a few months later. [DAVID LOW Liberal election poster]

1923

The Pipe of Prosperity

Less than a year after the Conservatives had won an election with a comfortable majority, Stanley Baldwin, who had replaced the dying Andrew Bonar Law as Prime Minister, called a snap General Election on the issue of protection. According to Baldwin, 'The only reason for the election is that we promised to have one before any fundamental change in tariff policy.' [DAVID LOW Star 19 November]

The Glove-stretcher Grin!

After the Conservatives won the 1922 General Election, the little-known Stanley Baldwin was appointed Chancellor of the Exchequer and negotiated an agreement with America whereby British war debts of $4,600 million were to be paid back over 62 years. Here, Frank Holland shows Britain being forced to acquiesce to the arrangement. [FRANK HOLLAND Reynolds's News 18 February]

Foggy Weather

The General Election was held on 5 December. The Conservatives won the most seats, but Labour, led by Ramsay MacDonald, and Herbert Asquith's reunited Liberal party gained sufficient to produce a hung Parliament. Having failed to obtain the electoral mandate he sought, Stanley Baldwin declined to form a government. [News of the World 9 December]

MR. STANLEY BALDWIN, CHANCELLOR OF THE EXCHEQUER, BROUGHT BACK AMERICA'S BEST TERMS, WHICH HAVE BEEN ACCEPTED.

Der Münchner ('Munich Man')

'What I want is a bit of peace and a revolution, law and order and a pogrom for the Jews. We should get hold of a dictator and then get rid of him. We'll show you how to build up Germany.' This cartoon was inspired by Adolf Hitler's attempt the previous month to overthrow the regional government in Munich, which was intended to be the first step towards taking over the national government. The so-called Munich Putsch resulted in a short jail sentence for Hitler. This cartoonist, although at the time anti-Nazi, remained working for *Simplicissimus* after the Nazis seized power and ultimately produced pro-Hitler cartoons. [KARL ARNOLD *Simplicissimus* (Germany) 3 December]

Removing the Treasures

When, in the midst of growing economic problems, Germany defaulted on its war reparation payments, the French prime minister Raymond Poincaré (seen here) ordered French troops into the Ruhr, centre of German coal, iron and steel production, to collect reparations. Widespread strikes followed. Poy's cartoon was inspired by the recent discovery of Tutankhamun's tomb in the Valley of the Kings, near Luxor, and the three 'pharaohs' shown are major German industrialists. [PERCY FEARON 'Poy' *Daily Mail* 30 January]

Napoo!

'Ex-Kaiser Bill, gloomily: "There is no room for Napoleons today, Mussolini. Look at me."' Mussolini, who had taken power in Italy in 1922, became embroiled in a dispute with Greece over the murder of an Italian general and four other members of an Italian boundary commission that had occurred on the Greek side of the Albanian frontier. Although those responsible were in fact Albanian bandits, Mussolini threatened Greece with a humiliating ultimatum, making war between the two countries seem inevitable. [ERNEST GOODWIN *News of the World* 9 September]

1924

The Gentleman with a Duster

Liberal leader Herbert Asquith, having refused overtures from the Conservatives to join a new coalition government, decided that Labour should be given a chance in office. He was convinced that an inexperienced socialist administration would collapse, leaving a rejuvenated Liberal party ready to step in. He was also confident that the Liberals could control Labour's legislative agenda. 'Poy' is less confident, showing Asquith opening the door to a thuggish Labour leader, Ramsay MacDonald. [PERCY FEARON 'Poy' *Daily Mail* 8 January]

The Situation is Well in Hand

Labour supporters hoped that MacDonald's government would introduce a radical programme of new legislation, but MacDonald was anxious not to alienate middle-class voters. In the eleven months in which Labour remained in office the only significant piece of legislation that they were able to pass was the Wheatley Housing Act, which began a building programme of 500,000 homes for rent to working-class families. [JACK WALKER *Daily Graphic* 12 January]

Well, We've Got a Labour Government Now

As David Low caustically shows here, the right-wing press had frightened the electorate into thinking that Labour was unfit to govern and that it would all end in a Bolshevik-style revolution, in which private property and even the sanctity of marriage would disappear. The reality was rather different. [DAVID LOW *Star* 23 January]

Shall a Bogy Bar the Way to Freedom?

This cartoon, published on the day of the 1924 General Election, shows the fiercely anti-socialist Tories, Winston Churchill and the then Secretary of State for India Lord Birkenhead, looking down on the people as press barons Beaverbrook and Rothermere assist Lloyd George, Herbert Asquith and former Liberal but now Tory MP Sir Alfred Mond in hoisting the 'Bolshevik Bogy'. Huge damage to Labour had been done by the publication of the Zinoviev Letter in the Beaverbrook and Rothermere press. Purportedly written by the Russian chairman of the Communist International, it instructed British communists on how to promote revolution in Britain. In fact it was a forgery. [*Daily Herald* 29 October]

The Bolshie and the Socialist

The Zinoviev Letter and the fears instilled by the press of a Labour party in collusion with communists – as suggested in this cartoon – led directly to Labour losing the 1924 General Election. But while the Conservatives formed the new government with an overall majority of 200, Labour had now clearly supplanted the Liberals as the party of opposition. [JACK WALKER *Daily Graphic* 3 November]

Enter Mr – Churchill

The new Prime Minister Stanley Baldwin unexpectedly appointed Winston Churchill to be Chancellor of the Exchequer, even though Churchill had only just rejoined the party from the Liberals and knew very little about finance. Many of his new colleagues were unhappy and suspicious, but Baldwin reckoned that Churchill would be less of a problem within the cabinet than outside it causing mischief from the backbenches. [JACK WALKER *Daily Graphic* 5 December]

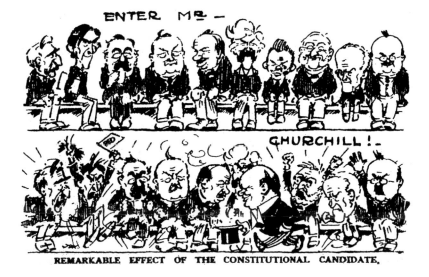

1925

Bee-keeping in England – The Drones

In the view of the cartoonist Sidney Strube, the 'little man' – i.e. the taxpayer – was forced to support the lazy unemployed – a fairly typical perception of the time. [SIDNEY STRUBE *Daily Express* 11 March]

A Guy to be Burned

Germany's gradual return to international favour was given a boost when, along with Belgium, France, Great Britain and Italy, it signed the Locarno Pact, a non-aggression pact that also sought to guarantee international boundaries. Illingworth's cartoon shows, however, that some popular mistrust of Germany still persisted. [LESLIE ILLINGWORTH *Western Mail* 5 November]

Finding a Substitute for 'The Red Flag'

The iconic song 'The Red Flag', written in 1889 by the Irish socialist Jim Connell, had quickly become an anthem of the international Labour movement and was traditionally sung at the end of the Labour party conference each year. Ramsay MacDonald held a competition to find something more 'inspired', but although there were over 300 entries 'The Red Flag' remained a key feature of party conferences until 1999, when New Labour decided that it was outmoded. [LESLIE ILLINGWORTH *Western Mail* 13 May]

Humpty Dumpty

By the end of 1925 the French economy was in trouble. The franc had depreciated significantly, and the French government was seemingly unable to agree on a course of action. Illingworth, conservative by nature, contrasts French internal squabbles with the situation in Italy where, by 1925, Mussolini had effectively forged unanimity by banning all opposition. [LESLIE ILLINGWORTH *Western Mail* 19 December]

Not Meeting Much Opposition

In his first budget the new Chancellor of the Exchequer Winston Churchill returned the pound to the gold standard at its pre-war level in a move he hailed as proof that the British economy was healthy once more. He also cut income tax by 6d. Shown here in the guise of Julius Caesar, he appears to have floored former Liberal MP Sir Alfred Mond and put Labour's leaders, Philip Snowden and Ramsay MacDonald, to flight. Less sympathetic observers felt that his move threatened to destroy the competitiveness of Britain's export trade. [LESLIE ILLINGWORTH *Western Mail* 6 May]

Winston Turpin

The Road Fund had been established solely to pay for road improvements, but Churchill announced in the House of Commons that he was a proposing to syphon £12 million off from it for the Exchequer. In so doing, he set a precedent that has lasted to this day. [LESLIE ILLINGWORTH *Western Mail* 6 November]

1926

Ready to 'Settle' Anything

Coalmines suffered a severe economic crisis in 1925, and Prime Minister Stanley Baldwin responded with a temporary subsidy to the mining industry to help support miners' wages. This was designed to buy time, and in early 1926 tensions rose as Baldwin and the mine owners started to demand major concessions from the miners. This cartoon argues that A J Cook, general secretary of the Miners' Federation, effectively refused to negotiate. In reality, the miners proved considerably less intransigent than the Government and the mine owners. [JACK WALKER *Daily Graphic* 12 February]

Take My Advice, Youngster, Don't Argue with Him

At the beginning of May talks between the Government and the Trades Union Congress broke down in the wake of the refusal by printers at the *Daily Mail* to print an article attacking the miners. The TUC then called a general strike in support of the miners but, in the face of stiff government resistance and crumbling union support, called it off after nine days. A victorious Baldwin is shown turning his attention to the miners again, who, by the autumn, would be suffering such hardship that they would be forced to go back to work. [LESLIE ILLINGWORTH *Western Mail* 18 May]

Votes of Thanks

Low took a conciliatory view of the short-lived general strike. Here we see (from left to right) a striker greeting one of the many volunteers who served as special constables or strike-breakers; Baldwin 'bagging' the die-hard Home Secretary Joynson Hicks who had wanted the strikers to surrender unconditionally; and Winston Churchill who, in the absence of ordinary newspapers during the strike, edited his own, officially approved *British Gazette*. [DAVID LOW *Star* 18 May]

There Must be Victims to Advance

The Scottish inventor John Logie Baird gave the first public demonstration of a working television system in 1925 using mechanical rotating disks to scan moving images and turn them into electronic impulses. His first television programme showed the heads of two ventriloquists' dummies, which he operated in front of the camera, out of view of the audience. [JACK WALKER *Daily Graphic* 26 January]

The New 'Custodian'

In a move that was generally welcomed Germany applied to join the League of Nations in February. This came in the wake of the Locarno Pact of the previous year, when Germany agreed not to seek to alter its western or eastern borders. Attitudes to Germany had softened considerably by the mid-1920s. [JACK WALKER *Daily Graphic* 26 February]

Into the Limelight

Bitter differences within the Liberal party over the general strike eventually drove the party's leader, Herbert Asquith, to resign. Lloyd George, who had brought his supporters back into the Liberal party fold in 1923, now took over as leader. [LESLIE ILLINGWORTH *Western Mail* 8 June]

1927

The Hospital Bed

Labour leader Ramsay MacDonald, dressed as a nurse, is shown rubbing his hands at the prospect of higher taxation to support the unemployed. In reality, Labour did not bring this in until after the Second World War. [PERCY FEARON 'Poy' *Daily Mail* 20 January]

Consolation

'Taxpayer: "I say, Winston, aren't you glad you haven't got to sit up all night counting money like that poor fellow over there?"' While Britain's economy struggled in the late 1920s, America's stock exchange continued to boom. Shown here next to Winston Churchill, Chancellor of the Exchequer, is Sidney Strube's hallmark 'little man', representing the man in the street. [SIDNEY STRUBE *Daily Express* 19 March]

The Eagle's Abdication

On 21 May Charles Lindbergh became the first pilot to fly non-stop across the Atlantic from New York to Paris in his aircraft, the Spirit of St Louis. It was a feat that made him an international hero. [PERCY FEARON 'Poy' *Daily Mail* 23 May]

And All the World Wondered!

In the 1920s Britain's motor industry was enjoying considerable success and was also technologically innovative, winning impressive overseas sales. The British Motor Show (soon to move to Earls Court) had been held at Olympia since 1903. [A W LLOYD *News of the World* 16 October]

Idols of Tuesday Next

'Chorus of candidates: "Are we wasting our time on you?"' Voter apathy is not a new phenomenon. This cartoonist bemoans the low turnout at local elections, as well as offering a snapshot view of 1920s fashions. [A W LLOYD *News of the World* 30 October]

How Long, O Lord, How Long?

A rather favourable view of the tenth anniversary of the Bolshevik revolution. In January Trotsky (seen in the cartoon exiting from the top window) had been expelled from the Soviet Union and Stalin had become the indisputable leader of the Communist party. [DAVID LOW *Evening Standard* 10 November]

1928

The Wooden Horse of Troy

In March the Home Secretary Sir William Joynson-Hicks ('Jix') introduced the Equal Franchise Bill, designed to give the vote to all women aged 21 and over. Here, while opponents of the Bill look on aghast, Labour and Liberal leaders Lloyd George and Ramsay MacDonald stand on the ramparts speculating which of them will attract the most women voters, while Prime Minister Baldwin perches on the back of the horse. [SIDNEY STRUBE *Daily Express* 12 March]

The Flapper

A French take on late 1920s high society. [ANDRÉE SIKORSKA *Fantasio* (France) September]

Bad Housekeeping

Secretary of State for India Lord Birkenhead had contributed an article to *Good Housekeeping* in which he had stated that 'the incursion of women into industry and politics has failed, is failing, and must of necessity fail.' This caused great embarrassment to Prime Minister Stanley Baldwin, who was hoping that the Conservatives would win a sizeable share of the female vote at the next election. Baldwin, alongside Home Secretary Joynson-Hicks ('Jix'), is shown holding the hand of that symbol of the liberated, party-loving woman of the 1920s, the 'flapper'. [PERCY FEARON 'Poy' *Daily Mail* 15 April]

Jerry's Lament

Foreign ministers Aristide Briand of France, Sir Austen Chamberlain of Britain and Dr Gustav Stresemann of Germany (shown watching the other two ice skate) met in Switzerland to discuss the possible removal from the Rhineland of Allied troops, which had been there since the end of the First World War. No agreement was reached, as Sir Austen was recalled to London. However, the following year, the British (Labour) government persuaded the sceptical Aristide Briand (now Prime Minister) that all Allied occupation forces should evacuate the Rhineland by June 1930. [A W LLOYD *News of the World* 16 December]

Visions

In 1928 the BBC was given permission to broadcast 'controversial' and political items. This meant that the next General Election would be the first to be covered by the new medium, a fact celebrated here by the three party leaders, MacDonald, Baldwin and Lloyd George. [A W LLOYD *News of the World* 30 September]

Hanging up the Mailed Fist

'Anxious foreigners: "Will that nail be strong enough?" John Bull: "It all depends on the man with the hammer."' Although America had refused to join the League of Nations after the First World War, it was actively involved in promoting the Kellogg Pact (named after the US Secretary of State who helped negotiate it), which denounced war and which was signed by 15 countries, including Britain, France and Germany. [A W LLOYD *News of the World* 2 September]

1929

Action Wanted

An example of an altered cartoon. David Low was impressed by Liberal leader Lloyd George's dynamic plans for dealing with high unemployment. He was less impressed with the Conservatives under Stanley Baldwin, who proposed to fight the next election under the cautious slogan 'Safety First'. Consequently, in his original version, the 'unemployed bystander's' response to the Prime Minister's casual remark is, 'I dare say. Your crowd are pretty good at ... thinking.' Low's editor, however, felt it was wrong to blame the Conservatives alone for unemployment, and so had the cartoon's caption altered to spread the blame equally among Baldwin, the Labour leader MacDonald and Lloyd George. [DAVID LOW *Evening Standard* 11 March]

The Gallant Five Hundred

'The vendor (in a reckless advertising mood): "Well, some must survive the traffic."' The Liberal party, thanks to Lloyd George's war chest, was able to field 512 candidates in the 1929 General Election, 150 more than in the previous General Election; but while it polled 5.3 million votes, it gained only 59 seats and remained doomed to be the third party in British politics. [WALTER HOLT *Western Mail* 18 May]

The Dangers of 'Cutting in'

Although the Conservatives polled 300,000 more votes than Labour at the General Election, the vigorous Liberal campaign lost them a number of seats, and Labour was able to form a minority government. Holt's cartoon, like 'The Gallant Five Hundred', reflects a contemporary obsession with the ever-rising number of road accidents, which killed over 5,000 people a year in the mid-1920s. [WALTER HOLT *Western Mail* 1 June]

Sixty Years Hence

In order to celebrate the *Western Mail*'s 60th anniversary, Illingworth drew a series of cartoons that looked 60 years into the future. This one predicts the rise of television (still called by an early name, 'televisor', here), a house husband and a working wife. Like so many attempts to look into the future, this cartoon says a lot about contemporary prejudices. The fact that there is a semi-abstract painting on the wall, an obsession with health food and a woman dressed as a man suggests that Illingworth is quietly disparaging 'progressive' elements of 1920s society. [LESLIE ILLINGWORTH *Western Mail* 3 May]

The Ship of the Desert Wants to Discharge Cargo

The British Government informed the League of Nations of its decision to end its mandate in Iraq, while recommending the entry of Iraq as an independent state into the League. Many in Britain felt that the mandate in Iraq was too costly to the British taxpayer, including T E Lawrence (Lawrence of Arabia), who asked: 'How long will we permit millions of pounds, thousands of Imperial troops, and tens of thousands of Arabs to be sacrificed on behalf of colonial administration which can benefit nobody but its administrators?' The 'Quit Mesopotamia' campaign persisted until the end of the British mandate in Iraq in 1932. [PERCY FEARON 'Poy' *Daily Mail* 22 September]

Shackled

The crash of the New York Stock Exchange in October heralded a worldwide economic slump. Prime Minister Ramsay MacDonald appointed the former Colonial Secretary and Railway Unions leader J H Thomas as Lord Privy Seal with responsibility for unemployment, but Thomas had little idea as to how to deal with this growing problem and later famously joked 'I broke all records in the number of unemployed.' [A W LLOYD *News of the World* 24 November]

By the early 1930s political cartoonists had become celebrities in their own right, hounded by autograph hunters and pestered by senior politicians for originals of cartoons in which they appeared. Arthur Christiansen, editor of the *Daily Express*, recalled that when he was introduced to Neville Chamberlain, the Prime Minister asked, 'How do you do?', then immediately went on to enquire, 'Where's Strube?'

With fame came money, and throughout the decade the top cartoonists were undoubtedly the best paid men in Fleet Street. They were also greatly coveted by rival newspapers. J S Elias of the *Daily Herald* believed that had he been able to persuade David Low or Sidney Strube to join him his paper's circulation would have gone up by at least 100,000. Sir Walter Layton, proprietor of the *News Chronicle*, reckoned that his paper's leader page received less attention than that of the *Daily Express* because of one man: Strube.

Given the attention paid to cartoons, it is not surprising to find that – probably more than at any other time – they could sometimes become a part of the events on which they commented. When, for instance, Low drew a cartoon linking Hitler with the burning down of the Reichstag in 1933, the *Evening Standard* was banned in Germany, and the paper's proprietor Lord Beaverbrook was informed that the Nazis would maintain the ban for as long as the paper continued to employ Low. Two years later Low brought down the wrath of the Italian government on his head when he drew a cartoon suggesting that the reason Hitler supported Mussolini's imperial ambitions in Abyssinia was that he wanted to be left free to take over Austria. Shortly before the Munich crisis of 1938 the *Westdeutscher*

1930–39

Beobachter (West German Observer) cast a sour glance in Low's direction:

> His craftsmanship is undoubtedly great, but he is a man without love, without admiration, without enthusiasm, without forbearance. A dangerous, obstinate, adversary … It is needless to add that Low is not one of Germany's friends. (28 June)

Strube was another cartoonist to fall foul of the Nazis. On 8 July 1936, during the Berlin Olympics, he drew a cartoon about the Nazi leadership that Hitler so disliked that he insisted that no German citizen should inspect the offending page in that day's *Daily Express*. The *Daily Herald*'s Will Dyson caused similar outrage with the work he produced until his tragically early death at 57, prompting a conversation between Britain's ambassador in Germany, Lord Halifax, and the Nazi propaganda minister, Joseph Goebbels, in which Goebbels revealed how sensitive the Führer was to criticism in the British press, particularly from cartoonists.

Complaints from abroad clearly rattled the British establishment on occasion. In an address to the Newspaper Society's annual dinner in May 1938, Neville Chamberlain appealed to newspapers to refrain from being overly critical of foreign dignitaries:

> Such criticism might do a great deal to embitter relations when we on our side are trying to improve them. German Nazis have been particularly annoyed by criticisms in the British press, and especially by cartoons. The bitter cartoons of Low of the *Evening Standard* have been a frequent source of complaint.

Newspaper proprietors sometimes showed concern, too. When Strube produced his Olympics Games cartoon, he did so expressly against the wishes of his employer Lord Beaverbrook, who did not want Anglo-German relations to be put under strain while the Games were being staged. At around the same time Low received a letter from the assistant editor of the *Evening Standard*, Stanley Tiquet, stating that while the Games were on it was of 'vital importance that nothing should appear in English newspapers which might tend to prejudice international peace and, particularly, the good relations between all the countries now represented in Berlin'. Low's response was to scribble '!!? To hell with Tiquet' on the offending correspondence.

Inevitably the deteriorating situation abroad increasingly occupied cartoonists' minds as the decade proceeded. They explored the failings of that supposed bastion against international aggression, the League of Nations, and traced the careers of Mussolini in Italy, Hitler in Germany and Franco in Spain. Their stance was generally strongly anti-fascist, even in papers, such as the *Daily Mail*, that supported appeasement until the eleventh hour. Among the major cartoonists only Leslie Illingworth showed a degree of support for Mussolini – and that was in the 1920s. All the major cartoonists were to find themselves on a Nazi hit-list when war finally broke out.

Domestic coverage tended to focus on the economic miseries of the 1930s. Cartoonists recorded the soaring levels of unemployment that came in the wake of the Wall Street Crash of 1929, the failure of the Labour government to agree an approach to the country's problems and the shortcomings of the National government, formed by Labour's Ramsay MacDonald but dominated by the Conservatives after 1931. Ironically, Britain's acute social problems were to be alleviated only by the outbreak of war in 1939, which brought full employment to the nation.

The Gathering Clouds

1930

Squally Weather!

'John Citizen (to Lord Passfield, Colonial Secretary): "Good heavens! What on earth are you going to do with them?"' Britain, which had controlled Palestine since the end of the First World War, had agreed to allow unlimited Jewish immigration, and the influx of Jewish settlers that resulted led to tensions with the local Arab population and, ultimately, to riots. Bowing to pressure from the Arabs, Lord Passfield (shown here pushing the pram) decided to restrict immigration, though it proved impossible to halt it. [A W LLOYD *News of the World* 16 March]

The New Knight Errant

The power of the newspaper baron is shown in a cartoon in which the hero, St George, is in reality the owner of the *Daily Express* and *Evening Standard*, Lord Beaverbrook. He had argued that the route to prosperity lay in closer economic links with the British Empire and, along with Lord Rothermere, owner of the *Daily Mirror*, *Daily Mail* and *Evening News*, established a new party, the United Empire Party. The fact that Lloyd George, Ramsay MacDonald and Baldwin are shown to be in cahoots with the 'dragon of unemployment' says much about Beaverbrook's attitude to the main political parties. [SIDNEY STRUBE *Daily Express* 28 February]

Fascism in England

Dressed as Italian fascists, press baron Lord Rothermere, his son Esmond and other members of the *Daily Mail*'s staff are seen administering the Empire Crusade's 'Food Policy' to Conservative leader Stanley Baldwin. Rothermere was not pleased, and got the editor of the *Daily Mail* to complain to Beaverbrook. Beaverbrook, delighted, apart from anything else, to see Baldwin being pilloried, responded, 'I must say I choked with laughter when I saw it.' Rothermere's right-wing sympathies were well known. In January 1934 he wrote an article in the *Daily Mail* entitled 'Hurrah for the Blackshirts', which was sympathetic to Oswald Mosley and the British Union of Fascists. [DAVID LOW *Evening Standard* 12 July]

The Elephant and the Mouse

Determined to win Indian independence from British control, Mahatma Gandhi embarked on a campaign of civil disobedience in March by organising a march to the sea to defy the Government's monopoly on salt production. 'With this,' he declared, 'I am shaking the foundations of the British Empire.' The David and Goliath nature of the struggle is nicely captured in this cartoon, which shows the Viceroy, Lord Irwin, later Lord Halifax (shown here being sheltered from the sun by the cartoonist himself), wanting to crush Gandhi while also accepting the need to negotiate. Gandhi was arrested the following month, but the Gandhi–Irwin pact was signed a year later. [PERCY FEARON 'Poy' Daily Mail 8 April]

An Extra One

Labour MP Oswald Mosley left the party after its rejection of his proposals for solving the growing unemployment problem. He went on to form the 'New Party', which he dedicated to 'complete revision of Parliament to change it from a talk-shop to a workshop'. Two years later he established the British Union of Fascists. In the cartoon, Lord Privy Seal J H Thomas, known as the 'Rt Hon. Dress Suit' by Low because of his fondness for dressing up in black tie, looks on bemused from a top window. [DAVID LOW Evening Standard 22 May]

Old Low's Almanack: Prophecies for 1931

In the wake of the Wall Street Crash of 1929 the Labour government struggled to deal with a worsening economic situation. Prophetically, Low suggests that Prime Minister Ramsay MacDonald will form a National government – which is exactly what he did do. Shown here seated at the table are (from left to right) Lloyd George, Lord Beaverbrook, Baldwin, James Garvin (editor of the Observer) and MacDonald. The trio of Labour ministers standing at the back are J R Clynes, Arthur Henderson and Philip Snowden. [DAVID LOW Evening Standard 8 December]

1931

Another Case of Civil Disobedience

In an attempt to deal with mounting nationalist unrest in India, Prime Minister Ramsay MacDonald tried, with the support of the leader of the opposition, Stanley Baldwin, to conciliate Indian leaders, releasing Gandhi from prison for his part in defying the salt laws. Winston Churchill's response was to resign in indignation from the Conservative shadow cabinet, so commencing his years in the political wilderness. Among those shown is Sir Samuel Hoare, in the fur-trimmed black coat, who was Secretary of State for India and who was hoping to introduce dominion status for India.
[SIDNEY STRUBE *Daily Express* 29 January]

Well What's it to be Boys?

'United States of Europe or Untied States of Eur'opeless?' Low had a reputation for contradicting the *Evening Standard*'s editorial stance in his cartoons. This one was referred by the editor to Lord Beaverbrook, the newspaper's proprietor, and while he did allow it to be published, it was printed half its normal size and with the heading 'Low on European Depression' to make it clear that this was the cartoonist's view, not the newspaper's.
[DAVID LOW *Evening Standard* 20 May]

Rest in Peace

'Here lies the League of Nations.' A German take on the weakness of the League of Nations.
[*Kladderadatsch* (Germany)]

Putting Him through it

'Arthur Henderson (to J R Clynes): "I don't like Phil's methods, Clynes, but there's no doubt about his courage."' In July, in response to Britain's continuing economic crisis, the May committee recommended that the Government should cut expenditure, including unemployment benefits. While most of the Labour cabinet opposed the committee's proposals, the Prime Minister and his Chancellor of the Exchequer, Philip Snowden, accepted them and proceeded to introduce them when MacDonald was then persuaded to head a new coalition National government. Labour MPs were furious, and MacDonald was expelled from the Labour party. Here Labour stalwarts Arthur Henderson and Joseph Clynes profess to admire Snowden's courage, but in reality they both resigned over the issue. [A W LLOYD *News of the World* 13 September]

Taking the Plunge

'Premier (to his companions) "Now then, altogether, boys, and good luck!"' Having formed a National government, MacDonald called a General Election to seek, in his own words, a 'Doctor's Mandate' to use any means necessary to deal with Britain's economic crisis. In the cartoon MacDonald (National Labour) is shown with coalition members and party leaders Stanley Baldwin (Conservative) and Herbert Samuel (National Liberal). Preparing to dive in are Liberal leader Lloyd George and Arthur Henderson, now leader of the Labour party. [A W LLOYD *News of the World* 11 October]

The Victory Celebration Dinner

'George Lansbury: "Waiter, I think I'll make a start; I don't think the boys will turn up now."' The result of the 1931 General Election was the greatest landslide ever, with the National government winning a total of 556 seats and a parliamentary majority of 500. Labour gained only 52 seats, and all former members of the cabinet, including Labour leader Henderson, failed to be returned to Parliament. Strube shows Labour's new leader, 72-year old George Lansbury, very much alone and wondering whether to invite the 'lady' at the next table (Lloyd George, whose Liberal party gained only 33 seats) to join him. [SIDNEY STRUBE *Daily Express* 31 October]

1932

What People in India Want Today is to Know Where They are

In January, after a second campaign of civil disobedience, the Indian National Congress party was declared illegal by the British authorities and their leader Gandhi was re-arrested. Here Low lampoons a remark made by the Under-Secretary of State for India, Lord Lothian. [DAVID LOW *Evening Standard* 23 May]

"With honourable compliments for distinguished foreign angel's use"

With Honourable Compliments for Distinguished Foreign Angel's Use

The League of Nations faced a real test of its resolve when large areas of the Chinese province of Manchuria were occupied by the Japanese army. The Chinese government appealed to the League of Nations, while Robert Cecil, Britain's official delegate to the League, proposed an inquiry to deal with the dispute. However, the US Secretary of State, Henry Stimson, advised against this. When, later in 1932, the League did eventually ask Japan to leave Manchuria, the Japanese responded by leaving the League. [WILL DYSON *Daily Herald* 24 February]

The Guardians of Art

'Epstein: "I may not have done much for Art, but they can't deny I have done a lot for letters."' Public controversy dogged sculptor Jacob Epstein's career to an exceptional and at times debilitating extent. In the eyes of many critics, his art consistently transgressed the laws of beauty and sexual propriety, and a number of conservative newspapers conducted vicious campaigns against him. Ironically, as a result, his originality made sculpture newsworthy in Britain to an extent it had never been before. [WILL DYSON *Daily Herald* 26 February]

The Lame Dog

'The German dachshund (to President Hindenburg): "These things won't help me over the stile, you know!"' By 1932 unemployment in Germany stood at around 3 million and civil unrest was growing. President Hindenburg was persuaded to ban the Nazi party's Brown Shirts (the SA) by Chancellor Bruning but then lifted the ban at the behest of Bruning's replacement, von Papen, who argued that, if concessions were made, the Nazis might be persuaded to support his new government. Elections were duly called on 4 June. Here the cartoonist blames virtually everyone: the government of Germany, the Nazis and the reactionary Junker social class. [A W LLOYD *News of the World* 12 June]

Putting Him in His Place ✒

'President Hindenburg (to Hitler): "And I think you'd better stop brandishing that sword!"' At the July elections to the Reichstag Hitler's Nazi party made sweeping gains, and Hitler, having earlier promised to support von Papen, demanded to be made chancellor in his place. Hindenburg, however, refused. [A W LLOYD *News of the World* 21 August]

That Musk-o Plant

A wry comment on Stalin's disastrous first five-year plan, launched in 1928 to boost the industrialisation of the Soviet Union. Part of the plan involved setting up collective farms to enhance agricultural output and free farm labourers to work in factories. However, bad planning and peasant resistance followed by state repression actually resulted in a drop in agricultural production by 40%, and famine ensued on a vast scale. [PERCY FEARON 'Poy' *Daily Mail* 28 July]

1933

The Next Test – Amazing Scoop!

The third Test of the 1933 Ashes series was dominated by the 'bodyline' controversy when English fast bowlers, including Harold Larwood, adopted a technique whereby they bowled on the line of the batsman's legs and body rather than at the wicket. As a way of restricting the batsman's options and forcing him to concede catches, it was effective, but it also caused injuries and prompted an outcry from Australian spectators. The media, which coined the term 'bodyline', joined the furore, with the English press branding the Australians 'squealers'. For their part, Australia's cricket board complained to the MCC that 'unless stopped at once, "bodyline" is likely to upset the friendly relations existing between England and Australia.'
[DAVID LOW *Evening Standard* 27 January]

THE NEXT TEST.– AMAZING SCOOP!
WITH CHARACTERISTIC ENTERPRISE THIS NEWSPAPER HAS ARRANGED WITH THE SUPERNATURAL AUTHORITIES (OLD LOW, LOCAL AGENT) TO PRESENT THESE SNAPSHOTS OF THE NEXT TEST EVEN BEFORE IT HAPPENS.

Bradman getting sock on jaw from Larwood.

Bradman's bat hurled at Larwood.

Fieldsmen stumping Bradman with himself.

Jardine bites Woodfull.

Australian Government considers cable from M.C.C. to say that biting is cricket and advising play-the-game-sir.

STOP PRESS – Australia declares war.

In the Moult!

Franklin Delano Roosevelt was inaugurated as President of the United States on 4 March and set about dealing with a country devastated by the fall-out from the 1929 Wall Street Crash. He sought to restore faith in a banking system that had seen a fifth of all banks close since the beginning of the Depression and announced federal schemes to deal with the problem of unemployment. As in contemporary photographs, there is no hint here that he had been crippled, probably by polio, over ten years previously. [A W LLOYD *News of the World* 12 March]

PHOENIX RISING FROM THE ASHES

These be Thy Gods, O Intelligentsia!

From 1933, in a move to remove dissident elements and consolidate his own leadership, Stalin proceeded to expel vast numbers of people from the Communist party, accusing them of counter-revolutionary activities. Additional campaigns of repression were carried out against other groups, including intellectuals, who were accused of opposing the state. The extraction of 'confessions' became a hallmark of Stalin's regime. [WYNDHAM ROBINSON *Morning Post* 12 April]

Rattling the Olive Branch

In the wake of the appalling casualties of the First World War a strongly pacifist sentiment became apparent in Britain, which Hitler's rise to power in Germany initially did little to shake. In February, for example, the Oxford Union passed a resolution stating that under no circumstances would the Union fight for King and Country – a resolution that was strongly criticised by, among others, Winston Churchill and his son Randolph, who even tried to get it expunged from the Union's records. It is the critical, Churchillian view of pacificism that is clearly reflected in this cartoon. [WYNDHAM ROBINSON *Morning Post* 17 May]

Justice at Stake

In February the German Reichstag went up in flames. Communists were blamed and President Hindenburg was prevailed upon to give Hitler dictatorial powers to deal with the situation. A Dutch communist, Marinus van der Lubbe, who was arrested at the scene, was put on trial in September, found guilty and executed the following year. Many believed, as the cartoonist here appears to, that the fire was a put-up job by the Nazis, though it is now generally accepted that van der Lubbe was involved in it. There is no doubt that Hitler made the most of the opportunities it presented. [*Daily Herald* 17 September]

The Secret Tippler

'The German mouse: "Now! Vere is dod blinkin' cat?"' In October Hitler announced that Germany would not only be withdrawing from the Geneva Disarmament Conference but also from the League of Nations. He then began a programme of rearmament in direct contravention of the Treaty of Versailles. [A W LLOYD *News of the World* 24 September]

91

1934

A Most Refreshing Draught!

By 1934 the British economy was showing some signs of recovery. In his annual budget as Chancellor of the Exchequer, Neville Chamberlain took 6d off income tax and raised unemployment benefit, announcing that the budget deficit of £32 million the previous year had been replaced by a budget surplus: 'Great Britain now has finished *Bleak House* and is sitting down to enjoy the first chapter of *Great Expectations*.' [A W LLOYD *News of the World* 22 April]

Haunted House

In 1932 Baldwin had made a strong plea for rearmament, pointing out that Britain was now vulnerable to air attack – as he put it, 'the bomber will always get through'. Will Dyson, though, was one of many to view him as a scaremonger. To avoid too much controversy, Baldwin soft-pedalled the issue at the 1935 General Election. Churchill later accused him of putting party before country, while Dyson's fellow cartoonist David Low argued that Baldwin was 'torn by a wish to lose neither the favour of the pacifist masses, nor the chance one day to begin a programme of rearmament.' [WILL DYSON *Daily Herald* 26 July]

Twenty-five Years on

'Pilots: "It's all very well to scoff, John, but remember we have only had 25 years' notice!"' As international tensions mounted in the 1930s, arguments grew about the state of Britain's defences. This cartoon argues the case for rearmament and should be compared with 'Haunted House', which represents a very different view. [PERCY FEARON 'Poy' *Daily Mail* 25 July]

They Salute with Both Hands Now

One of Low's most chilling cartoons reflects the aftermath of 30 June, when Himmler's SS and Goering's special police, on Hitler's orders, purged the Nazi party by arresting and executing the leaders of the Brown Shirts, or SA. A vital part of the Nazi organisation in the early years, the SA, under its head Ernst Röhm, were keen to see further changes in the power structure of Germany, changes that included taking over control of big businesses and enhancing the SA's military role. Hitler thought differently and increasingly felt that the SA threatened his leadership. Röhm was one of many to perish in the 'Night of the Long Knives'. [DAVID LOW *Evening Standard* 3 July]

It Fits Where it Touches

On 2 August the 87-year-old President Hindenburg died. Hitler had already obtained agreement that on Hindenburg's death the offices of president and chancellor would be combined, and now he went a step further by making the whole of the armed forces swear an oath of allegiance to him personally. The cartoonist sees him inadequately assuming Hindenburg's mantle. In reality, he was far more powerful. [ARTHUR GRIMES *Daily Herald* 3 August]

Godfathers

Strube's cartoon came in the wake of a declaration by Mussolini that all Italians between the ages of eight and 55 should have military training. [SIDNEY STRUBE *Daily Express* 21 September]

1935

Congratulations, Sir!

King George V's Silver Jubilee was celebrated in Britain and around the empire. The king was deeply moved by the tokens of goodwill and affection showered on him from all quarters and gave a radio broadcast thanking his subjects: 'I dedicate myself anew to your service from the years that may still be given to me.' Here we see Strube's famous 'little man' shaking the hand of the king. [SIDNEY STRUBE *Daily Express* 6 May]

Colours Run

In July the League of Nations Union, the largest and most influential organisation within the British peace movement, announced the results of its Peace Ballot, which showed strong support for the League of Nations. It also revealed that 11 million people in Britain supported sanctions against Italy if Mussolini carried out his threats to invade Abyssinia and that 9 million backed military sanctions. Chancellor of the Exchequer Neville Chamberlain described the ballot as being 'terribly mischievous' and would clearly have agreed with this cartoonist, who appears more concerned about the risk of Britain being dragged into a conflict with Italy than with preserving the independence of Abyssinia. [PERCY FEARON 'Poy' *Daily Mail* 25 July]

The Rush to Join the Ladies

The French and British governments did not want to upset the Italians over their imperial ambitions, so the British Foreign Secretary Sir Samuel Hoare and French Prime Minister Pierre Laval secretly agreed to allow Italy to annex most of Abyssinia. When the Hoare–Laval pact was leaked to the press in December, there was outrage and Hoare was forced to resign. The pact – and its secrecy – were a devastating blow to those who had hoped that the League of Nations would end war. This cartoon shows Hoare and Laval hesitating over imposing sanctions on Italy. [WYNDHAM ROBINSON *Morning Post* 17 September]

Still Altering the Map

'Japan: "Who says I have territorial designs on China? I am only straightening a few things out!"'
An aggressive Japan, continuing its expansion into Manchuria, now began to expand its borders southwards. In 1934 it also issued the Amau Declaration, declaring it had special rights in East Asia, which came within its 'sphere of influence'.
[A W LLOYD *News of the World* 29 June]

We Swear to Love, Honour and Obey Adolf Hitler …

On 15 September the Nazis passed the Nuremberg Law for the Protection of German Blood and German Honour, stating that: 'Marriages between Jews and nationals of German or kindred blood are forbidden.' [WILL DYSON *Daily Herald* 18 September]

Rise in Employment Figures (Official)

When Stanley Baldwin replaced Ramsay MacDonald as Prime Minister in June he immediately called a General Election. A few days before it was due to take place, the Ministry of Labour, for obviously political reasons, published its quarterly unemployment figures earlier than usual, claiming that unemployment had dropped by over 40,000. (The Labour-backed *Daily Herald* suggested that the Tories had in reality created some short-term employment.) David Low's depiction of Colonel Blimp talking through his hat is clearly a reference to what he regarded as Conservative dishonesty. The *Evening Standard* refused to publish the cartoon. Baldwin won the election comfortably. [DAVID LOW *Evening Standard* 11 November (unpublished)]

1936

Olympic Games, Berlin

Strube's cartoon about the 1936 Berlin Olympics, particularly his representation of Hitler, greatly offended the Nazis, resulting in a ban on that day's *Daily Express* throughout Germany. A *Daily Express* journalist reported back to London that Nazi officials who came across the newspaper 'scarcely dared to look'. As well as lampooning the Nazi leadership, Strube mocks the way in which the regime tried to appear benign while the Olympics were being staged (anti-Jewish activities, for example, were curbed) and points out that on 8 July the Polish government declared that German support for the independence of Danzig (at the time a free city under the auspices of the League of Nations) was a belligerent act that could lead to war. [SIDNEY STRUBE *Daily Express* 8 July]

Stepping Stones to Glory

In March Hitler had ordered the reoccupation of the Rhineland, in contravention of the Versailles Treaty. Even though he sent only a token military force there, Britain and France did not stop him, so further demonstrating in his eyes their timidity and the weakness of the League of Nations. Here Hitler walks across the backs of Anthony Eden, Stanley Baldwin and French Prime Minister Léon Blum. [DAVID LOW *Evening Standard* 8 July]

The Price of 'Sound' Government

One consequence of the economic problems of the 1930s was that many potential military recruits from deprived areas suffered from malnutrition and so had to be rejected as unfit. The version of David Low's cartoon shown here is the one that appeared in the early edition of that day's *Evening Standard*. In later editions, the caricature of Diana Cooper, the wife of the then Minister of War Alfred Duff Cooper, had disappeared, probably because the proprietor of the *Evening Standard*, Lord Beaverbrook, who had been having an affair with her, did not want her to be depicted in this way. [DAVID LOW *Evening Standard* 20 May]

The Ghost Walks

The coalmining and shipbuilding industries in the northeast of England were hardest hit by the 1930s economic depression. On 5 October 207 unemployed men set out from from Jarrow to lobby Parliament over their plight, and when the Jarrow marchers arrived in London on 31 October a petition with 12,000 signatures was handed into Parliament by Jarrow's Labour party MP, Ellen Wilkinson. Prime Minister Stanley Baldwin, however, refused to see any of the marchers' representatives, a decision pilloried here by Wyndham Robinson. It would take the Second World War to bring full employment back to Jarrow. [WYNDHAM ROBINSON *Morning Post* 6 November]

The Spanish Civil War

In July civil war erupted in Spain when the army rose up against the Republican government. This Italian postcard presents the fascist view, showing the Republican President Manuel Azaña about to be crushed by a heroic figure. [ROBERTO TAFURI (Italy)]

The Little Pigs!

The Spanish Civil War may have dominated the international scene, but on the domestic front the end of the year was dominated by the constitutional upheaval brought about by King Edward VIII's decision to marry his mistress, Mrs Wallis Simpson, a twice-divorced American socialite. There was a news blackout in Britain until 3 December. Eight days later, at Prime Minister Baldwin's urging, Edward VIII abdicated in favour of his brother. Here the left-wing cartoonist Jimmy Friell caustically contrasts the obsession with the king shown by Baldwin and his colleagues with what Friell regards as the real threat to stability – fascism. [JIMMY FRIELL 'Gabriel' *Daily Worker* 5 December]

1937

The New Diplomacy

The hostility that Russia and Germany felt for each other was demonstrated by their support of opposite sides in the Spanish Civil War. As this cartoon suggests, they both also had their own plans for the future of their shared neighbour Poland. [WYNDHAM ROBINSON *Morning Post* 5 January]

A Suggestion for the Representation of both Italy and Abyssinia at the Coronation Pageant

Despite appeals to the League of Nations by Abyssinia's Emperor Haile Selassie, by 1937 Mussolini's troops were in control of the country, creating an Italian East African Empire. Haile Selassie fled to Britain where he spent five years in exile before returning to Abyssinia after the British had expelled the Italian forces. [WILL DYSON *Daily Herald* 25 February]

But Bless You – Ducks Don't Care!

While President Roosevelt pledged a huge aid package for American cities such as Cincinnati, which had been overwhelmed by flooding, the National government in Britain seemed to be doing little to alleviate domestic 'black areas' of high unemployment. Here the swans – Home Secretary Sir John Simon, Prime Minster Stanley Baldwin, Minister for Labour Ernest Brown and, behind him, Chancellor of the Exchequer Neville Chamberlain – swim complacently by. [WILL DYSON *Daily Herald* 5 February]

Their Only Hope

The Peel Commission was established at a time of increased violence between Arabs and Jews in Palestine, and in July it recommended that Palestine should be partitioned to create separate Jewish and Palestinian states, and areas of strategic or religious importance, including Jerusalem and Bethlehem, governed under a separate mandate. [WYNDHAM ROBINSON *Morning Post* 22 July]

🌊 Taking the Plunge

Ernest Bevin, seen here in a bathing suit labelled TUC, pushes the Labour leadership of Arthur Greenwood, Hugh Dalton, Herbert Morrison and Clement Attlee down the waterslide towards rearmament. Bevin, a staunch anti-fascist, had attacked the pacifists in the party two years earlier, resulting in the resignation of the pacifist George Lansbury as Labour leader and his replacement by Clement Attlee. However, Labour continued to oppose rearmament. Neville Chamberlain, seen in the water doing the crawl along with John Citizen and John Bull, followed a two-track foreign policy of appeasement and rearmament, though he hoped that the former would make the latter unnecessary. [PERCY FEARON 'Poy' *Daily Mail* May]

The Role of the Black Races

Foreign Secretary Lord Halifax was concerned that this cartoon would damage Anglo-German relations. In a letter to the British ambassador in Berlin, Neville Henderson, he wrote: 'The *Daily Herald* had what I considered a very objectionable cartoon on Wednesday and I immediately wrote to Southwood [editor of the *Daily Herald*] following our interview and have had a reply of a character which gives me to hope that we shall not have reason to complain again of this sort of thing in that quarter at any rate.' [WILL DYSON *Daily Herald* 1 December]

1938

The New Cloak

Imitating Hitler, Mussolini introduced anti-Jewish legislation, depriving Italian Jews of their rights and their livelihoods. He also expelled all Jews who had entered Italy after 1918. [JIMMY FRIELL 'Gabriel' *Daily Worker* 6 September]

Shiver Sisters Ballet

David Low was deeply critical of the 'Cliveden Set', a group of upper-class people generally in favour of appeasement and of friendly relations with Germany. Shown here being conducted by Hitler's propaganda minister, Joseph Goebbels, are J L Garvin, editor of the *Observer*; politician and socialite Nancy Astor; Geoffrey Dawson, editor of *The Times*; and Philip Kerr, Marquess of Lothian and future ambassador to Washington. The Cliveden Set got its name from the stately home in Buckinghamshire that was then the Astors' country residence. [DAVID LOW *Evening Standard* 3 January]

Get a Move on – You Guys

The international crisis in 1938 did much to raise concerns and awareness in Britain of the need to make preparations for war. As a consequence, the Air Raid Precautions (ARP) Act was introduced and an Air Raid Warden service was set up, along with other Civil Defence services. The Home Secretary, Sir John Anderson, was responsible for civil defence, while Leslie Hore-Belisha was brought in as Secretary of State for War and carried out urgent reforms in the armed services. [J C WALKER *South Wales Echo* 4 November]

The Mark of Cain

A left-wing view of Prime Minister Neville Chamberlain's mission to Godesberg to negotiate a peaceful settlement with Hitler, following Hitler's demand that the Sudeten area of Czechoslovakia (which had a sizeable German population) should be ceded to Germany. Here he is depicted as a Nazi sympathiser. [*Daily Worker* 22 September]

Mr Chamberlain Leaves for Berchtesgaden

Chamberlain refused to give in to Hitler at Godesberg and returned to London believing that war was inevitable. Then, at Mussolini's suggestion, a four-power conference made up of Germany, Italy, Britain and France came together, and Chamberlain flew to Munich to meet with Hitler again. Strube's cartoon represents Chamberlain's mission very positively. Mrs Chamberlain liked it so much she asked if she could have it as a present for her husband to give him on his return. [SIDNEY STRUBE *Daily Express* 15 September]

Horrible and Fantastic

An alternative view of the Munich summit, at which it was agreed that the Sudetenland should be given to Germany immediately and that if the Czechs rejected this solution neither Britain nor France would support them. Jimmy Friell mocks Chamberlain's famous radio broadcast about 'a quarrel in a faraway country' and shows his suspicion of the motives of the European great powers. [JIMMY FRIELL 'Gabriel' *Daily Worker* 29 September]

1939

A Glutton for Punishment

Despite Britain's inability to stop Mussolini invading Abyssinia or sending aid to the Nationalists in Spain, Neville Chamberlain and Foreign Secretary Lord Halifax visited Rome in the hope of achieving a rapprochement with Italy. No agenda was set and the visit produced no visible result. This American cartoonist takes a less than favourable view of British diplomacy. [JERRY DOYLE *Philadelphia Inquirer* (USA) 6 January]

The Double Cross

At Munich Hitler had given assurances that the Sudetenland was his last territorial demand and guaranteed that he would not seek further revisions to the Treaty of Versailles. Despite this, on 14 March the Czechoslovak president, Emil Hácha, was informed by Hitler that Prague would be immediately destroyed by bombing if Czechoslovakia did not accept German rule. The next day German troops occupied Prague and declared Bohemia and Moravia a German protectorate. Slovakia became a puppet state. [TAC *Sunday Pictorial* 10 March]

Quite a Change in Chamberlain

Chamberlain, now realising that Hitler could not be trusted, promised to defend Poland in the event of a Nazi invasion. He had been badly shaken by the invasion of Czechoslovakia, which had proved that Hitler's ambitions extended to non-Germanic people. [*Detroit News* (USA) 28 March]

Guardian John Bull

This German cartoon scoffs at Britain's guarantee to Poland, suggesting that Stalin was the far greater threat to its independence. Stalin, in fact, did not think Britain would honour its promise to Poland and thought that any pact with the British would mean in reality Russia fighting Germany alone. [*Der Angriff* (Germany) 27 April]

I Have Just Dispatched Our Latest Proposals

'Yes, lovely weather, isn't it?' In April Stalin had proposed an alliance of the Soviet Union, France and Britain to combat any further German aggression. However, negotiations dragged on because Chamberlain distrusted the Russians, and nothing came of them. [KIMON MARENGO 'Kem' *Daily Sketch* 20 June]

The Light of Hope Still Burns

Unknown to the cartoonist, Germany invaded Poland on the day this cartoon was published, dashing any hope of a last-minute deal with Hitler. Chamberlain still prevaricated over a declaration of war on Germany, but his hand was forced when the members of his cabinet threatened to resign if he did not. Wells, an Australian, had supported Chamberlain's policy of appeasing Hitler, feeling that if it came to war with Germany, Britain stood little chance. He returned to Australia after war was declared. [SAM WELLS *Daily Dispatch* 1 September]

NAPOLEON 'DON'T LET THE DISTANCE DECEIVE YOU — I THOUGHT HIS GREAT-GRANDFATHER LOOKED SMALL TOO'

The Great Delusion

Napoleon and Hitler consider their British foe, a few weeks after the evacuation of Allied forces from the beaches of Dunkirk. [PETER WALMESLEY 'Lees' *Sunday Graphic* 23 June 1940]

In the Second World War, as in the First, cartoons were important propaganda tools. They may not have been able to conceal the long litany of Allied military disasters that dogged the early part of the war, but they did at least help to underplay or minimise them. All cartoonists set out to make it clear that this was a war to the death between right and wrong. 'The political cartoonist,' Sidney Strube wrote, 'is a powerful weapon for good or evil and in a righteous cause should be used like a giant.' At the same time, they sought to use ridicule to render the enemy less terrifying. Hitler, Mussolini, Goebbels, Goering, Himmler and the Japanese Prime Minister Tojo were the butts of constant jokes and made to seem absurd, childish and irrational. Winston Churchill, by contrast, who became Prime Minister in May 1940 after the resignation of Neville Chamberlain, was depicted as the epitome of the stoic,

never-say-die bulldog spirit that was going to pull Britain through. His visual armoury – the cigar, the V-sign, the siren suit, the bow tie – were godsends to cartoonists.

The British and their cartoonists prided themselves on their sense of humour and made much of the belief that the Axis powers were singularly lacking in an ability to make light of themselves. Renowned actor Sir Seymour Hicks said of Hitler in a radio broadcast: 'This poor man is deficient in the greatest essential needed to achieve victory – a sense of humour. This he can neither manufacture nor buy.' Strube similarly felt a sense of humour to be a crucial weapon in wartime:

During these long years of tragedy, juggling with forms and coupons, standing in queues and stumbling in the blackout, humour has been a great relief. What an opportunity Goebbels

1939–45

missed! If only he had persuaded Hitler to write and ask for a Low, people would have said, 'Why, this man Hitler has a sense of humour after all – he can't be so bad!' But the Nazis couldn't laugh at themselves. As they goose stepped along to their downfall, we in this country laughed our way through our difficulties.

Among the well-known cartoonists at work during the Second World War, the *Daily Worker*'s Jimmy Friell was one of the comparatively few who served at the front. Called up in September 1940, he was posted to an anti-aircraft battery. However, he continued to send drawings when he could to the communist *Daily Worker* until it was closed down by Home Secretary Herbert Morrison between January 1941 and September 1942 for spreading 'defeatist' propaganda at a time when Russia and Germany were nominally friends. He also produced cartoons for the army and in 1944 was appointed art editor of *Soldier* magazine.

Other cartoonists who applied to join up found that they were covered by Britain's Schedule of Reserved Occupations, which allowed the exemption from military service of key figures in newspapers aged 30 or over. Both Zec and Butterworth, for example, had applied to join the RAF but, in the event, neither served. As Zec recalled:

I was already virtually in the RAF. I'd been passed A1. I waited for my damned ticket but it never turned up. I didn't get into the RAF. The Government decided I was more useful where I was.

A number of cartoonists kept back from military service volunteered to become ARP wardens – a dangerous occupation during the Blitz. For his part, Illingworth joined the Home Guard and worked as a gunner on night duty with an anti-aircraft unit in Hyde Park.

New artists came to swell the ranks of political cartoonists. With sport curtailed during the war, a number of cartoonists who had previously covered local and national sporting events for the provincial press found themselves switched to drawing political cartoons. Two of the most successful were Arthur Potts at the *Bristol Evening World* and George Butterworth at the *Manchester Daily Dispatch*. At the same time, some national newspapers that had not previously run political cartoons now decided to do so for the first time. The *Daily Mirror*, for example, promoted Philip Zec, who had been illustrating two strips in the paper, to be its first political cartoonist. He thought they were mad, but he proved to be highly adept.

As victory approached in 1945, cartoonists started to turn their attention to what would happen once peace was re-established, focusing on the General Election of that year and then on the new Labour government's major programme of social and political reform.

The War for Civilisation

1939

Putting a Kick in it

Despite the claims of this cartoon, depicting various British and French politicians (with Churchill in the forefront) defeating Goering, Goebbels and Hitler, attempts to blockade Germany in the Second World War were far less successful than the ones that had nearly starved Germany into defeat in the First World War. This was largely because, as a result of the Nazi–Soviet Pact, the Germans were being supplied with oil and food by the Russians.
[LESLIE ILLINGWORTH *Daily Mail* 2 December]

Oh, Go Away, We're Busy!

On 30 November the Soviet Union invaded Finland after the Finns had refused to give in to Stalin's territorial demands. The League of Nations ineffectually expelled the Soviet Union from the League and urged other countries to send help to Finland.
[LESLIE ILLINGWORTH *Daily Mail* 12 December]

Rendezvous

David Low's greatest cartoon has also been the most frequently reprinted of all British cartoons. It is a superbly conceived attack on the Nazi–Soviet Pact, pointing up the cynicism of two bitterly opposed regimes that, for entirely pragmatic reasons, had agreed to a non-aggression pact in August. Unknown to the rest of the world, the Germans and Russians had also signed a secret protocol that stipulated that they would divide Poland between them. Low later recalled in his autobiography: 'Hitler divided his opponents … Britain and France were dragged to war under such uninspiring and disadvantageous circumstances that it seemed hardly possible for them to win. What a situation! In gloomy wrath at missed opportunity and human stupidity I drew the bitterest cartoon of my life.' [DAVID LOW *Evening Standard* 20 September]

Cockney Kids in the Country

'Coo lummy, Emily. Look wot's 'ere … the local United Dairy.' The fear of air attacks on British cities led to the evacuation of nearly 2 million school children to rural areas from 3 September. As this cartoon suggests, many urban children, especially those from London, found it hard to acclimatise to the country, especially as their hosts were not always welcoming, believing the children would be dirty, ill-mannered and lice-ridden. When the expected bombing failed to materialise many children returned to the cities, to be caught up in the 1940 Blitz. [JOSEPH LEE *Evening News* 6 September]

An American on Neutrality

'Congress: "Nothing wrong with that hose!"' In America the 1937 Neutrality Act meant there was an embargo on the export of US arms to belligerent countries. Three weeks after this pro-Allies cartoon was published, President Roosevelt repealed the embargo and released the £44 million of arms ordered by Britain and France before the declaration of war had brought the original embargo into effect. [MARCUS *New York Times* (USA) 14 October]

One for All and All for One

The British Empire followed Britain into the Second World War, with vast numbers of soldiers from the colonies and dominions rallying round the Union flag. The Australian Prime Minister Robert Menzies announced, 'We are in this most holy war with you … One King, One Flag, One Cause.' The New Zealand Prime Minister Michael Savage asked the governor general for a formal declaration of war before proclaiming, 'Where she goes, we go; where she stands, we stand'. But while the dominions were given a choice whether or not to fight, in India the viceroy Lord Linlithgow declared war without consulting any of the major political or cultural figures. Indian Congressional leaders consequently refused to participate in government. [CON *Daily Sketch* 6 September]

1940

Complacency Black-out

'Mr C.: "Oh, I thought I was sitting in a bus!"'
Neville Chamberlain had confidently told
Parliament that Hitler had 'missed the bus' just
days before Nazi Germany invaded Denmark and
Norway, and there was, as a result, much criticism
of the Government's complacency and lack of
initiative. The 'black-out' referred to here, involving
turning off street lamps and so forth, had been
introduced the year before to make it difficult for
night-time German bombers to find their targets.
[GEORGE WHITELAW *Daily Herald* 7 May]

Churchill Takes the Lead

Following the British military debacle in Norway,
Chamberlain came under increasing political
pressure and was forced to step down on 10 May.
Winston Churchill replaced him as Prime Minister
and immediately formed a coalition government.
Uptton's cartoon captures the spirit of Churchill's
speech to the House of Commons on 13 May:
'I have nothing to offer but blood, toil, tears and
sweat … You ask, what is our aim? I can answer in
one word: Victory.' [CLIVE UPTTON *Sunday Graphic*
19 May]

Who is to Blame?

On 26 May the British Expeditionary Force, which
had been sent to France the previous autumn,
withdrew to the port of Dunkirk to avoid encircle-
ment by the German army. Over 300,000 British
and French troops were then successfully evacu-
ated across the Channel in a move that Churchill
described as 'a miracle of deliverance'. Most of the
media presented the evacuation as a successful and heroic adventure, but, as this left-wing
cartoonist correctly implies, Dunkirk was in reality
a monumental defeat. [JIMMY FRIELL 'Gabriel' *Daily
Worker* 3 June]

WHO IS TO BLAME?

The Big Let-down

German attempts to gain control of the skies during the Battle of Britain that raged during the summer and autumn of 1940 ended in failure and severely damaged the reputation of the Luftwaffe's commander, Hermann Goering. Depicted here as a barrage balloon, his stoutness and love of extravagant clothes made him a gift to cartoonists. [PETER WALMESLEY 'Lees' *Sunday Graphic* 18 August]

Blitz Bus 'Drive to the East'

Mussolini, having grown jealous of Hitler's conquests, wanted to prove to his Axis partner that he could lead Italy to similar military successes. Since he regarded southeastern Europe as lying within the Italian sphere of influence, he duly invaded Greece on 28 October. The Greek army counter-attacked and forced the Italians to retreat – a temporary success that had wider repercussions, as Hitler felt compelled to bail out the Italians and, as a result, delayed his offensive against the Soviet Union. [PETER WALMESLEY 'Lees' *Sunday Graphic* 3 November]

The Hold-up Behind

Food profiteering thrived as a result of wartime food rationing. Yet, although this cartoon by Low makes a perfectly valid point, the owner of the *Evening Standard*, Lord Beaverbrook, refused to publish it. According to the journalist Bruce Lockhart, Beaverbrook was himself strict about using rationed food ('Very angry if anyone suggests that he can buy better food than other people or that he deals with black marketeers'), so his objection was presumably that such an acknowledgement of food profiteering would have an adverse effect on public morale. [DAVID LOW *Evening Standard* December (unpublished)]

1941

Turning on the Tap

Despite strong opposition from the isolationist lobby, President Roosevelt persuaded Congress to pass the Lend-Lease Act, allowing the selling or lending of military equipment vital to Britain's war effort. In a 'fireside chat' broadcast to the American people, Roosevelt explained his reasoning: 'Your neighbour's house is on fire. He comes to you and asks if he can have your hose. You say, "I will not give you my hose but I will lend it to you. You can borrow it to put out your fire. And when the fire is out, you will return it to me."' [A W LLOYD *News of the World* 16 March]

On, On, Invincible Italy

At the start of the war Italian troops in North Africa massively outnumbered British forces in Egypt. By April, however, the British had not only routed the Italian army but had taken over 100,000 prisoners. In the Mediterranean British warships destroyed a large part of the Italian fleet in a battle off the island of Crete without suffering a single casualty themselves. [PETER WALMESLEY 'Lees' *Sunday Graphic* 6 April]

Anti-Jairminy Calling

The caption to Low's cartoon refers to the distinctive opening to Nazi broadcasts to Britain made by 'Lord Haw-Haw', the nickname given to a number of German propagandists, most notably William Joyce (executed for treason in 1946). The broadcasts, typically sneering in tone, ran throughout the war, and began with the words 'Germany calling, Germany calling', pronounced in a rather nasal way ('Jairminy'). They proved strangely popular with the British public. For those in Nazi-occupied Europe, by contrast, it was illegal to listen to Allied broadcasts. [DAVID LOW *Evening Standard* 12 September]

The Mask Off

On 22 June 1941 Operation Barbarossa, the German codeword for the invasion of the Soviet Union, was put into effect. Hitler had told one of his generals, 'We have only to kick in the door and the whole rotten structure will come crashing down.' Stalin, although warned by his own security agencies that an attack was imminent, refused to believe it. His catastrophic blunder proved costly. [A W LLOYD *News of the World* 29 June]

The Hess Message

On 10 May Hitler's deputy, Rudolf Hess, flew to Scotland with the intention of persuading the British to make peace so that Germany could concentrate on defeating the Soviet Union. He landed by parachute just outside Glasgow, was immediately arrested and was then incarcerated in the Tower of London. Hitler's response was to declare Hess insane and insist that he had acted on his own accord. [FLATTER *Reynolds's News* 29 June]

Summer/Winter

At first Operation Barbarossa went smoothly, and German forces soon occupied a large area of Soviet territory. They also destroyed most of the Red Army and the Russian air force. However, as this cartoonist correctly predicts, their failure to gain an outright victory before the onset of the Russian winter was to have disastrous consequences. [CLIVE UPTTON *Sunday Graphic* 24 August]

Death Takes a Holiday

On 7 December Japanese bombers and torpedo-carrying planes made a surprise attack on the American naval base at Pearl Harbor in Hawaii. News of the raid shocked members of Congress, particularly as it came at a time when Japanese officials in Washington were negotiating for the lifting of US sanctions that had been imposed in the wake of continuing Japanese aggression against China. President Roosevelt called the attack 'a day that will live in infamy' and, in declaring war on Japan, ended America's policy of isolationism. Churchill's reaction was one of joy: 'So we had won after all!' [LESLIE ILLINGWORTH *Daily Mail* 9 December]

1942

Fun While it Lasts

Illingworth's cartoon attempts to make light of one of Britain's worst military defeats: the loss of Singapore to the Japanese army on 15 February. A strategically vital military base, which protected Britain's possessions in the Far East, it had supposedly been an impregnable fortress. [LESLIE ILLINGWORTH *Daily Mail* 18 February]

Tell 'im!

Gandhi was arrested, along with 50 other leaders of the All-India Congress, after they had passed a 'Quit India' resolution by a 20–1 majority and had started to organise a massive campaign of civil disobedience. At a time when the Japanese were sweeping all before them, the British government were worried that Gandhi's campaign would undermine both war production and the defence of India – a view this cartoon clearly endorses. [PHILIP ZEC *Daily Mirror* 17 July]

The Gap

In July British forces under General Bernard Montgomery defeated Erwin Rommel's Africa Korps at El Alamein in what would become the decisive battle of the North African campaign. With victory at El Alamein and with the German advance in Russia halted, the war appeared to have tilted for the first time in favour of the Allies. [GEORGE WHITELAW *Daily Herald* 29 October]

How Long, O Lord?

In the course of 1942 various accounts of Nazi atrocities against the Jews circulated. A week after this cartoon appeared Foreign Secretary Anthony Eden told a shocked House of Commons that, according to Polish sources, mass executions of Jews were taking place in occupied Europe, that Jewish ghettos were being 'systematically emptied' and that the able-bodied were being sent to labour camps. After his announcement the House rose and held a one-minute silence in sympathy for the victims. [VICTOR WEISZ 'Vicky' *News Chronicle* 10 December]

The Big Round Up

The Minister of Food, Lord Woolton, enlisted the support of the country's leading cartoonists to encourage the public to eat more potatoes and also to discourage food wastage. Strube produced three posters entitled 'The Three Salvageers', this one urging people to recycle their waste. [SIDNEY STRUBE Ministry of Food December]

When They Pursue, When They're Pursued

In the autumn and winter of 1942 the German invasion of Russia was effectively broken at Stalingrad. Stalin had insisted that it should be held at all costs, knowing that if the Germans broke through they could attack Moscow from the east. The Red Army therefore resisted strongly, forcing the Germans to fight street by street, usually at close quarters and, ultimately in January 1943, to surrender. This Soviet cartoon depicts the turning of the tide on the Eastern Front. [KUKRYNIKSY, the collective name of three caricaturists, Mikhail Kupriyanov, Porfiri Krylov and Nikolai Sokolov *Pravda* (USSR) December]

1943

Beveridge Report Dynamite

In December 1942 Sir William Beveridge's report on reforms of social services for post-war Britain was published. He took it for granted that the Government would accept the need for family allowances, for a national health service and for the maintenance of full employment. However, Churchill warned against 'dangerous optimism'. 'Ministers,' he said, 'should be careful not to raise false hopes as was done last time [i.e. after the First World War] by speeches about "Homes for Heroes"'. [LESLIE ILLINGWORTH *Daily Mail* 17 February]

The Unexpected Encore

Throughout 1943 the Royal Air Force bombed German cities at night while the United States Army Air Force bombed during the day. For Zec, as for many others, this was justified retaliation. [PHILIP ZEC *Daily Mirror* 9 March]

Ssh, They're Rising

In April, in Katyn Forest in German-occupied Russia, the Germans discovered a mass grave containing the bodies of 4,500 Polish soldiers. The German claim that responsibility for the massacre lay with Russia's secret police embarrassed Stalin's regime, but, since it came from Goebbels's propaganda ministry, was treated with scepticism by the Allies. Here Illingworth accepts the (false) Russian version of events: that the German themselves were guilty of the atrocity. [LESLIE ILLINGWORTH *Daily Mail* 28 April]

Mein Kampf

In July Mussolini was dismissed from office by the Italian king, Victor Emmanuel III, after the Allies had taken Sicily and had started to plan an invasion of mainland Italy. In September Mussolini's successor, Marshal Pietro Badoglio, signed an unconditional armistice with the Allies. Mussolini was rescued from captivity by German paratroopers, but the Italian government nevertheless declared war on Germany on 13 October. [PHILIP ZEC *Daily Mirror* 2 October]

History Class

'If any boy wishes to leave the room he has only to hold up his hand.' In November Hitler called his henchmen and many of his senior generals to a special meeting in his Berlin bunker. It started peacefully enough but degenerated into a two-hour rant in which Hitler railed against those he felt had let him down. Osbert Lancaster's cartoon includes a sly reference to 11 November – the day on which Germany surrendered in the First World War. [OSBERT LANCASTER 'Bunbury' *Daily Express* 7 November]

Getting Warmer

By the end of 1943 the Allies – both the British and the Americans on the Italian Front and the Russians on the Eastern Front – were beginning their advance on Germany. Six months later a third front would be opened on the northern coast of France. [GEORGE BUTTERWORTH *Daily Dispatch* 15 December]

1944

Marshall Islands

The Marshall Islands, which consist of hundreds of coral atolls and islets scattered over some 400,000 square miles in the central Pacific, had been occupied by the Japanese army since 1941. After the capture of the Gilbert Islands in November 1943, the United States Army Air Force was able to launch air attacks on Japanese positions on the Marshall Islands, and in February US soldiers and Marines successfully took control of most of them. In the process, they came a step closer to their next target, the Philippines, and so to mainland Japan.
[GEORGE BUTTERWORTH *Daily Dispatch* 6 February]

Bayeux Tapestry of D-Day

Operation Overlord, the long-anticipated Allied invasion of Nazi-held Europe, was launched on 6 June with an invasion of the Normandy beaches by Allied troops. That night Churchill reported to the House of Commons that the operation was 'proceeding in a thoroughly satisfactory manner'.
[LESLIE ILLINGWORTH *Daily Mail* 9 June]

Another Job for the Home Guard

Moon's cartoon was drawn in response to Churchill's avoidance of a parliamentary question whether he was planning to visit France in the wake of the D-Day invasion. In fact, he had wanted to be present when the landings took place and was dissuaded only when King George VI said to him, 'Well, as long as you feel that it is desirable to go along, I think it is my duty to go along with you.' It was not until six days after D-Day that Churchill visited Normandy; four days later the king followed him. [SID MOON *Sunday Dispatch* 11 June]

Only the Nazis are Nasty

'As there is a Nazi flying bomb over at the moment we will adjourn to the basement to continue the discussion on how to be kind to Germany after the war.' D-Day prompted some premature rejoicing that the war was as good as won and discussion as to what attitude the victorious Allies should adopt towards the Germans. One strand of opinion was that it was important not to make the German people as a whole accountable for the crimes of the Nazis. Then on 13 June the first V1 rockets, or 'doodlebugs', were launched on southern England from German-occupied France and Holland. Almost 9,250 were aimed at London, but fewer than 2,500 reached their targets, British defences over time becoming adept at spotting and destroying them. [SID MOON *Sunday Dispatch* 23 June]

Well – Forever More!

Hitler had assumed complete command of the German army in December 1941. Stubborn and distrustful, he relied too much on his own instincts, and his meddling in military operations did much to hamper German efforts in the later stages of the war. [KIMON MARENGO 'Kem' *Daily Sketch* 13 June]

The Spinning Ball

On 16 December Field Marshal von Rundstedt launched a powerful counter-offensive in the wooded Ardennes region of southern Belgium, initially catching American forces off guard and making a significant 'bulge' in the Allied line. The German advance was eventually halted by reinforcements led by General Patton and by the fact that the German Panzers simply ran out of petrol. The 'Battle of the Bulge', as it became known, was the last German offensive of the war. [GEORGE WHITELAW *Daily Herald* 21 December]

1945

Unpublicised Ceremony in Germany

'The Nazi party welcome to the man who forgot to blow up the Remagen bridge.' The one major obstacle to the final Allied advance into Germany was the river Rhine. Capturing its bridges intact therefore became a major priority for the Allies, and in March American forces were able to take the Ludendorff railway bridge at Remagen following two abortive attempts by the Germans to blow it up. Its capture gave the Allies a crucial bridgehead on the eastern bank of the river. [SID MOON *Sunday Dispatch* 18 March]

Concentration Camps

As the invading Allies liberated the death camps of Belsen, Dachau and Buchenwald, the full horror of the atrocities inflicted on Europe's Jews became all too apparent. Here Vicky, who was himself Jewish and who had fled Hungary to escape the Nazis, seems slightly coy in using 'anti-fascists' to characterise the victims of Hitler's regime. [VICTOR WEISZ 'Vicky' *News Chronicle* 24 April]

Both Hands Up, Please

Following Hitler's suicide on 30 April, Stalin, Montgomery and Eisenhower awaited the final and unconditional surrender of Nazi Germany. This came two days after this cartoon appeared. [J C WALKER *News of the World* 6 May]

No, No, Not Yet

At the 1945 General Election, Churchill seemed to be the Conservative party's best weapon, and indeed he was cheered almost everywhere he went. However, the Conservative party itself was deeply unpopular, remembered for its appeasement of Hitler and its inability to deal with the high unemployment of the 1930s. Sid Moon, who was sympathetic to the Conservatives, fails to realise here that while the electorate were indeed cheering Churchill (at the top of the cartoon) they were about to vote against him. [SID MOON *Sunday Dispatch* 1 July]

The Bomb

This cartoon appeared the day the US dropped an atomic bomb on the Japanese city of Nagasaki, and three days after a similar device was dropped on Hiroshima. Japan surrendered on 15 August. [LESLIE ILLINGWORTH *Daily Mail* 9 August]

Press the Button. Doc ☞

New Labour Prime Minster Clement Attlee and Minister of Fuel and Power Manny Shinwell preside over the Labour government's nationalisation programme. Although the coal industry was nationalised in 1945, the steel industry was not nationalised until 1951 and was then denationalised by the Conservatives in 1953. [STEPHEN ROTH *Sunday Pictorial* 19 August]

But What's Your Programme?

The diminutive Lord Beaverbrook (far left) was Conservative party chairman and responsible for the party's rather negative election strategy. Rather than advance a Conservative programme, he attacked the Labour party, while Churchill for his part insinuated that the Labour leader, Clement Attlee, would, if elected, have to fall back on some form of Gestapo in order to create a socialist state. When the election results were eventually announced, they were not as expected. There was no victory for the man who had won the war, but instead a landslide victory for the Labour party. Harold Laski was chairman of the Labour party. [GEORGE WHITELAW *Daily Herald* 4 July]

The euphoria that accompanied the end of the Second World War did not last long. War with Germany was soon replaced by the Cold War with the Soviet Union. On the domestic front initial optimism about the Labour government's plans to build a 'New Jerusalem' crumbled as the US curtailed financial aid to its wartime ally, leaving Britain virtually bankrupt and facing shortages and rationing. Not surprisingly, therefore, the cartoons of the immediate post-war period were dominated by austerity at home and the spectre of war (even nuclear war) abroad.

One or two of the cartoonists who had made their names in the inter-war years were now starting to fade from sight. Sidney Strube, for example, who had been such a dominant figure for such a long time, was forced to retire from the *Daily Express* in 1948 after 36 years' continuous service. It broke his heart. The *Daily Mail*'s 'Poy' died in 1949, having retired ten years earlier. Even David Low was eclipsed for a while. In 1950, having been deliberately deprived of the space he had once commanded in the *Evening Standard*, he joined a newspaper more in tune with his own political sympathies, the Labour-backed *Daily Herald*. However, preaching to the converted did not really suit a man who thrived on being edgy and contentious, and it was not until he joined the *Manchester Guardian* three years later that his work recovered much of its old bite.

As for those cartoonists who had been asked to produce political cartoons as part of the war effort, they now generally found themselves surplus to requirements and took on different work. Arthur Potts was made redundant by the *Bristol Evening World* and in 1945 joined the *Daily Mail* to

Noel

The late 1940s and early 1950s were characterised by continued food rationing and shortages. It was to be several years before Britain recovered from the Second World War. [HAROLD HOAR 'Acanthus' *Daily Graphic* 18 December 1946]

1946–55

draw the 'Teddy Tail' strip (which had been running since 5 April 1915). In 1946 Zec stopped producing his own work when he became a director of the *Daily Mirror* with responsibility for its strip-cartoon department. Butterworth was forced to stop drawing political cartoons in early 1953 when a new editor at the *Daily Dispatch*, arguing that readers needed 'cheering up', insisted that he produce a strip based on the *Daily Express*'s highly successful 'Gambols'. Out of financial necessity Butterworth grudgingly agreed.

Of course, some well-established cartoonists continued to work throughout the 1950s, and new talent came in to swell their numbers. Jimmy Friell, discharged from the army in January 1946, was soon back at the communist *Daily Worker*, toeing the party line and depicting the Americans and the British as warmongers, the Russians as peace-lovers and the new West Germany as a potential Nazi state. Meanwhile, Victor Weisz (better known by his pseudonym 'Vicky'), who had fled from Hungary to escape the Nazis, was starting to win a following. He was greatly influenced by Low both politically and artistically, although, unlike Low, Vicky was a lifelong pacifist who was later to design the iconic CND logo. Recognising his talents, his editor at the *News Chronicle*, Gerald Barry, sent him on a crash course in English culture, winning him over to just about everything except cricket.

A new, rather more right-wing recruit to the cartoon ranks was the son of a former editor of the *News Chronicle*, Michael Cummings, who ironically got his first break in cartooning when Michael Foot employed him on the distinctly left-wing *Tribune*. Throughout the late 1940s Cummings tore into the Labour government with a vengeance, not even letting up when Labour was driven from government in late 1951. His editor at the *Daily Express* once commented: 'He reserves most of his venom for Labour leaders. Every day he submits five or six rough outlines, and I select the one which seems least cruel.'

In addition to charting Britain's years of austerity after the war, along with the Labour government's nationalisation programme and establishment of the welfare state, cartoonists inevitably focused on the unfolding of the Cold War: Churchill's speech in March 1946 warning of an 'iron curtain' that had descended across eastern Europe; Stalin's direct challenge to the West in 1948 when he blockaded West Berlin; and the detonation of the Soviet Union's first atomic bomb in 1949. Communism took on a global dimension in October 1949 when Mao Zedong's Red Army took power in China, and then in 1950 the Korean War broke out – the first major conflict with international implications since the Second World War. Given all this, and Senator Joseph McCarthy's communist witch-hunt in the US in the early 1950s, it is scarcely surprising that David Low should have described the decade as the 'Fearful Fifties'. 'On January the first 1950,' he wrote, 'we were fearful of the H-bomb, of the arms race, of spies, of communism, of Russia and the Chinese.'

The Years of Austerity

1946

'Old Glory' – or a New Shame?

In the wake of the Second World War came a severe food shortage throughout Europe. Britain even prepared to ration bread for the first time. Despite its involvement in the setting up of the International Monetary Fund and the World Bank at Bretton Woods in New Hampshire in July 1944, the United States did not at this stage offer financial help to alleviate Europe's post-war difficulties, hence Zec's critical cartoon. [PHILIP ZEC *Daily Mirror* 18 May]

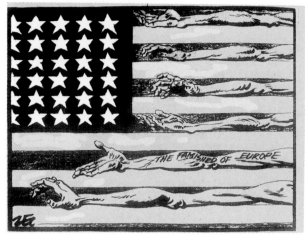

Bevan's Suit

Minister for Heath Aneurin Bevan's decision not to wear a dinner suit at a state banquet caused quite an outrage at the time. Over 50 years later Chancellor of the Exchequer Gordon Brown similarly refused to don formal evening wear at the annual Lord Mayor's banquet at the Mansion House. Both men opted instead for lounge suits. [SID MOON *Sunday Dispatch* 13 January]

Through which Needle's Eye?

Appalled at the wartime suffering of Europe's Jews, US President Truman put pressure on the British to allow some of the 250,000 displaced survivors of the Holocaust to settle in Palestine. The British refused, but because they were anxious to obtain a loan from America suggested setting up an Anglo-American Committee of Inquiry. On 30 April Truman publicly backed the committee's request for 100,000 refugees to be immediately allowed to enter Palestine. Britain, however, ignored the recommendation. As with many other cartoons from this period, newsprint from the next page is visible in the background: a sign of post-war austerity, since paper remained rationed and of poor quality for some time after 1945. [VICTOR WEISZ 'Vicky' *News Chronicle* 4 July]

Account Settled?

The Nuremburg trials of Nazi war criminals lasted until 1 October when eleven of the Nazi leaders were sentenced to death by hanging, and one – Martin Bormann – was sentenced to death *in absentia*. Hermann Goering committed suicide the day before the executions were due; the other ten were hanged in the early hours of Wednesday, 16 October. Zec's caption questions whether, given the enormity of their crimes, even the execution of these Nazi leaders could ever settle the 'account'. [PHILIP ZEC *Daily Mirror* 16 October]

Our Object All Sublime

Labour, under Clement Attlee, continued to carry out its election commitment to nationalise Britain's principal industries. The Bank of England was nationalised in 1946; then came Cable and Wireless Ltd (the dominant force in long-distance communications in Britain). The coal industry followed in 1947, railways in 1948, and iron and steel in 1949. There was little opposition to the nationalisation of coal and the railways, since neither had been profitable, but the nationalisation of iron and steel proved highly contentious. [HAROLD HOAR 'Acanthus' *Daily Graphic* 15 November]

Churchill and Russia

Vicky nicely summarises Churchill's attitude to Soviet Russia: hostility in the aftermath of the 1917 revolution, when Churchill had wanted the Allies to intervene on the side of the anti-Bolshevik White Armies; friendship in the wake of Germany's invasion of the Soviet Union in June 1941, when Churchill's hatred of Nazism made him prepared to befriend any country that would resist it ('if Hitler invaded Hell, then I would at least make a favourable reference to the Devil in the House of Commons'); hostility again by March 1946 when, in a speech at Fulton, Missouri, he warned the West that the Soviet Union's territorial ambitions had caused an 'iron curtain' to descend across eastern Europe. His speech heralded the beginning of the Cold War. [VICTOR WEISZ 'Vicky' *News Chronicle* 30 October]

1947

Division of Labour

A critical view of the Government's nationalisation programme, which, opponents said, seemed to need an ever larger army of bureaucrats to run it.
[OSBERT LANCASTER *Daily Express* 25 January]

Economic Blizzard

Between January and March the British Isles experienced one of its worst ever winters, with record low temperatures and persistent heavy snowfall. Coinciding with a serious fuel shortage, it caused Britain's economy to stall, and over 4 million workers were laid idle by power cuts.
[LESLIE ILLINGWORTH *Daily Mail* 7 February]

Freeway to the Marshall Plan

A West German poster welcoming the plan devised by US Secretary of State General George C Marshall to bring economic help to a Europe stricken by war. Billions of dollars in aid were given between 1948 and 1951 to 16 non-communist European countries, including Britain.

The Old Master

Despite Churchill's continued attacks on government bureaucracy, planning and controls, he did not appear to have an alternative programme to offer – at least in the eyes of those on the left, such as Vicky. [VICTOR WEISZ 'Vicky' *News Chronicle* 29 September]

Just Fancy, Kate

'This is where they make those crises and shortages.' Britain came close to bankruptcy in the immediate post-war period. Shown here is the House of Lords chamber, which had been taken over by MPs when the House of Commons was destroyed by a German bomb in May 1941. [SID MOON *Sunday Dispatch* 19 October]

Funnier than the Flicks

The House of Un-American Activities Committee (HUAC) had originally been established in 1937. In 1947 it began an investigation into the film industry and in September interviewed 41 people who were working in Hollywood. The president of the Screen Actors Guild, Ronald Reagan, warned of the dangers of a witch-hunt: 'I hope that we are never prompted by fear or resentment of communism into compromising any of our democratic principles in order to fight them.' [GEORGE WHITELAW *Daily Herald* 28 October]

1948

Blessed are the Peacemakers

In the wake of the end of British rule in India in 1947 came conflict between Hindus and Muslims and the creation of the separate state of Pakistan. Gandhi embarked on a fast to try to reconcile the two sides. Eleven days after this cartoon was published, he was assassinated by a fanatical Hindu who detested the tolerance he displayed towards Muslims. His murder caused such widespread revulsion that, ironically, it ushered in a period of stability. [VICTOR WEISZ 'Vicky' *News Chronicle* 19 January]

The National Health Service

'Even if it's not appendicitis, I think I'd rather have it out now before it's nationalised.' Vehemently opposed by the British Medical Association, which resented the prospect of seeing the medical profession lose its independence, the National Health Service came into being in July. Perhaps the Labour government's most radical reform, it offered free healthcare to all for the first time and free prescriptions. [OSBERT LANCASTER *Daily Express* 10 February]

Who's Next?

A severe labour shortage in post-war Britain led the Government to encourage immigration, and around 345,000 Germans, Italians, Ukrainians, Austrians and Poles were recruited through work permit schemes. When the supply of European labour proved insufficient, immigration from the fast-disappearing empire was encouraged. Under the British Nationality Act of 1948 workers from the colonies could migrate to Britain without restriction. The xenophobia on display here was fairly typical of the period. [SID MOON *Sunday Dispatch* 29 February]

There'll be Some Commotion this Side of the Ocean

'They can't blame us now – bless 'em all!' Following the establishment of the state of Israel and the end of the British mandate in Palestine on 15 May, the country was invaded by armies from Jordan, Egypt, Lebanon, Syria and Iraq. The war ended the following year with an Israeli victory. The cartoon's caption is an allusion to a popular Second World War song, 'The Long and the Short and the Tall', and strongly implies that Britain was relieved to be able to wash its hands of Palestine – British rule and policies had met with the approval of neither the Arabs nor the Jews. [SID MOON *Sunday Dispatch* 16 May]

That's the Third Tin of Corned Beef that's Dropped on Me this Week!

In June Stalin ordered East German troops to blockade Allied railway and road access to West Berlin in what was to become the first major crisis of the Cold War. The Berlin Blockade lasted until May the following year, during which time the Americans, British and French airlifted supplies of food and other provisions to the Western-held sectors of Berlin. [SID MOON *Sunday Dispatch* 4 July]

I'm Afraid of the Olympic Games. Some of Them will Cheat. Dagoes!

This cartoon derives its title from a speech made a few days before by a Church of England bishop in which he had suggested that while the British would never stoop so low as to cheat at the Olympics, being held that year at Wembley Stadium in London, foreign competitors might well do so (except, that is, for Germany and Japan – who were not invited). Vicky's version shows Foreign Secretary Ernest Bevin's struggles with various international problems. [VICTOR WEISZ 'Vicky' *News Chronicle* 17 June]

1949

Escorting Ernie to the Poll

Foreign Secretary Ernest Bevin had strongly resisted Zionist calls for the creation of a state of Israel, arguing that it would be 'carved out of Arab land by a foreign force, against the wishes and over the protests of the native population'. Winston Churchill, on the other hand, argued that the Labour government should recognise Israel's legitimacy as a sovereign state: 'They have a victorious army at their disposal and they have the support both of Soviet Russia and the United States. The government of Israel cannot be ignored and treated as if it did not exist.' Although the Attlee government survived a parliamentary vote of confidence on Palestine, 150 Labour MPs, including Crossman, Silverman and Stanley, joined the opposition or abstained. Four days after this cartoon appeared, Britain recognised the state of Israel. [DAVID LOW *Evening Standard* 25 January]

You Feed the Cow and I Milk it

Because of General Franco's sympathies for Germany and Italy during the Second World War, Spain found itself isolated in the post-war world. It was not included in the list of countries to benefit from the US Marshall Aid programme and, when NATO was founded, Spain was not invited to join. However, because of worsening relations with the Soviet Union, American Secretary of State Dean Acheson not only established diplomatic relations with Spain but also opened discussions on an American loan to help the struggling Spanish economy. [VICTOR WEISZ 'Vicky' *News Chronicle* 6 May]

I've Got it, Dickens, Old Boy!

When David Lean's film of *Oliver Twist* appeared, Alec Guinness's portrayal of Fagin evoked furious accusations of anti-Semitism in Britain and West Germany. Lean had used George Cruikshank's original illustrations to establish a look for Fagin, failing to appreciate that such a caricature would cause outrage in a world recently scarred by the Holocaust. The film was not shown in America until three years after its British release. In the cartoon film tycoon J Arthur Rank attempts to persuade Charles Dickens to adopt a less controversial Fagin. [DAVID LOW *Evening Standard* 24 February]

The Champ who won't Retire

The Labour government's determination to maintain existing strategic and military commitments created an imbalance of trade and an increasing shortage of dollars – the 'dollar gap'. Further rationing, an American loan and Stafford Cripps's reluctant devaluation of the pound helped to ease the situation a little, but the Prime Minister here looks distinctly the worse for wear. [VICTOR WEISZ 'Vicky' *News Chronicle* 10 August]

Magnificent View, isn't it?

'On a clear day one can see eight satellite town sites and 26 Regional Board Headquarters.'
To help deal with the chronic post-war inner-city housing problem, various New Towns were developed, the first eight of which (including Stevenage, Crawley and Hemel Hempstead) were in the London area. The idea was not initially welcomed by local people, who felt that their traditional way of life and communities were being taken away. [ALBERT EDGAR BEARD *Daily Graphic* 20 June]

We Have Stood Up

In September Mao Zedong's communist armies finally gained control of China, and on 1 October he proclaimed the establishment of a People's Republic. Speaking from the balcony overlooking the entrance to Beijing's imperial palace, he declared: 'The Chinese have always been a great, courageous and industrious nation; it is only in modern times that they have fallen behind. And that was due entirely to oppression and exploitation by foreign imperialism and domestic reactionary governments ... Ours will no longer be a nation subject to insult and humiliation. We have stood up.' [JIMMY FRIELL 'Gabriel' *Daily Worker* 26 September]

1950

⚜ Look Dear, There's the Third Man

Labour and the Conservatives entered the 1950 election campaign in good heart, both believing (unlike the Liberals) that they stood a good chance of winning. During the previous five years the Government had not lost a single by-election and the Tories had thoroughly revamped both their polices and grassroots organisation (not that the cartoonist here seems to think so). In the event Labour squeezed an election victory, while Clem Davies's Liberals were virtually wiped out, taking only nine seats. Rodger's pre-election cartoon was inspired by Carol Reed's internationally successful film *The Third Man*, which had appeared the previous year. [RODGER *People* 5 February]

Now is the Time for All Good Men to Come to the Aid of the Party

Despite having gained more votes than in 1945, Labour was left with a Commons majority of just five seats after the General Election. Many of the cabinet, such as Foreign Secretary Bevin and Chancellor Cripps who had been in office since the beginning of the war, were now in poor health and would soon be forced to resign. Even Attlee's health was beginning to deteriorate. Herbert Morrison, leader of the House of Commons, was responsible for making sure that Labour did not lose any votes in the Commons. [VICTOR WEISZ 'Vicky' *News Chronicle* 19 September]

The Missing Spy

'Oh dear! Here's that bloke from MI5 again to ask if his missing atom scientist has turned up yet.' Bruno Pontecorvo, a scientist working on Britain's atomic bomb project, fled to the Soviet Union while on holiday in Italy. Coming in the wake of the arrest and imprisonment of his colleague Klaus Fuchs, convicted of passing atomic secrets to the Russians, his abrupt disappearance caused considerable embarrassment to the British government and security services. [JOSEPH LEE *Evening News* 30 October]

History Doesn't Repeat Itself

On 25 June the North Koreans, with the tacit approval of the Soviet Union, unleashed a surprise attack on South Korea. The United Nations Security Council met in emergency session and passed a resolution calling for the assistance of all UN members in halting the North Korean invasion. As the Soviet Union was boycotting the Security Council at the time, it was unable to veto this decision. On 27 June President Truman, without asking Congress to declare war, ordered United States forces to come to the assistance of South Korea as part of the UN police action. Low, mindful of the fate of the ineffectual pre-war League of Nations, shows here his belief that Truman, for one, had learned the lessons of the past. [DAVID LOW *Daily Herald* 30 June]

Chinese Willow Pattern

In November China entered the Korean War, pushing the UN forces back beyond the 38th parallel. The following year, the UN forces turned the tide, but the war dragged on until 1953. Here Stalin opens the gate to Chinese forces. [SID MOON *Sunday Dispatch* 11 February]

1951

Sweeney Attlee, the Demon Barber of Westminster

The last industry to be nationalised by the Labour government of 1945–51 was iron and steel. The move was strenuously resisted by the Conservative-dominated House of Lords and met with considerable opposition even from within Labour's own ranks, not least from within the cabinet. [SID MOON *Sunday Dispatch* 11 February]

The Festival of Britain

'Well, Persia's taken the oil, Egypt wants the Sudan, and Cuba wants the Havana railway – what say we claim the Festival of Britain?' The Festival of Britain, on London's South Bank, was the brain-child of Gerald Reid Barry and the Labour deputy leader Herbert Morrison, who described it as 'a tonic for the nation'. Here, Stalin and his hench-men look across the Thames to the Royal Festival Hall, the Skylon and the Dome of Discovery, while commenting on Britain's struggles to cope with various international problems. Herbert Morrison became Foreign Secretary in March and proved totally ineffectual, later joking: 'Foreign policy would be OK except for the bloody foreigners'. [SID MOON *Sunday Dispatch* 6 May]

Bevan through the Looking-glass

On 21 April Aneurin Bevan resigned as Minister of Labour, along with Harold Wilson and John Freeman, when Hugh Gaitskell, the Chancellor of the Exchequer, announced that he intended to introduce charges for dentures, spectacles and prescriptions. (Defence spending – and the Korean War – lay behind the need to raise extra revenue.) Bevan's decision to resign was strongly criticised by deputy Labour leader, Herbert Morrison, who disliked Bevan and felt that his move would damage a government that had only a small major-ity in the House of Commons. [LESLIE ILLINGWORTH *Daily Mail* 25 April]

132

You Have Been Warned

By 1951 the Labour government, having carried out most of its 1945 manifesto promises, had run out of steam. However, its attacks on what it regarded as a warmongering Conservative party and its reminders of the Tories' record on unemployment ensured that by polling day the Conservative lead in the opinion polls had dropped to just 2.5%. Accusations of warmongering were very apparent in the left-leaning *Daily Mirror*, one of whose headlines, 'Whose Finger is on the Trigger', so infuriated Churchill that he later sued the paper; criticism of the Conservatives' record on social policies lie at the heart of this cartoon by David Low (now working for the Labour-backed *Daily Herald*), which appeared on polling day. [DAVID LOW *Daily Herald* 25 October]

As Jon Sees it

Labour stalwarts Attlee, Morrison and Shinwell are depicted as sheep, while Iranian Prime Minister Mohammad Mosaddeq and King Farouk of Egypt remove Nelson from his column, replacing him with the Sphinx. King Farouk was not only demanding British withdrawal from Sudan but also denounced the 1936 treaty that defined British rights in the Suez Canal zone. In Iran Mosaddeq had just nationalised the British-owned oil industry against Britain's wishes. In the course of the 1951 election, called by Attlee in an attempt to increase his majority, the Conservative opposition made much of the Government's record on foreign affairs, claiming it damaged British prestige in the Middle East. [WILLIAM JONES 'Jon' *Daily Graphic* 15 October]

Power Politician

John Foster Dulles, a consultant to US Secretary of State Dean Acheson, believed America should control Soviet ambitions by threatening massive retaliation in the event of a war, and in 1950 he published *War or Peace*, which criticised the then favoured – and less aggressive – policy of containment. In 1953 he was appointed Secretary of State by the new president, Dwight D Eisenhower. Dulles's critics would later accuse him of being inflexible, arguing that his 'brinkmanship' raised international tensions. [JIMMY FRIELL 'Gabriel' *Daily Worker* 24 November]

As Jon Sees it

Despite polling fewer votes than the Labour party, the Conservatives won the election with an overall majority of 17. Churchill, now back in office at the age of 77, committed himself to championing private enterprise, ending austerity and, above all, increasing British prestige abroad. Jon therefore restores Nelson's Column, which he had rearranged in cartoon form less than two weeks before. [WILLIAM JONES 'Jon' *Daily Graphic* 27 October]

1952

What Names Would You Add to Those who Inherit the Nation's High Honours?

George VI died on 6 February, and his daughter succeeded to the throne as Elizabeth II. With rationing having ended and the British economy showing signs of revival, many commentators optimistically heralded the dawn of a new Elizabethan age. In this snapshot view of the great and the good of the early 1950s are (from left to right): actors Gielgud, Olivier and Evans; artists Moore and Sutherland; dancer Fonteyn; scientists Watson-Watt (radar), Whittle (jet) and Fleming (penicillin); engineer Nuffield; (on the queen's right) economist Beveridge; Archbishop of Canterbury; Churchill; Admiral Vian; Lord Chancellor; military leaders Dowding and Montgomery; historian Trevelyan; writers Fry and Eliot; pianist Hess; composers Britten and Vaughan Williams. [MICHAEL CUMMINGS *Daily Express* 11 February]

Attention! Eyes Right

In March Aneurin Bevan initiated a split within the Labour party between the right and the left after he and 57 fellow MPs defied the party whips on a defence vote. The 'Bevanites' criticised the high cost of rearmament, especially the expenditure on nuclear weapons. [VICTOR WEISZ 'Vicky' *News Chronicle* 21 March]

Further Outlook: Continuing Cold

On 29 March, while Britain was experiencing blizzard conditions, President Truman, having lost the New Hampshire primary, announced that he would not stand for re-election as US president. In Vicky's view, this left two snowmen in the Cold War – Churchill and Stalin. [VICTOR WEISZ 'Vicky' *News Chronicle* 31 March]

Infant in Peril

On 21 October British troops were flown to Kenya to deal with an insurgency by Kenyan rebels against the British colonial administration – the Mau Mau uprising. It did not succeed militarily, but did cause considerable loss of life and created a rift between the white settler community in Kenya and the Home Office in London. Kenyan independence followed in 1963. [LESLIE ILLINGWORTH *Daily Mail* 22 October]

Coronation Television

Public opinion was such that the Government decided that the following year's coronation of Elizabeth II in Westminster Abbey should be televised. Churchill, however, made it clear that the BBC would be allowed to show only the congregation's view of the ceremony and would not be permitted any close-ups. He explained: 'The congregation in the Abbey does not see all the ceremony. Much of it is restricted to dignitaries of Church and State who are close to the Sovereign.' [DAVID LOW *Daily Herald* 31 October]

Vote for Ike

On 5 November Dwight D Eisenhower, having campaigned on a promise to bring an end to the Korean War, defeated his Democratic challenger, Adlai E Stevenson, to become the 34th president of the United States. With the support of President Truman, he flew to Korea two weeks later on a fact-finding mission. [MICHAEL CUMMINGS *Daily Express* 6 November]

1953

Churchill Visits America

'Say, boss, I'm kinda suspicious of dis guy, he says he knows Joe Stalin!' In January, before the presidential inauguration, Churchill flew to New York to tell Eisenhower that he was thinking of setting up a meeting with Stalin. The McCarran Immigration Act referred to here was passed in 1950 and stipulated that all 'subversives' at large in the US should be registered and fingerprinted. It also authorised the establishment of concentration camps 'for emergency situations'. [SID MOON *Sunday Dispatch* 4 January]

The Condemned Cell

Julius and Ethel Rosenberg were American communists who had been found guilty of passing nuclear weapons secrets to the Soviet Union and were sentenced to death. Despite several appeals and a worldwide campaign for mercy, they were executed at Sing Sing prison in New York on 19 June 1953, the only American civilians ever executed for espionage. [JIMMY FRIELL 'Gabriel' *Daily Worker* 13 January]

The Doctors' Plot

'Frankly, I think the hammer and sickle are the only safe things to use at the moment!' On 13 January the Soviet press announced the uncovering of a 'conspiracy' by prominent medical specialists to murder leading government and party officials. Nine doctors, at least six of them Jews, had been arrested and had reportedly confessed their guilt. The Doctors' Plot, as it became known, marked the culmination of state-sponsored anti-Semitism under Stalin. After his death in March *Pravda* announced that the charges had been false and the doctors' confessions obtained by torture. Stalin's successor Nikita Khrushchev asserted that Stalin had intended to use the doctors' trial to launch a massive party purge. [SID MOON *Sunday Dispatch* 18 January]

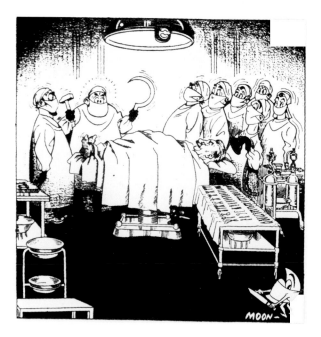

God Save the People!

On the day this cartoon was published, Queen Elizabeth II was crowned in Westminster Abbey in London. Gabriel was less than impressed. [JIMMY FRIELL 'Gabriel' *Daily Worker* 2 June]

Suez Styles

Under pressure from the Egyptian government, Foreign Secretary Anthony Eden had agreed to withdraw British troops from the Suez Canal and, in so doing, had incurred the wrath of a number of Conservative backbenchers, led by Julian Amery and Enoch Powell, known as the Suez Group. 'There could be no solution of the Egyptian problem,' said Amery, 'which endangered the security of the Middle East.' Churchill found himself in a quandary, sympathetic to both sides. Amery and Colonel Blimp are seen measuring Churchill up for his uniform. [DAVID LOW *Manchester Guardian* 18 November]

Down to Earth

The cartoonist Vicky, decked with coronation flags, returns from holiday and surveys the year's events: the ascent of Everest (conquered by Edmund Hillary and Tenzing Norgay on 29 May); the continuing anti-communist witch-hunts of Senator McCarthy in the US; and, in particular, the continuing Korean crisis. South Korean President Syngman Rhee, seen here with Churchill and Eisenhower, had made it clear that he opposed any truce that would leave Korea divided. He proceeded to sabotage a possible armistice by releasing more than 24,000 North Korean anti-communist prisoners as a protest and prepared to pressgang them into the South Korean army. Eisenhower and Churchill feared this would make a peaceful settlement impossible, but a ceasefire was eventually established on 27 July. [VICTOR WEISZ 'Vicky' *News Chronicle* 9 June]

1954

The Right to Hee-Haw

'Those in the artistic vanguard may chide us undeveloped morons for our failure to appreciate "modern art", but let them not try to prohibit our innocent merriment at it.' A recurrent theme in the history of modern art. [DAVID LOW *Manchester Guardian* 16 March]

The Nyeti

The ideological division between East and West became only too apparent when foreign ministers from Russia, the USA, Britain and France met in Berlin to discuss the possibility of free elections in a re-united Germany. While Britain's Anthony Eden proposed free elections in East and West Germany for an all-German government, Molotov, Soviet minister of foreign affairs, sought to give legitimacy to the unelected East German government by insisting on forming a government before any elections took place. The Yeti references in the cartoon reflect the fascination with this supposed ape-like creature that accompanied the exploration of the Himalayas and the conquest of Mount Everest in the 1950s. [LESLIE ILLINGWORTH *Daily Mail* 27 January]

It's All Right

'It's only Old Joe's candy-floss machine got out of control!' On 1 March the USA tested a hydrogen bomb in the Bikini Atoll. Up to 1,000 times more powerful than the atomic bomb that had destroyed Hiroshima, it overwhelmed measuring instruments and vaporised one of the atolls, creating a gigantic mushroom cloud that spread at least 100 miles (160 km) wide and dropped back to the sea in the form of radioactive fall-out. [SID MOON *Sunday Dispatch* 18 April]

Someone Talking about Me?

In 1946 a struggle had begun in Indo-China to overthrow French rule, and it culminated in the fall of Dien Bien Phu to the communist Viet Minh on 7 May after a 55-day siege. The defeat signalled the end of French rule in Indo-China and, following an agreement reached in Geneva in July, the division of Vietnam along the line of the 17th parallel. Ho Chi Minh's communists now controlled the North, while Bao Dai's regime was granted the South. [JIMMY FRIELL 'Gabriel' *Daily Worker* 19 May]

A Fourpenny Fig Leaf

A critical left-wing view of the decision by the Labour opposition to support German rearmament during the Cold War. Clement Attlee, shown here brandishing a pamphlet, had hoped – in vain – for a less emotional response. [JIMMY FRIELL 'Gabriel' *Daily Worker* 21 June]

Smog!

Smog was a major health hazard, particularly in London. One 'pea souper' in December 1952 brought the capital to a standstill for five days and caused the deaths of around 12,000 people. Two years after this cartoon appeared the first Clean Air Act was passed, authorising local councils to set up smokeless zones and make grants to householders to enable them to convert their homes from traditional coal fires to heaters fuelled by gas, oil, smokeless coal or electricity. [JOSEPH LEE *Evening News* 22 November]

1955

You Really Must not be Led Away by All the Chatter in the Press

Aged 80, an increasingly frail Churchill resigned as Prime Minister. Ironically, this occurred during a newspaper strike in London, and so caused little immediate comment. In the view of David Low, 'Churchill had governed too long, but the British people still revered him as the man whose spirit saved them from the Nazis. As he tiptoed out of office he could reflect that his monument lay all around him.' The cartoon caption quotes from a statement made by Churchill on 22 March, dismissing rumours of his impending resignation. [VICTOR WEISZ 'Vicky' *Daily Mirror* 9 April]

Labour vs Conservative: Into Battle

As expected, Anthony Eden succeeded Churchill as Prime Minister and immediately called a General Election. Eden had plenty of reasons to be optimistic. Wartime rationing was over, the Government's house-building programme was running ahead of target, Chancellor 'Rab' Butler had just passed a tax-cutting budget and the Labour party was in disarray. The election campaign of 1955 was singularly uneventful. One journalist described its early stages as 'the lull before the lull'. [DAVID LOW *London Illustrated* 28 May]

Monday Morning at No. 10

After his election victory Anthony Eden faced growing difficulties both at home and abroad. Illingworth lists several here: economic problems (not helped by the Chancellor's poor handling of the economy), demonstrations against British rule in Cyprus and the admission by the Foreign Office that Burgess and Maclean, who had fled from Britain in 1951, were spies. As problems crowded in on him Eden was increasingly perceived as weak and indecisive, the 'firm smack of Government', as the *Daily Telegraph* put it, clearly being lacking in his administration. [LESLIE ILLINGWORTH *Daily Mail* 17 October]

The US Takes over the World

Friell shows the commonly held far-left Cold War view of the Americans as militaristic warmongers attempting to destroy the peace-loving communist states of the Soviet Union and China so that they can dominate the world.
[JIMMY FRIELL 'Gabriel' *Daily Worker* 12 January]

Here We Go Again

A year after the Americans tested a hydrogen bomb on the Bikini Atoll, the Soviet Union followed suit, on 22 November. Here the Russians face Eden and Eisenhower. [VICTOR WEISZ 'Vicky' *Daily Mirror* 29 November]

Labour Leaders

On 7 December Clement Attlee retired as leader of the Labour party. Deputy leader Herbert Morrison, considered by some as too old at 67, stood against Hugh Gaitskell and Aneurin Bevan. Illingworth obviously thought Gaitskell the clear favourite to win the leadership, and, in fact, on the day this cartoon was published he won easily, gaining 157 votes in the ballot of Labour MPs. Bevan and Morrison received only 70 and 30 votes respectively.
[LESLIE ILLINGWORTH *Daily Mail* 14 December]

As the 1950s progressed, the British economy started to recover. Rationing finally came to an end, unemployment levels remained low and there was relatively little industrial tension. Soon a boom in consumer goods took hold, helped by a relaxation on credit and reflected in a sharp rise in the sales of television sets and the arrival of commercial television in 1955.

Politically, the decade was dominated by the Conservatives, who had won the 1951 election and who were to remain continuously in power until 1964. Moderate in tone, they decided to retain many of the changes initiated by the previous Labour administration, including the welfare state and most of Labour's nationalisation programme, and despite the debacle of the Suez crisis in 1956 they proved popular, increasing their majority at two consecutive General Elections in 1955 and 1959.

Their success posed a real challenge to the Labour party and to cartoonists sympathetic to it. Labour became split between 'modernisers' on the right and full-blooded socialists on the left, while their cartoonist supporters, such as Low and Vicky, found themselves having to deal with party in-fighting and simultaneously struggling to find suitable Conservative targets. Vicky's attempt to lampoon Harold Macmillan as 'Supermac', for example, actually backfired and served to increase the Prime Minister's prestige. That said, there were still plenty of targets for left-leaning cartoonists, including the growing spectre of racism in Britain following the arrival of immigrants from the West Indies and the continuing Cold War.

Meanwhile, on the communist fringes of the left Jimmy Friell ('Gabriel') faced a major dilemma when in November 1956 the *Daily Worker* refused to publish his cartoon criticising the Soviet invasion of Hungary. He chose to resign

Vicky vs Harold Macmillan
Vicky sits at his desk, plotting ridicule for Conservative Prime Minister Harold Macmillan. [VICTOR WEISZ 'Vicky' *Evening Standard* 30 October 1958]

but found that his 'extreme' left-wing views made him less than attractive to other newspapers. After being unemployed for six months, he accepted Lord Beaverbrook's offer to work for the *Evening Standard*, where his cartoons appeared under his own name: he had told his former *Daily Worker* colleagues that he would never use the pseudonym 'Gabriel' in another paper. He was, after all, starting a new life.

In the 1950s Vicky's career changed direction several times. In 1954, after a number of his cartoons had been rejected, he left the *News Chronicle* to join the *Daily Mirror*.

1956–64

He soon regretted the move, however, feeling that no one in political circles read the *Daily Mirror* and believing that his style did not fit in with the *Mirror*'s glaring headlines. When his contract ended in 1958 he replaced Friell at the *Evening Standard*. Here, like David Low before him, he was in his element, his contentious and innovative cartoons gaining a wide following while simultaneously antagonising readers sympathetic to the Conservative party. However, as cartoonist Stanley Franklin said, his move did not bring with it the greater political leverage he craved. 'He really wanted to use the cartoon to change the world, to try and engineer opinions,' Franklin recalled, 'but even he had to admit in the end that he had failed … He hoped he would have an influence over the more informed members of the Labour party who did read the *Standard*. But he had none.' In 1964 Lord Beaverbrook attempted to replace Vicky, still at the height of his popularity, with the *Toronto Star* cartoonist Duncan Macpherson. Macpherson, though, turned the job down.

As for Stanley Franklin, he was Vicky's replacement at the *Daily Mirror*. He had first applied for a political cartooning job on the *Evening Standard* after leaving school in 1944, when he 14 years old, only to be informed that 'a chap called David Low already held the post and intended keeping it'. When he arrived at the *Mirror* in 1959 he was asked to adopt a lighter tone and more humorous approach than his predecessor, and he soon found himself reaching a huge audience as sales of the *Mirror* soared. Another major talent to arrive on the scene was John Musgrave-Wood ('Emmwood'), who joined the *Daily Mail* in 1956 as deputy political cartoonist to Leslie Illingworth. The two men made a formidable team, more than matching their rivals Carl Giles and Michael Cummings at the *Daily Express*.

The 1950s may have been the decade of the Conservatives, but by the early 1960s things were starting to go wrong for them. As Britain's rate of social change gathered momentum Prime Minister Harold Macmillan began to seem complacent – an old Etonian aristocrat out of touch with the present. Growing economic difficulties, a panicked decision to sack a third of his cabinet in one fell swoop in 1962 and the scandal over the Profumo affair in 1963 fatally undermined Macmillan and his party. As they went into the 1964 election, now with old Etonian Alec Douglas-Home as leader, they faced a major challenge from a resurgent Labour party led by Harold Wilson.

'You've Never Had it So Good'

1956

No More Personality Cult ♟

'And now, comrades, let us stand in silence for two minutes in memory of all those comrades who criticised comrade Stalin while he was alive.' Nikita Khrushchev finally became Soviet leader following two years of 'collective leadership' after Stalin's death in March 1953. In a speech at the Twentieth Congress of the Communist Party he shocked his audience by bitterly attacking Stalin's rule, exposing its excesses and mistakes and accusing Stalin of 'flagrant abuses of power and brutality for the mass arrests [the purges] which caused tremendous harm to our country and to the cause of socialist progress.' He announced a change in policy and gave orders for the Soviet Union's political prisoners to be released. [VICTOR WEISZ 'Vicky' *Daily Mirror* 20 March]

The Missing Diver

'Quick, Selwyn – two hon. membership cards for the Tory party, and a couple of freedoms of the Carlton Club.' In April Soviet leaders Khrushchev and Bulganin arrived in Britain on a goodwill visit on the Soviet cruiser *Ordzhonikidze*. While their ship was moored in Portsmouth harbour, a former Royal Navy frogman, Commander Lionel 'Buster' Crabb, was instructed by MI6 to examine the ship's special anti-sonar equipment and mine-laying hatches. He disappeared during the mission. On 9 June a body in a frogman's suit was found floating in the sea nearby and, although missing its head and hands, was judged to be that of Crabb. The incident did little for Anglo-Soviet relations, which had in any case been strained throughout the visit – at a dinner organised by the Labour party (whose leader, Gaitskell, is shown here holding a mine), Khrushchev had an altercation with shadow cabinet minister George Brown and reportedly said afterwards that if he lived in Britain he would vote Conservative. Shown on deck is Conservative Foreign Secretary Selwyn Lloyd. [MICHAEL CUMMINGS *Daily Express* 14 May]

Egyptian Mirage

In July, after the US and Britain had turned down President Nasser of Egypt's request for a loan to fund the building of the Aswan Dam, he nationalised the Suez Canal, saying that he would use the revenue raised to help finance the dam. Britain and France, determined to regain control of the canal, hatched a secret plan with Israel whereby Israel would invade Egypt and an Anglo-French force would then intervene to 'restore' peace. Israel duly invaded Egypt on 29 October, and the British and French then moved in, swiftly achieving all their early military objectives. [NEVILLE COLVIN *Daily Sketch* 7 November]

Yah! You're an Aggressor

On 23 October the Hungarian people began a revolt against the pro-Soviet regime in Budapest. On 4 November, taking advantage of international disunity over the Suez crisis, Khrushchev sent Russian tanks and troops to Hungary. The uprising was crushed, and many Hungarians lost their lives. When the *Daily Worker* refused to publish this cartoon because it equated Russian actions in Hungary with French and British actions in Suez, Friell resigned. 'I couldn't conceive carrying on cartooning about the evils of capitalism and imperialism,' Friell later wrote, 'and ignoring the acknowledged evils of Russian communism.' [JIMMY FRIELL 'Gabriel' *Daily Worker* (unpublished)]

Petrol Prospects

Although the British government denied collusion with Israel over Suez, it soon became apparent that some sort of deal had been done. Here an angry President Eisenhower confronts the leader of the House of Commons, 'Rab' Butler, French premier Guy Mollett and Israeli Prime Minister David Ben Gurion. [DAVID LOW *Manchester Guardian* 23 November]

Anglo-American Rift

'I heard that things were so strained at one time that the Yanks threatened to withhold supplies of Elvis Presley … Johnny Ray… Roberto Brassie …' Eisenhower was furious with the British for having kept the US in the dark over the Suez invasion, particularly as it came at a time when he was campaigning for re-election. Pressure from the US – including a threatened run on the pound – ultimately forced the withdrawal of the Anglo-French force. In Britain, the crisis divided public opinion and ultimately precipitated Anthony Eden's resignation as Prime Minister. [JOSEPH LEE *Evening News* 3 December]

1957

The Shame of Little Rock

'Education, yeah? This'll teach you that I'm a supe-
rior human being!' The governor of Arkansas had
refused to accept a 1954 ruling by the US Supreme
Court that segregated schools were unconstitutional and used state troops to stop nine black children
attending the all-white high school at Little Rock.
On 23 September the children managed to gain
access by a delivery entrance, sparking a riot
outside the school among white segregation-
ists. When another mob turned up at the school
the following day President Eisenhower was
forced to send in 1,100 paratroopers to establish
law and order. [VICTOR WEISZ 'Vicky' *Daily Mirror*
25 September]

Marx and Spencer

New Labour leader Hugh Gaitskell (shown here
reading the *Financial Times*), along with his
shadow Chancellor Harold Wilson, set out to
reform the Labour party. By 1959 he was seeking to
repeal Clause IV of its constitution, which committed the party to wholesale public ownership.
The issue proved hugely divisive, however, and
Gaitskell was unable to push the change through.
[VICTOR WEISZ 'Vicky' *Daily Mirror* 3 October]

⚑ De-Flagged

'Er … with or without the Union Jack?' A case
of history repeating itself. In the aftermath of
the Suez debacle of the previous year, British
European Airways (BEA) decided to drop the
Union Jack from all its aircraft. There was a public
outcry, and the decision was reversed. Forty years
later British Airways (BEA and BOAC had become
British Airways in 1974) also removed the Union
Jack from its aircraft, replacing it with art from
the many countries that BA served. A less than
impressed Prime Minister Margaret Thatcher
famously draped a handkerchief over the design
on a model plane, and, in the wake of another
public outcry, BA reinstated the Union Jack.
[SID MOON *Sunday Dispatch* 9 June]

The Brighton Bucks

'Stop nagging, d-d-dear! I keep telling you that you've never had it so good!' At a Conservative rally in Bedford in July Harold Macmillan, who had taken over as Prime Minister in January when Anthony Eden resigned, had optimistically proclaimed 'most of our people have never had it so good' (often quoted as 'you've never had it so good'). Accusations of complacency followed – picked up here by Vicky in a cartoon drawn at the time of the Brighton Conservative party conference. In fairness to Macmillan, it should be noted that he had actually added the warning: 'What is beginning to worry some of us is … "Is it too good to last?"'
[VICTOR WEISZ 'Vicky' *Daily Mirror* 10 October]

Curly

This cartoon appeared on the day that Laika (a dog previously named Kudryavka, Russian for Little Curly) became the first mammal to be launched into space. The dog died a few hours after launch, causing a storm of protest from animal lovers and a riposte from Moscow Radio: 'We in Russia love dogs, too, but the dog in space is a real hero.' The experiment proved that it was possible to survive in space; a year later two monkeys became the first animals actually to survive a space flight.
[LESLIE ILLINGWORTH *Daily Mail* 4 November]

Anything You Can Do

Soviet successes in space, including the launch of a second satellite, Sputnik 2, on 3 November, prompted the US to compete with the launch of its own satellite aboard a Vanguard rocket (the first US rocket programme not to be tied to a weapons system). In the event, though, the mission proved a humiliating disaster – the rocket exploded a few seconds after lift-off on 6 December.
[JOHN MUSGRAVE-WOOD 'Emmwood' *Daily Mail* 9 November]

1958

Soccer Mourns

On 6 February a British European Airways flight crashed in a blizzard on its third attempt to take off from an icy runway at the Munich-Riem airport in Germany. On board was the Manchester United football team. Nicknamed the Busby Babes, in reference to their manager Matt Busby and their unusually low average age, they had been flying home from Belgrade after their European Cup match against Red Star Belgrade, and the plane had made a scheduled stop in Munich to refuel. Twenty-three of the 43 passengers on board died in the disaster, including seven members of the squad. [ROY ULLYETT *Daily Express* 7 February]

Don't Care who You are

'You'll carry your rifle the same way as everyone else!' Elvis Presley, the unchallenged king of rock 'n' roll, with nine US chart-topping hits in less than two years, arrived at the draft board office in Memphis on 24 March to start his two-year national service in the army. His unit, the 1st Battalion, US 32nd Armored Regiment, was posted to Ray Barracks, Friedberg, Germany, and while serving there, Presley met his wife-to-be, the 14-year-old Priscilla Beaulieu. [KEITH WAITE *Daily Sketch* 25 March]

They're Quite Right, You Know

'Before the H-bomb we *always* had good weather at Easter.' On the day this cartoon was published 3,000 anti-H-bomb demonstrators arrived at Aldermaston after a three-day march from London. Twelve thousand supporters of the new Campaign for Nuclear Disarmament then attended the final rally at the gates of the Atomic Weapons Research Establishment at Aldermaston. Vicky the cartoonist was responsible for designing the famous CND symbol. [LESLIE ILLINGWORTH *Daily Mail* 7 April]

Oh, No, Not Another Man of Destiny!

Conflict between Algerian separatists and French settlers threatened to bring civil war to a France divided between those who wanted to retain the French colony and those who wanted to see it become independent. Consequently, in an attempt to bring stability to the country, Charles de Gaulle was invited, some twelve years after he had previously relinquished power, to become premier (replacing Pflimlin, shown here) and to form a new government. He demanded special powers for at least six months to restore order and unity, pledging to draft a new constitution for a Fifth Republic and to submit it to the people in a referendum. [JIMMY FRIELL *Evening Standard* 27 May]

Accelerator ... Brakes ... Accelerator – and Look, No Hands!

Vicky created Supermac to ridicule Harold Macmillan – and this cartoon is the character's second outing. Here he sits alongside Chancellor of the Exchequer Heathcoat Amory. Despite the affluence felt by many Britons at the time, the Government's stop-go economic policies came under fire from the opposition. Ironically, Vicky's Supermac figure actually enhanced the public's perception of the Prime Minister. [VICTOR WEISZ 'Vicky' *Evening Standard* 7 November]

Just Ignore that Move – it's Only One of His Pawns

Khrushchev demanded a formal German peace treaty that would enshrine the principle of a permanently divided Germany and the transformation of West Berlin into a 'demilitarised free city'. He also said that if changes were not brought about within six months, the Soviet Union would feel obliged to seek an independent solution. 'Get out of Berlin or be kicked out,' Khrushchev bluntly told the West. Walter Ulbricht, the pawn in Khrushchev's hand, was the East German communist leader. [VICTOR WEISZ 'Vicky' *Evening Standard* 28 December]

1959

They Just ain't Civilised
– Like We are …!

Racial tensions in Notting Hill Gate, west London, had spilled over into rioting after white youths had taunted black residents with racist slogans. On 17 May a 32-year-old Antiguan carpenter, Kelso Cochrane, was set upon by six white youths in Notting Hill Gate, knifed and left to die in the street. Witnesses came forward with names, but no one was ever prosecuted. The attack caused widespread revulsion. [VICTOR WEISZ 'Vicky' *Evening Standard* 19 May]

The Deterrent that Doesn't Work

Six men were hanged in 1959, including Ronald Marwood, aged 25, who had stabbed a policeman while drunk, and Michael Tatum, aged 24. In Zec's view, though, hanging was not an effective deterrent – as the mention of 'Jamaican knifed by thugs' (a reference to the murder of Kelso Cochrane) makes clear. The death penalty for murder was not abolished until 1965. [PHILIP ZEC *Daily Herald* 21 May]

Just One Big Happy Family

The Morris Mini Minor was launched in August to great reviews from the motoring press, which were impressed by Alec Issigonis's stylish and affordable design. Sales were sluggish at first but picked up in the 1960s, stimulated by the Mini's popularity with film and music stars, such as Peter Sellers and the Beatles. Franklin's cartoon was not the first – nor the last – to express worries about road congestion. [STANLEY FRANKLIN *Daily Mirror* 4 September]

I Intend to Remain Entirely Unflappable

Harold Macmillan had a reputation for calmness and kept a placard in his office in 10 Downing Street that read 'Calm cool deliberation disentangles every knot'. (He admitted to his wife, though, that that he was always terrified before Prime Minister's question time.) He also had a reputation for being able to find time to enjoy himself – pheasant and grouse shooting being one of his favourite pastimes. [GEORGE CHRYSTAL 'Chrys' *Daily Mail* 13 August]

I've Never Had it So Good

Macmillian had come to power in the wake of the disastrous Suez crisis, but soon restored the Conservatives' fortunes, taking them from being 13 points behind Labour in the opinion polls to seven points ahead immediately before the 1959 General Election. After years of post-war austerity, many Britons now found themselves able to afford such consumer durables as televisions, washing machines, cars and fridges for the first time, and so, not surprisingly, Macmillan focused on the economy in his election campaign. He also sought to make political capital from President Eisenhower's visit to Britain in August. At the election the Conservatives increased their majority. [FRANK BROWN 'Eccles' *Daily Worker* 1 September]

Opening the M1

'Its 'ousmaid's elbow … salutin' every thirty seconds at 120 flippin' miles an 'our.' The M1, Britain's first substantial motorway, was officially opened on 2 November 1959 by the Minister for Transport Ernest Marples. He described it as a 'magnificent motorway opening up a new era in road travel, in keeping with the new, exciting, scientific age in which we live.' In the early days there was no speed limit, no central reservation, no crash barriers and no motorway lighting. A mere 13,000 vehicles were estimated to use the M1 on a daily basis in 1959 compared with today's figure of just over 88,000. AA and RAC men were expected to salute members who had a badge on the front of their cars. [JOHN MUSGRAVE-WOOD 'Emmwood' *Daily Mail* 3 November]

1960

The Bigger Bomb Goes Off

Zec's cartoon came at a time when France was preparing to explode its first atom bomb, in southwestern Algeria. However, in his view, this was overshadowed by the continuing separatist struggle in the French colony, where violence was occurring on an appalling scale. Eventually, after six years of conflict and yet another revolt, negotiations began, and Algeria achieved independence in 1962. [PHILIP ZEC *Daily Herald* 26 January]

And May I Say to Hon. Members Opposite Me ...

As Vicky's cartoon shows, Labour leader Hugh Gaitskell's support for nuclear weapons placed him in an awkward position with his own party. At the Labour party conference later that year he opposed a motion to abandon the H-bomb, arguing that he and his supporters would 'Fight, fight and fight again to save the party we love'. He lost the vote. [VICTOR WEISZ 'Vicky' *Evening Standard* 3 March]

Gale Warning!

During a tour of Africa Prime Minister Harold Macmillan received a frosty reception in South Africa when, in a speech to Parliament in Cape Town, he criticised the country's system of apartheid. He also spoke of a 'wind of change' blowing through the continent of Africa as more and more majority black populations in European colonies claimed the right to rule themselves. South African Prime Minister Dr Hendrik Verwoerd, seen in the cartoon with his finger to his mouth, thanked Macmillan for his speech but said he could not agree. [PHILIP ZEC *Daily Herald* 4 February]

The Hard Way

On 21 March between 5,000 and 7,000 people gathered in the South African township of Sharpeville to protest against the pass laws. These required all black men and women to carry personal documentation and stipulated that anyone found in a public place without their pass could be arrested and detained for up to 30 days. The police opened fire, killing 67 and wounding nearly 200. Police Commander D H Pienaar said: 'If they do these things, they must learn their lessons the hard way.' [FRANK BROWN 'Eccles' *Daily Worker* 23 March]

More than Twelve on this Jury

Adolf Eichmann, the SS officer who had been dubbed the 'Chief Executioner of the Third Reich' for his involvement in the Holocaust, had fled from Europe in 1947 and settled in Buenos Aires. The Israeli Secret Service (Mossad) eventually tracked him down, however, and on 21 May kidnapped him, flying him to Israel to stand trial for crimes against humanity. He was sentenced to death and hanged in 1962. [STANLEY FRANKLIN *Daily Mirror* 27 May]

🏛 Trip-up

On 1 May an American U2 spy plane was shot down over Russia. The US State Department at first claimed that it was simply an aircraft that had gone astray. Then, when Khrushchev produced photos of military installations taken by the pilot, President Eisenhower admitted he had authorised the flight but refused to apologise. Not surprisingly, a summit planned to take place in Paris that month between Eisenhower, Khrushchev, de Gaulle and Macmillan never got beyond the preliminary procedural meetings. [STANLEY FRANKLIN *Daily Mirror* 9 May]

The Holes are Left Behind

On 9 November Democratic candidate John F Kennedy became president-elect of the United States after narrowly defeating Republican candidate Richard Nixon by two tenths of a percentage point in the popular vote. Here he is seen contemplating some of the challenges that face him, while his predecessor, Eisenhower, leaves the room with his beloved golf clubs after his eight-year term as president. [STANLEY FRANKLIN *Daily Mirror* 15 November]

1961

The Exploding Cigar

Cuba had been viewed as a thorn in the side of the US since Castro's guerrillas had taken power in 1959. In April 1961 Kennedy backed an attempt by Cuban exiles to oust Castro and his Marxist regime, but the attempted invasion via the Bay of Pigs was a fiasco, driving Castro closer to the USSR and strengthening the view of Nikita Khrushchev that Kennedy was a weak and inexperienced leader. [LESLIE ILLINGWORTH *Daily Mail* 21 April]

Algeria ✈

When it became clear that de Gaulle intended to resolve social and political turmoil in Algeria by granting the country independence, French settlers there reacted with fury. The climax came on 22 April when four French generals in Algeria launched a coup. It collapsed four days later, but unrest and violence persisted. Algeria became independent in 1962. [LESLIE ILLINGWORTH *Daily Mail* 25 April]

A Question of 'Face'

Kennedy's humiliation over the Bay of Pigs fiasco was compounded by the Soviet Union's success in being the first nation to get a man into space. On 12 April Soviet cosmonaut Yuri Gagarin successfully orbited the earth in a Vostok spacecraft and returned safely to earth in a flight that lasted 108 minutes. Khrushchev rushed to Gagarin's side to bask in a little reflected glory. [MICHAEL CUMMINGS *Daily Express* 21 April]

The Communist Paradise

By 1961 around 3 million people had left East Berlin to share in the growing prosperity of West Germany. Among them were many highly qualified workers the East could ill afford to lose. The Soviet Union under Khrushchev therefore approved plans proposed by East German leader Walter Ulbricht to halt the exodus by building a wall. In the early hours of 13 August 'shock workers' shut off the border between East and West Berlin using barbed wire. By 16 August the barbed wire had been replaced by a wall of concrete blocks, and soon West Berlin found itself surrounded by a wall 13 feet (4 m) high and 69 miles (111 km) long. Here Khrushchev is shown hugging cosmonauts Yuri Gagarin and Herman Titov. [MICHAEL CUMMINGS *Daily Express* 14 August]

Stand-off

One particular crossing point between East and West Berlin, Checkpoint Charlie, gained worldwide notoriety in October when American and Soviet tanks confronted each other across the divide. The stand-off ended peacefully 16 hours later when Kennedy and Khrushchev agreed to pull back their forces. [KEITH WAITE *Daily Sketch* 30 October]

No Longer in Our Top Ten

Immigration remained a major political issue throughout the 1960s, and the 1961 Commonwealth Immigration Bill sought to place restrictions on the rights (granted in 1948) of Commonwealth citizens to settle in Britain. Here, in a reference to the popular 1960s BBC programme *Juke Box Jury*, Conservative stalwarts Selwyn Lloyd, Macmillan, Butler, Maudling and Duncan-Sandys vote to keep Commonwealth citizens out. Butler, who was Home Secretary at the time, said of the legislation: 'Although the scheme purports to relate solely to employment and to be non-discriminatory, the aim is primarily social and its restrictive effect is intended to, and would in fact, operate on coloured people almost exclusively.' [GLAN WILLIAMS *Reynolds's News* 5 November]

1962

By 1962 the Conservative government had lost much of its popular appeal, and this led Prime Minister Harold Macmillan to take drastic action: on 13 July he abruptly dismissed seven cabinet members in what became known as the Night of the Long Knives (a reference to the 1934 Nazi party purge). Liberal MP Jeremy Thorpe was quoted at the time as saying: 'Greater love hath no man than this, that he lay down his friends for his life.' [LESLIE ILLINGWORTH *Daily Mail* 14 July]

Come in, Stupid, They're Ever So Friendly

Britain's first attempt to join the Common Market, established by six European nations in 1957, was negotiated by the Lord Privy Seal Edward Heath. German Chancellor Konrad Adenauer (on the left) and French President Charles de Gaulle (on the right) were, however, both suspicious of British intentions, and de Gaulle vetoed the move in January 1963. [GLAN WILLIAMS *Reynolds's News* 19 August]

What We Object to, Bud, is the Idea of Foreign Bases in Cuba!

The dominating international crisis of 1962 began when the Soviet Union started to install near-range nuclear missiles just 90 miles (145 km) off the coast of the United States, in Cuba. The US reacted with outrage. Here, though, Frank Brown takes the view that the US line was hypocritical, given that a US naval station had been established at Guantanamo Bay in 1898 when the US had obtained control of Cuba after the Spanish-American War. [FRANK BROWN 'Eccles' *Daily Worker* 24 October]

I'll See You

As the Cuban missile crisis intensified, President Kennedy declared a naval blockade of Cuba and threatened the USSR itself with attack if any Cuban missile were ever launched against any country. With further Soviet ships already on their way to Cuba and apparently prepared to ignore the block-ade, nuclear war started to seem a real possibility. In this cartoon, international leaders Mao Zedong, Nehru, Harold Macmillan, de Gaulle and Adenauer watch anxiously as Khrushchev and Kennedy raise the stakes. [LESLIE ILLINGWORTH *Daily Mail* 26 October]

Just ...

Khrushchev eventually backed down on 28 October, ordering Soviet vessels to turn back and agreeing to dismantle all Soviet missiles based in Cuba and ship them back to the Soviet Union. For his part, Kennedy promised that the United States would not invade Cuba. Rather less publicly he decided that US nuclear weapons would be withdrawn from Turkey. [MICHAEL CUMMINGS *Daily Express* 29 October]

1963

C'est Bon (That's Good)!

On 14 January General de Gaulle (described by the Foreign Office as an 'almost impossible ally') brutally vetoed Britain's bid to join the Common Market. It was a blow that delayed Britain's entry for a decade and hastened the end of Harold Macmillan's political career. [PETER CLARKE *Daily Sketch* 30 January]

The Other Woman in Orbit

John Profumo, Secretary of State for War, had a brief affair with model and showgirl Christine Keeler. When it became public much was made of the fact that Keeler had also had a relationship with a naval attaché at the Soviet embassy. But what proved more serious was that a panicked Profumo initially lied to Parliament about the allegation, before owning up and resigning. This cartoon showing Macmillan and Keeler, which appeared nearly two weeks later, reflects the enormous damage done to Macmillan's premiership by the affair. It appeared the day after Russian cosmonaut Valentina Tereshkova became the first woman and the fifth Soviet cosmonaut to travel in space. [LESLIE ILLINGWORTH *Daily Mail* 17 June]

Test Ban Hope

This cartoon appeared the day that President Kennedy, visiting the Berlin Wall, made his famous morale-boosting 'Ich bin ein Berliner' speech to West Germans ('All free men, wherever they may live, are citizens of Berlin'). At the same time as this hardline rhetoric, though, negotiations between the nuclear powers to ban nuclear tests (except underground) seemed to herald a thawing in the Cold War. [VICTOR WEISZ 'Vicky' *Evening Standard* 26 June]

Into Whose Hands … ?

Macmillan suddenly resigned as Prime Minister when diagnosed with prostate cancer from which he was not expected to recover (an incorrect diagnosis, as it turned out). At the time, the Conservative party had no formal procedure for selecting a leader, and as would-be candidates made their ambitions known at the annual party conference, four front-runners appeared: R A Butler, Reginald Maudling, Lord Hailsham and Lord Home. To many people's surprise, Macmillan suggested to the queen that Home should succeed him. [LESLIE ILLINGWORTH *Daily Mail* 11 October]

LBJ

On 22 November President Kennedy was assassinated by a gunman in Dallas, Texas. His vice-president, Lyndon Baines Johnson, was sworn in as president just two hours later. Cartoons of the assassination did appear, but they tended to be mawkish or clichéd. This one, by contrast, focuses on Johnson, seen here under the microscope of international scrutiny. On arriving in Washington he announced, 'I will do my best. That is all I can do.' [MICHAEL CUMMINGS *Daily Express* 25 November]

The Lab Men/The Con Men

'Better change it to TORY men – our abbreviation doesn't look too good.' Before assuming the premiership, Lord Home renounced his hereditary title, becoming Sir Alec Douglas-Home. The Labour opposition attacked both his aristocratic background and his perceived lack of a public profile (deputy leader George Brown referred to him as the 'lowest common denominator'). Harold Wilson was presented as Douglas-Home's opposite – an ordinary bloke whose dynamism would transform Britain socially and economically. [STANLEY FRANKLIN *Daily Mirror* 12 November]

1964

Punish Me?!!

'I'm only a poor suffering victim of an acute attack of boredom.' On 29 March Mods and Rockers clashed for the first time on Clacton beach. The Mods, often armed with coshes and flick-knives, generally wore designer suits protected by parka jackets, rode scooters bedecked with mirrors and mascots and listened to soul music. The Rockers rode motorbikes, wore leathers and listened to the likes of Elvis and Gene Vincent. [MICHAEL CUMMINGS *Daily Express* 1 April]

Alec Douglas-Home

'When I have to read economic documents I have to have a box of matches and start moving them into position to simplify and illustrate the points to myself.' As Alec Douglas-Home had spent most of his political career in the House of Lords he was unused to the cut and thrust of life in the Commons. The depth of his inexperience became apparent when he remarked casually that he used matchsticks to help him understand economic problems. The press had a field day. Shown next to him here are (from left to right) Chancellor of the Exchequer Reginald Maudling, Foreign Secretary 'Rab' Butler and Leader of the Commons Selwyn Lloyd. [MICHAEL CUMMINGS *Daily Express* 15 April]

Mandela Sentenced

'Johannes Vorster, South African Minister of Justice: "Is it anybody's right to oppose or campaign against apartheid?"' On 12 June the leader of the anti-apartheid struggle in South Africa, Nelson Mandela, was jailed for life for sabotage. He told the court: 'I do not deny that I planned sabotage. I did not plan it in a spirit of recklessness nor because I have any love of violence. I planned it as a result of a calm and sober assessment of the political situation that had arisen after many years of tyranny, exploitation and oppression of my people by the whites.' [GLAN WILLIAMS *Sunday Citizen* 14 June]

Salute in Passing

American involvement in Vietnam stretched back to the 1950s, but it escalated following an incident in early August involving the US destroyer *Maddox* and North Vietnamese torpedo boats in the Gulf of Tonkin. President Johnson asked for and gained from Congress approval to take 'all necessary action' against the communist North Vietnamese, hoping that by bombing North Vietnam the US could persuade its leader Ho Chi Minh to cut off all aid to the National Liberation Front that was seeking to overthrow the South Vietnamese regime. [GLAN WILLIAMS *Sunday Citizen* 9 August]

Olympic Games

In the lead-up to the 1964 General Election Labour under Harold Wilson were initially ahead in the opinion polls, but started to slip as Douglas-Home's Conservatives fought back, helped by Chancellor of the Exchequer Reginald Maudling's 'run for growth' pre-election budget. With the two main parties running neck and neck as polling day (15 October) approached, the result rested on a knife edge. On 10 October the 18th Olympic Games, the first to be televised in colour, opened in Tokyo. [LESLIE ILLINGWORTH *Daily Mail* 12 October]

Did You Hear Someone Laugh?

On 14 October Khrushchev was deposed as Soviet leader by the Politburo. He had become increasingly out of favour since backing down over the Cuban missile crisis, and his hastily prepared reforms of agriculture and industry had been unsuccessful. He was succeeded as Communist party leader by Leonid Brezhnev and spent the rest of his life in quiet retirement in Moscow. This cartoon recalls his attacks on Stalin after Stalin's death. [JOHN MUSGRAVE-WOOD 'Emmwood' *Daily Mail* 31 October]

The new Labour government of 1964 faced the twin challenges of a tiny majority in the House of Commons and a struggling economy. To remedy the former problem, the new Prime Minister Harold Wilson called an election in March 1966 and managed to increase Labour's majority to 96, but thereafter things began to go wrong for him. He was forced to devalue the pound in November 1967, his attempt to join the Common Market was vetoed by France and plans for trade union reform were shelved when the Government came under pressure from the unions. Labour did enjoy something of a revival in 1969 but went on to lose the 1970 election to Edward Heath and the Conservatives.

For a left-wing cartoonist such as Vicky the Government's record was a disappointing one, and he also found it hard to forgive Wilson for his moral (though not military) support of the Americans during the Vietnam War. He also had his own personal demons in the 1960s, worrying that the quality of his work might be on the decline. Caricaturist Ralph Sallon believed that eventually Vicky began to take himself 'too seriously': 'Everything he drew had to be a touch of genius.' Suffering from worsening depression as well as insomnia, Vicky committed suicide on 23 February 1966.

Wilson may have proved a disappointment to Vicky, but for other cartoonists the problems he posed were more practical: he was quite hard to portray, certainly in comparison to his predecessors Harold Macmillan and Alec Douglas-Home. 'I realise I'm unpromising material,' he admitted to cartoonist Stan McMurtry ('Mac') in May 1970. Cummings, for his part, struggled to come up with a caricature that was recognisable, reckoning that Wilson had a face like the underside of a chamber pot. 'I had to give him black and heavy bags under the eyes to make him look distinctive,' he recalled. 'Thank God he began to smoke a pipe.'

In many ways the 1960s was a decade of opportunity for political cartoonists. Although the *Guardian* had taken on David Low on a permanent basis in 1953, other broadsheets had shied away from employing them, but this changed in 1966 when the *Daily Telegraph* employed Nick Garland as its first political cartoonist and Ken Mahood became the first political cartoonist of *The Times*. There were other changes in personnel. In 1969 Illingworth retired from the *Daily Mail* and recommended Wally Fawkes ('Trog') as his successor (Trog had been producing the 'Flook' strip on the paper since 1947). Two years later the *Daily Mail* absorbed the old *Daily Sketch*, whose editor David English now took over the combined paper and, in the process of transforming it into a tabloid, elected to bring on board his old *Daily Sketch* cartoonist Stan McMurtry in place of Trog. Trog, who had, in any case, often found himself out of sympathy with the paper's politics, left for the *Observer*, and McMurtry began alternating with Emmwood on the redesigned *Daily Mail* until Emmwood's retirement in 1975. McMurtry was urged by his editor to be 'more politically minded', but he saw himself as a gently mocking cartoonist whose job was 'to make the dreary news copy of the daily paper brighter by putting in a laugh'.

The 1970s were certainly in need of a laugh or two, for it was a challenging decade for Britain. The winner of the 1970 General Election, Edward Heath, managed to negotiate Britain's entry into the Common Market, but his time in office coincided with an upsurge in violence in Northern Ireland, and his attempts to curb trade union power led to strikes by the miners. When the oil crisis that followed the

1965–78

"Help! Our civilised society is being menaced by savages . . ."

Yom Kippur War of 1973 was followed by another miners' strike, the resulting energy shortages led to power cuts and a three-day week. Failing to secure a majority at the 1974 election and to negotiate a deal with the Liberals, Heath resigned, and Harold Wilson formed a government, calling another election later in the year to try to shore up his power base – a largely ineffective move, as it turned out. He retired in May 1976, to be replaced as Prime Minister by James Callaghan.

Stanley Franklin, who joined the *Sun* in 1974, got considerable mileage out of portraying Callaghan as Wilkins Micawber, the eternal optimist in Charles Dickens's *David Copperfield*. But optimism was something that Callaghan

needed. With no overall majority and having to work with the Liberals to stay in power, he faced a major sterling crisis that was alleviated only by an IMF rescue package, and his attempts to enforce pay restraint were challenged during the 'winter of discontent' in 1978–9 as a succession of strikes broke out. On 28 March 1979 Labour lost a vote of confidence by just one vote, and Callaghan called a General Election. The result was a Conservative victory, with Margaret Thatcher, who had replaced Heath as Conservative leader in 1975, becoming Britain's first female Prime Minister.

From Boom to Bust

1965

On Safari in Darkest Westminster

After narrowly losing the 1964 General Election to Labour, many Conservative backbenchers felt they needed new, more rigorous leadership. Here Alec Douglas-Home imagines bagging the new Prime Minister, Harold Wilson. His colleagues, Edward Heath, Iain MacLeod (who had refused to serve under Home) and Reginald Maudling have a different victim in mind. Heath was elected leader when Home resigned in July. [MICHAEL CUMMINGS *Daily Express* 18 January]

Churchill

Winston Churchill died, aged 90, on 24 January. His body lay in state for three days at Westminster Hall before his state funeral took place. It attracted millions of mourners. Illingworth's depiction of Churchill is prophetically close to the statue by Ivor Roberts-Jones that was unveiled in Parliament Square in 1975 by Lady Churchill. [LESLIE ILLINGWORTH *Daily Mail* 29 January]

Civil Rights

President Johnson's Voting Rights Act sought to transform the status of African Americans by enhancing their political power. Prior to it only an estimated 6.7% of those theoretically eligible to vote were actually registered in the southern states. By 1969 the number had jumped to 66.5%. Various landmark moments in the history of the civil rights movement are referred to here, including the three Selma to Mongomery marches that took place in March. During a radio speech urging the passage of the Voting Rights Act, Johnson stunned many of his listeners when he closed with the civil rights phrase, 'And we shall overcome'. [LESLIE ILLINGWORTH *Daily Mail* 22 March]

The Beatles

'What are we pushing for, Mummy … the Beatles will come out on the balcony, won't they?' The day this cartoon appeared the Beatles went to Buckingham Palace to receive MBEs while, outside, a crowd of 4,000 young people chanted 'Long live the Queen, long live the Beatles.' Not everyone was pleased. The following day the first of many awards to be returned by disgruntled recipients arrived back at the palace. The former Canadian MP Hector Dupuis, for example, sent back his award, complaining, 'The British House of Royalty had put me on the same level as a bunch of vulgar numskulls', while author Richard Pape, on returning his MBE, wrote, 'If the Beatles and the like continue to debase the Royal honours list, then Britain must fall deeper into international ridicule and contempt.' [JOSEPH LEE *Evening News* 26 October]

Continuing Our Thrilling Serial

Britain's attempts to give the black majority population of its last African colony, Rhodesia, a fair share of power was challenged by the country's leader Ian Smith, who threatened to declare unilateral independence. Last-minute negotiations and the threat of sanctions failed, and Smith duly declared independence on 11 November, leaving the minority white population of 220,000 Rhodesians governing the majority black population of nearly 4 million. [VICTOR WEISZ 'Vicky' *Evening Standard* 8 November]

Of Course it Should Have been Held in Camera

In October Ian Brady and Myra Hindley were arrested and accused of the murders of Edward Evans (17), Lesley Ann Downey (10) and John Kilbride (12). The 'Moors Murders' dominated the media even after Brady and Hindley's conviction in May 1966. Here Harold Wilson complains that the case has kept developments in Rhodesia – especially the Government's oil embargo – off the front pages. [WALLY FAWKES 'Trog' *Observer* 12 December]

1966

Dammit, Angus!

'After Eden, Mac and Douglas-Home, maybe we Tories should have given Lady Lewisham a chance.' With Nehru's daughter Indira Gandhi becoming Prime Minister of India on 19 January and Golda Meir set to become Prime Minister of Israel three years later, the 1960s was a decade of real political achievement for women, but it must have seemed somewhat unlikely that the Conservatives would consider appointing a female leader. Here the suggestion is being made to a *Spectator*-reading Angus Maude, Conservative party chairman and thorn in the side of Edward Heath. Nine years later, he was to be a key member of Mrs Thatcher's leadership campaign. Lady Lewisham was the daughter of Barbara Cartland and, later, the stepmother of Princess Diana. In 1966 she was serving as a Conservative member of the Greater London Council. [GLAN WILLIAMS *Sunday Citizen* 23 January)

Vietnam Escalation

Harold Wilson's policy of providing moral, but not military, support to the United States during the Vietnam War caused anger and disillusionment among many Labour party members and activists, who were fiercely opposed to US policy. As the war escalated, he continued to resist persistent US pressure to send British troops to Vietnam, though, at the same time, he was able to preserve Britain's 'special relationship' with the United States – no mean achievement. Here he is seen parachuting from President Johnson's plane. [KEN MAHOOD *The Times* 1 July]

V for Victory

On 30 July England won the World Cup for the first time, beating West Germany at Wembley 4–2. Here Jon suggests that Wilson is trying to cash in on England's football success, and by showing him making a V for victory sign alludes to President Johnson's description of Wilson as 'another Churchill' for his support of the US in Vietnam. [WILLIAM JONES 'Jon' *Daily Mail* 1 August]

Concorde

'Is it no longer possible to design anything that becomes obsolete *before* millions have been spent on it?' Four years into the Anglo-French project to build *Concorde*, the first prototype took off from Bristol airport. Originally expected to cost between £150 and £170 million, by 1966 estimates had sky-rocketed, topping £1 billion by 1976. [KEN MAHOOD *The Times* 10 September]

I Will Walk Further along the Road Set by Hendrik Verwoerd

South Africa's Prime Minister Hendrik Verwoerd was assassinated by a mentally unstable parliamentary clerk on 6 September. He was succeeded by B J Vorster who enforced racial segregation even more strictly. [STANLEY FRANKLIN *Daily Mirror* 15 September]

Remember the Days When it was Only Bottles and Toilet Rolls?

According to the 1966 Chester report, incidences of football-associated violence doubled in the first five years of the 1960s. Many sociologists blamed television for this, suggesting that because it publicised hooliganism it also helped fuel it. When a riot broke out after Sunderland equalised against Spurs in 1961, and it was shown on television, the *Guardian* suggested that the broadcast 'provided … encouragement to others'. [STANLEY FRANKLIN *Daily Mirror* 27 September]

If You Become President You'll Need a Vice-President

On 8 November former movie actor Ronald Reagan was elected governor of California. He went on to seek the Republican nomination, unsuccessfully in 1972 and 1976, successfully in 1980 when he proceeded to defeat the incumbent Jimmy Carter for the presidency. [STANLEY FRANKLIN *Daily Mirror* 10 November]

1967

Don't Pat it, Hit it for Six

Basil D'Oliveira was a South African cricketer of mixed blood. Under apartheid rules, he was not allowed to play for the South African cricket team, so, encouraged by John Arlott, he came to Britain in 1960 to join the Lancashire League Club. By 1966 he was both a key member of the England team and a British citizen. In 1967, though, he was omitted from the team scheduled to tour South Africa in 1968, an act that provoked a storm of anger. South African Prime Minister Vorster made it very clear that the tour would be cancelled if D'Oliveira were selected. [GLAN WILLIAMS *Sunday Citizen* 29 January]

What on Earth Did We Do with Ourselves before the Cultural Revolution?

Mao Zedong declared a Cultural Revolution in 1966 to reinvigorate revolutionary fervour and ferret out 'revisionists'. The result was political and social turmoil as foreigners were reviled and millions of supposed urban 'bourgeois reactionaries' banished to the countryside for 're-education'. [KEN MAHOOD *The Times* 13 January]

The Frightened Capitalist ✒

A Soviet postcard showing a pot-bellied capitalist concerned by industrial progress in the USSR.

14. Перед нашею
    республикой
    стоят богатые.
    Но как постичь ее!
    В. Маяковский

Colour Television

In 1967 BBC2 became the first British television channel to broadcast regularly in colour. Shown at the back of this cartoon is the broadcaster and political interviewer Robin Day. [Stanley Franklin *Daily Mirror* 17 February]

Man! Whatever are We Going to Do until We're 65?

This cartoon is both a homage to the 65-year-old Sir Francis Chichester who, on 28 May, became the first man to sail around the world single-handed, and a snapshot view of London's Carnaby Street in the mid-1960s when it was, briefly, the centre of the fashionable world. Unisex styles are very much in evidence here. [JOHN MUSGRAVE-WOOD 'Emmwood' *Daily Mail* 30 May]

Gaza Strip

Egyptian President Gamal Nasser, vowing both to avenge Arab defeats at the hands of the Israelis in 1948 and 1956 and press the cause of Palestinian nationalism, organised an alliance of Arab states surrounding Israel and mobilised for war. On 5 June, however, Israel pre-empted the planned invasion and in the space of six days drove Arab armies from the Sinai Peninsula, Gaza Strip, West Bank and Golan Heights. It also reunited Jerusalem, the eastern half of which Jordan had controlled since the 1948–9 war. A huge victory for Israel, the Six Day War was a disaster for Nasser. [STANLEY FRANKLIN *Daily Mirror* 8 June]

Try to Think of it as a Golden Opportunity to Learn How to Swim

On 19 November the British government, after weeks of increasingly feverish speculation and a day in which the Bank of England spent £200 million trying to shore up the pound, was forced to devalue it. Prime Minister Harold Wilson famously sought to calm any public anxiety as follows: 'From now the pound abroad is worth 14% or so less in terms of other currencies. It does not mean, of course, that the pound here in Britain, in your pocket or purse, or in your bank, has been devalued.' [KEN MAHOOD *The Times* 21 November]

Spot the Ball

By April 1968 President Johnson's attempts to force a victory in Vietnam by escalating the conflict had failed, his popularity at home was at an all-time low, and anti-war demonstrations were an almost everyday fact of life. Announcing on 31 March that he would not run again for president, he set about organising peace negotiations with Ho Chi Minh's North Vietnam. A conference in Paris went ahead in May but made little progress. This cartoon draws attention to the appalling casualties on both sides of the conflict: by April 1968, 40,000 American soldiers had died and 250,000 had been wounded; by the end of the war it is estimated that up to 4 million Vietnamese civilians had either been killed or wounded. [LESLIE ILLINGWORTH *Daily Mail* 17 April]

Pow! Wham!

On 20 April Conservative MP Enoch Powell made a speech attacking what he regarded as the Government's disastrously lax immigration policy. Addressing a Conservative association meeting in Birmingham, Powell warned of the consequences of continuing immigration from the Commonwealth in apocalyptic terms: 'As I look ahead, I am filled with foreboding. Like the Roman [Virgil], I seem to see "the River Tiber foaming with much blood". This 'River of Blood' speech achieved immediate notoriety, leading to Powell's sacking from the shadow cabinet by Edward Heath. [LESLIE ILLINGWORTH *Daily Mail* 24 April]

The Mini-skirt

Perhaps the defining fashion item of the 1960s was the mini-skirt, invented (possibly) by either Frenchman Jean Courrèges or Mary Quant. In New York the norm was to have a skirt that reached 4–5 inches (10–12 cm) above the knee; London tended to be more daring, with skirts commonly stopping 3–4 inches (8–10 cm) shorter. When, in 1968, Jackie Kennedy wore a white Valentino mini-skirt for her wedding to Aristotle Onassis its place at the pinnacle of fashion was confirmed. Not everyone approved. [STANLEY FRANKLIN *Daily Mirror* 5 June]

A Black Spot in Our Sunshine

'Carlyle: "Always there is a black spot in our sunshine – it is the shadow of ourselves."' On 4 April the American black civil rights leader Dr Martin Luther King was assassinated in Memphis, Tennessee, where he was about to lead a march of sanitation workers protesting against low wages and poor working conditions. Two months later, on 5 June, Senator Robert Kennedy was killed by an obsessed Palestinian immigrant, Sirhan Sirhan, shortly after giving a victory speech in a Los Angeles hotel to celebrate his win in the California primary. Kennedy had been a strong favourite to win the Democratic nomination in the lead-up to the 1968 presidential election. [STANLEY FRANKLIN *Daily Mirror* 6 June]

A Psychedelic Non-cartoon

The psychedelic movement had been born on the west coast of America and had travelled rapidly across the Atlantic. Fuelled by drugs, particularly the newly popular LSD, it became strongly embedded in the late 1960s counter-culture and had a strongly social and political aspect. Emmwood's cartoon appeared during a summer of student unrest, with riots in Paris in May and sit-ins at a number of British universities. [JOHN MUSGRAVE-WOOD 'Emmwood' *Daily Mail* 8 August]

The End of the Prague Spring

In January Alexander Dubček became leader of the Communist party in Czechoslovakia and introduced a series of liberalising reforms. By June many Czechs were calling for more rapid political progress, and while Dubček believed he could control the situation, his Warsaw Pact neighbours became alarmed. In August Soviet troops invaded Czechoslovakia, Dubček was deposed and hardliners put in his place. Later that year the Soviet leader Leonid Brezhnev, seen here as a giant, formulated what became known as the Brezhnev doctrine, asserting the right of the Soviet Union to intervene in the internal affairs of Warsaw Pact countries. [LESLIE ILLINGWORTH *Daily Mail* 25 August]

1969

White Heat or White Elephant?

The Anglo-French *Concorde* project was well advanced when Tony Benn became Minister of Technology in 1966. The Treasury wanted to cancel the project because of spiralling costs, but Benn played a major part in persuading them not to. In April *Concorde* took off on her maiden flight. The 'white heat' element of the caption is a reference to a speech made by Harold Wilson in 1963, extolling scientific innovation. [EDWARD MCLACHLAN *Sunday Mirror* 25 May]

WHITE HEAT or ..

WHITE ELEPHANT?

Careful, Harold, He's Still Very Much Alive!

Emmwood's tribute to Rembrandt's *The Anatomy Lesson* records the dissension within Labour ranks over 'In Place of Strife', a government white paper designed to create a new framework for industrial relations by proposing that, for example, unions should always hold a ballot before striking and that a board should be established to enforce settlements where required. Put forward by Secretary of State for Employment and Productivity Barbara Castle, it was opposed by, among others, Home Secretary James Callaghan and was eventually abandoned. Here the Labour cabinet (with union leader Hugh Scanlon at the back) watches Wilson as he operates on the Trades Union Congress. [JOHN MUSGRAVE-WOOD 'Emmwood' *Daily Mail* 3 June]

Biafra

'Maybe they'll discover it is made of cheese, and bring some back for us to eat!' By July the Biafran War, which had begun two years earlier with the secession of the southeastern provinces of Nigeria, was causing misery and suffering on an appalling scale. Nigeria had banned all Red Cross aid in the region in its attempts to defeat the Biafran regime and only partly relented in the face of international condemnation. It has been calculated that up to a million people died, many of them of starvation and illness. This cartoon appeared the day after the launch of *Apollo* 11. [JOHN MUSGRAVE-WOOD 'Emmwood' *Daily Mail* 17 July]

Nixon Celebrates

On 20 July American astronauts became the first to land on the moon. Here Nixon celebrates not only the success of the mission but also the disaster that had befallen his likely Democratic rival for the 1972 presidential election, Senator Ted Kennedy. Shortly before the moon landing, Kennedy had left a party on Chappaquiddick Island, Martha's Vineyard, and driven his car off the road into a creek. His passenger, Mary Jo Kopechne, was drowned. [WALLY FAWKES 'Trog' *Daily Mail* 23 July]

Why Go to the Moon for Rocks?

August saw the 'Battle of Bogside' – a three-day confrontation between Irish Nationalist residents and the Royal Ulster Constabulary. Riots followed elsewhere, leading to the deaths of seven people in Belfast and hundreds of casualties. British troops were sent in to quell the unrest and were at first welcomed by Catholic residents, but the events of August 1969 can be seen as heralding the beginning of the 'Troubles' in Northern Ireland. [WALLY FAWKES 'Trog' *Daily Mail* 15 August]

So it wasn't the H-bomb that Finished off the Earth People, After All!

Space continued to offer inspiration to cartoonists long after the moon landing in August. The occasion for this cartoon by Cummings was an international convention, being held in London, that was looking at the problems of oil pollution. [MICHAEL CUMMINGS *Daily Express* 10 November]

173

1970

And this One's Gonna Take Care of Them Campus Bums!

On 4 May, during a Vietnam War demonstration at Kent State University in Ohio, four students were killed and a number of others injured when the National Guard opened fire. Nixon's White House deplored the incident but also criticised the students – 'when dissent turns to violence it invites tragedy'. Just over a week earlier Nixon had given his approval for US and South Vietnamese ground forces to enter Cambodia in a campaign aimed at destroying North Vietnamese army bases there. South Vietnamese troops invaded the Parrot's Beak region – a strip of land jutting from Cambodia towards Saigon – while US troops entered the Fish Hook area to the north. [RAYMOND JACKSON 'JAK' *Evening Standard* 6 May]

But What about Next Week, if Bobby Moore Misses the World Cup?

At the start of the World Cup in Mexico, the England captain Bobby Moore was detained after being accused of stealing an emerald bracelet from a shop in Bogota, Colombia. He was cleared, but England went on to lose in the quarter-finals. [WILLIAM JONES 'Jon' *Daily Mail* 27 May]

Waterloo Day 1970

'Stop worrying about the future – we might lose!' A good showing in the local elections in May, as well as signs that the economy was picking up, persuaded Harold Wilson to call an early election, and he set polling day for 18 June. Most opinion polls predicted a comfortable Labour victory, but in the event a late swing to the Conservatives gave them a Commons majority of 30. Commentators believed that an unexpectedly bad set of balance of payments figures released in polling week and England's defeat in the World Cup contributed to Labour's downfall. Wilson astride the TUC horse, first created by David Low to represent the trade unions, addresses (from left to right): Roy Jenkins, Richard Crossman, James Callaghan, Barbara Castle, George Brown, Denis Healey and Michael Stewart. [JOHN MUSGRAVE-WOOD 'Emmwood' *Daily Mail* 18 June]

Yesterday's Men

Labour's attempt to portray the Conservatives as 'Yesterday's Men' during the election campaign backfired badly on them, as this cartoon shows. The following year 'Yesterday's Men' was to be the title of a BBC programme about Harold Wilson and his shadow cabinet – much to Wilson's fury. Huw Wheldon, managing director of BBC Television, later conceded that it was like making a programme about doctors and calling it 'Quack, Quack'. [LES GIBBARD *Guardian* 20 June]

It's not Every Arab that Can Boast a £10m Home ... eh, Ahmed?

On 12 September three hijacked planes that had been forced to land in Dawson's Field, Jordan, were destroyed by Palestinian extremists who had issued a 72-hour deadline for the release of seven militants. The rebels had blown up the airliners before the deadline had passed because they believed they were about to be attacked. In the aftermath, insurance cover for commercial aircraft went up as much as five times. Plane hijackings became all too common in the 1970s. [BERNARD COOKSON *Evening News* 15 September]

And My Dad's Bigger than Your Dad

In 1968 Egypt began a military struggle with Israel to regain the Sinai Peninsula, which it had lost in the Six Day War of 1967. As the 'War of Attrition' dragged on, the US under Richard Nixon sent military aid to Israel, led by Golda Meir, while Egypt's President Nasser looked to Soviet leader Leonid Brezhnev for support. A few weeks after this cartoon appeared, Nasser died of a heart attack. Vice-president Anwar al-Sadat took over and agreed to end the 'War of Attrition'. [WALLY FAWKES 'Trog' *Daily Mail* 4 September]

1971

No, No Stringbold – NEW Pence, HOT Pants

On 15 February decimal currency replaced pounds, shillings and pence. At around the same time, hot pants replaced the mini-skirt as the must-have fashion item for young woman. Even Royal Ascot felt obliged to allow them, though it added the proviso: 'Ladies in hot pants should only be allowed to enter the Royal Enclosure at Ascot if the "general effect" is satisfactory'. [KEITH WAITE *Sunday Mirror* 14 February]

Coming Home to Roost

By 1971 President Lyndon Johnson's Vietnam War strategy was in tatters. More and more dollars were being printed in Washington to pay for the Vietnam War, resulting in a currency crisis. At the same time, anti-war protesters were becoming more vocal, their numbers now swelled by many Vietnam veterans, who even formed an organisation, Vietnam Veterans Against the War. In April thousands of them converged on the White House and then threw their war medals on the Capitol steps. [CLIVE COLLINS 'Collie' *People* 9 May]

What Inquiry?

On 14 July the IRA claimed responsibility for shooting and killing a British soldier in Belfast who had been guarding an observation post overlooking the peace line separating Roman Catholics from Protestants. The incident was the latest in a series of killings of British soldiers and came at a time when Northern Ireland republican political activist and MP for Mid-Ulster Bernadette Devlin was holding an unofficial inquiry into the deaths of two men shot by British troops in Londonderry. Emmwood's cartoon shows that Devlin was pregnant at the time. Since she had conceived out of wedlock, she lost the support of the more conservative of her Catholic constituents and went on to lose her seat in the 1974 General Election. [JOHN MUSGRAVE-WOOD 'Emmwood' *Daily Mail* 16 July]

Stinker Thatcher, Milk Snatcher

Education Secretary Margaret Thatcher introduced legislation to put an end to free school milk for children over the age of seven, intending to release funds for other areas of education, like new school buildings. The Bill was passed by 281 votes to 248 but gained her considerable unpopularity, Labour's education spokesman Edward Short attacking the move as 'the meanest and most unworthy thing' he had seen in his 20 years in the House of Commons. [WALLY FAWKES 'Trog' *Observer* 12 September]

The Post Office Tower

In the early hours of 31 October a bomb exploded on the 31st floor of the Post Office Tower, which had been opened five years before. No one was injured in the blast but the damage took two years to repair. The IRA claimed responsibility. [KEITH WAITE *Daily Mirror* 2 November]

Mum! We Thought You were Creating Havoc down at the Albert Hall

A 'second wave' of feminism spread from the US in the late 1960s as women started to campaign increasingly vigorously for political and social equality. This cartoon refers to events at the Albert Hall in London in 1970 when protesters threw flour bombs during the Miss World pageant. The BBC stopped televising the event in 1979. [STAN MCMURTRY 'MAC' *Daily Mail* 11 November]

1972

He Fired First!

On 30 January 13 civil rights protesters were shot dead by members of the 1st Battalion of the Parachute Regiment during a Northern Ireland Civil Rights Association march in the Bogside area of Londonderry. The official army position, backed by the Home Secretary, was that the paratroopers had reacted to the threat of gunmen and nail-bombs from suspected IRA members. However, many witnesses, including bystanders and journalists, maintained that all those shot had been unarmed. A tribunal held in the immediate aftermath of the events of Bloody Sunday largely cleared the soldiers and British authorities of blame but was itself criticised as a 'whitewash'. [RAYMOND JACKSON 'JAK' *Evening Standard* 31 January]

Heath and Pompidou

'I was going to ask about all that technological know-how Britain will bring into Europe.'
In January the miners went on strike over take-home pay. As a result, factories were forced to lay off workers and, because of power cuts, many homes and businesses had to go without electricity for up to nine hours a day. Meanwhile Prime Minister Edward Heath was negotiating with French President Georges Pompidou over Britain's third attempt to join the EEC. [WALLY FAWKES 'Trog' *Observer* 20 February]

The Vietnam War

An American progaganda leaflet from the late 1960s/early 1970s claiming that Vietcong bases in the north and south of Vietnam had been destroyed. In reality, even though President Nixon escalated the bombing of North Vietnam in April, victory seemed as far away as ever.

Munich 1938. Munich 1972

During the 1972 Olympics in Munich, West Germany, members of the Israeli Olympic team were taken hostage by the Palestinian Black September organisation, a militant group with ties to Yasser Arafat's Fatah group. Two Israeli athletes died in the initial attack, and a further nine perished in a botched rescue attempt by the German authorities. According to author and television presenter Simon Reeve, the Munich massacre 'thrust the Palestinian cause into the world spotlight, set the tone for decades of conflict in the Middle East, and launched a new era of international terrorism'. [KEITH WAITE *Daily Mirror* 31 October]

MUNICH 1938

MUNICH 1972

Me Found Him Velly Nice Fella, Zhou

'He sell me velly nice second-hand car this morning!' Chairman Mao Zedong and Chinese Prime Minister Zhou Enlai wave President Nixon goodbye after his historic visit to China. The summit ended 20 years of tension between China and the United States that had largely been due to American support for Chinese nationalists in Taiwan. The cartoon contains a reference to a 1960 televised presidential debate when an unshaven Nixon was said to look like a 'truth-less second-hand car salesman'. [JOHN MUSGRAVE-WOOD 'Emmwood' *Daily Mail* 26 February]

Departheid

Uganda's President Idi Amin announced in August that he was expelling 50,000 Asians from the country. He subsequently seized their businesses, handing them over over to his supporters. He also ordered the British High Commissioner to Uganda, Richard Slater, to leave with the last group of Asians. [KEITH WAITE *Daily Mirror* 19 December]

1973

Cummings

The Sunnier Side of the Street

The engagement of Princess Anne to Lieutenant Mark Phillips of the Queen's Dragoon Guards was announced on 29 May, but as this cartoon shows what was really gripping public attention at the time was a sex scandal involving Lord Lambton, Parliamentary Under-secretary for Defence, and Earl Jellicoe, Lord Privy Seal and Tory leader in the House of Lords, both of whom admitted associating with prostitutes. The two men resigned. [WALLY FAWKES 'Trog' *Observer* 3 June)

I Wonder, Kosygin, if We Should Stop Backing Camels

On 6 October a coalition of Arab states led by Egypt and Syria launched a surprise attack on Israel on the Jewish holiday of Yom Kippur. Israel swiftly recovered, however, and, under the military leadership of Moshe Dayan (shown here with his distinctive eyepatch), pushed the Syrians entirely out of the Golan Heights and crossed the Suez Canal to cut off the Egyptian third army. Here Soviet Premier Leonid Brezhnev and Prime Minister Alexei Kosygin look on in despair as Egypt – which they supported – loses to Israel for the second time since 1967. [WALLY FAWKES 'Trog' *Observer* 28 October]

Final Gamble

The Watergate scandal had its origins in an apparently minor episode in June 1972 when there was a break-in at the Democratic party's national committee offices in the Watergate Hotel in Washington. By the time this cartoon appeared, though, controversy as to how much President Richard Nixon had known about the break-in was building inexorably, fuelled by the revelation that conversations were routinely recorded in the White House and that the tapes of these would almost certainly prove or disprove Nixon's much-proclaimed innocence. Nixon finally and reluctantly agreed to hand over the tapes on 23 October. [JOHN MUSGRAVE-WOOD 'Emmwood' *Daily Mail* 25 October]

Oil Crisis

Arab members of OPEC announced that they would no longer ship petroleum to those Western nations that had supported Israel in the Yom Kippur War. As oil became more expensive and its supply dwindled, the economic health of the industrialised nations started to suffer, and by November Britain was struggling with a huge balance of trade deficit. The helpless drivers here are Brandt (West Germany), Pompidou (France), Heath (Britain) and Nixon (US). [MICHAEL CUMMINGS *Daily Express* 2 November]

Here's a Light, Brother!

The autumn saw a wave of industrial action in Britain, while a ban on overtime by the miners, combined with escalating oil prices in the wake of the Yom Kippur War, resulted in a severe energy shortage. The Government's response was to introduce the three-day week, whereby commercial users of electricity were limited to three days' consecutive consumption each week. The fact that leader of the opposition Harold Wilson backed the miners clearly irked Emmwood, who shows him supplying a light to Joe Gormley, president of the National Union of Mineworkers. The Phase III code book that sits on top of the bomb is a reference to the Government's 'Phase III' counter-inflation proposals that included limiting pay raises to 7%. [JOHN MUSGRAVE-WOOD 'Emmwood' *Daily Mail* 19 November].

Boom! Boom!

The oil crisis and the miners' strike brought to an end the brief economic boom that Edward Heath and his Chancellor of the Exchequer Anthony Barber had overseen in 1972–3. [NICK GARLAND *Daily Telegraph* 17 December]

1974

No, We're not Police – We're Psychiatrists

The worsening economic climate in Britain did not deter continuing immigration from Pakistan. Many immigrants arrived illegally, crossing the Channel in small boats to arrive, unnoticed, on British beaches. [STAN MCMURTRY 'MAC' *Daily Mail* 16 January]

Caesar's Triumph

In the wake of the three-day week and with no end in sight to industrial action taken by the miners, Edward Heath called a General Election on the issue of 'Who rules Britain?' He failed to gain a majority, and the Labour party, led by Harold Wilson, accordingly formed a government. On 6 March Wilson brought the strike to an end by agreeing to the miners' demands for a 35% pay increase. Here, along with Michael Foot, James Callaghan and Tony Benn, he bows in front of the chariot of the president of the National Union of Mineworkers, Joe Gormley, while Edward Heath walks disconsolately behind. [MICHAEL CUMMINGS *Daily Express* 8 March]

Well Done, Robin

In Denis Healey's first budget as Chancellor of the Exchequer, he announced increases in income tax, corporation tax and stamp duty, a new wealth tax and the extension of VAT to sweets, soft drinks and ice cream. Trog is sceptical as to whether the money from the rich will actually end up in the pockets of the poor as it seems to be going straight into government coffers. [WALLY FAWKES 'Trog' *Observer* 31 April]

FORCED FEEDING

Forced Feeding

Sectarian violence in Ireland escalated on 17 May when car bombs were set off in Dublin and Monaghan, killing 33 people. A week later Sean Byrne and his brother, Brendan Byrne, both Catholic civilians, were shot dead by the Ulster Defence Association (UDA). [WALLY FAWKES 'Trog' *Observer* 26 May]

And Finally, I Hereby Pardon Myself for Pardoning Richard Nixon

On 8 September, one month after Richard Nixon had resigned the presidency in order to avoid impeachment over the Watergate affair, his successor Gerald Ford announced his decision to grant Nixon a full pardon for any crimes he might have committed while in office. The low-profile timing of the announcement (it was made on a Sunday morning) came in for severe criticism, while the decision itself proved highly controversial and almost certainly put an end to any chances Ford might have had to be re-elected in 1976. [KEITH WAITE *Daily Mirror* 12 September]

Palace of Wombleminster

'We had to do something! We couldn't allow the Labour party to win the prize for absurdity for 1974!' Having lost two General Elections in 1974 (in March and October), a number of right-wing Conservatives plotted to end Edward Heath's leadership. Here Margaret Thatcher, Edward Du Cann, William Whitelaw and Sir Alec Douglas-Home are shown in the guise of the eco-friendly Wombles, popular hits on BBC children's television in the early and mid-1970s. [MICHAEL CUMMINGS *Daily Express* 18 December]

1975

One Small Step for Woman – a Giant Leap for Womankind

In January Margaret Thatcher challenged Edward
Heath for the leadership of the Conservative party,
defeating him by 130 votes to 119 on 4 February and
becoming in the process the first woman leader
of a major British political party. Heath took the
defeat badly, refused to serve in Thatcher's shadow
cabinet and began what Robin Oakley in the *Daily
Mail* described as the 'longest sulk in history'.
Thatcher is seen here climbing over the backs
of fellow contenders Ted Heath, Geoffrey Howe,
Hugh Fraser, James Prior and William Whitelaw.
[STAN MCMURTRY 'MAC' *Daily Mail* 12 February]

Peace

The war in Vietnam finally ended in humiliation for
the United States as the South Vietnamese government in Saigon announced its unconditional
surrender to North Vietnamese forces. The capitulation came just four hours after the last frenzied
helicopter evacuation of Americans from the city.
[WALLY FAWKES 'Trog' *Observer* 6 April]

With a Left Wing like Mine, Who Needs an Opposition?

Labour's General Election manifesto of October
1974 committed the party to allow a referendum on
whether Britain should stay in the Common Market
on renegotiated terms or leave it entirely. In the
run-up to the referendum Wilson announced that
the Government had decided to recommend a 'yes'
vote, but it emerged that the cabinet was split, with
seven of its 23 members seeking British withdrawal.
The 'no' faction was led by Michael Foot, Secretary
of State for Employment, Tony Benn, Industry
Secretary, and Peter Shore, Secretary for Trade. The
day before this cartoon was published, Leeds had
lost to Bayern Munich 2–0 in the European Cup
Final. In the event, the overwhelming majority of
the electorate cast a 'yes' vote. [JOHN MUSGRAVE-
WOOD 'Emmwood' *Daily Mail* 29 May]

There's no Business like …

On 19 July the highly symbolic first Soviet–American joint spaceflight ended when an American *Apollo* and Soviet *Soyuz* undocked and went into separate orbits. Both craft returned safely to earth. [WALLY FAWKES 'Trog' *Observer* 20 July]

What Kept You?

On 20 November General Francisco Franco, who had ruled Spain with an authoritarian hand for 39 years, died at the age of 82. During the Spanish Civil War he had received important support from Hitler and Mussolini and, while remaining emphatically neutral in the Second World War, had nonetheless been sympathetic to the Axis powers, allowing Spanish soldiers to volunteer to join the German army in its struggle with the Soviet Union. [WILLIAM JONES 'Jon' *Daily Mail* 21 November]

North Sea Oil

'Under our devolution proposals, North Sea oil would become Scottish, but yon Chrysler plant would remain British.' The first underwater pipeline to bring North Sea oil to shore was opened on 3 November by the queen. Oil revenue was to prove crucial in propping up Britain's economy at a time when traditional areas of manufacturing, such as car-making, were on the decline. [KEITH WAITE *Daily Mirror* 19 November]

1976

Wilson Resigns

On 16 March Harold Wilson, Labour leader for 13 years and Prime Minister for almost eight, surprised the political world by resigning. This cartoon, showing those contending to succeed him, is reminiscent of the famous photograph of an eight-year-old Harold Wilson on the steps of 10 Downing Street. Shown here are (from left to right), Anthony Crosland, Michael Foot, James Callaghan, Roy Jenkins, Tony Benn and Denis Healey. [NICK GARLAND *Daily Telegraph* 19 March]

Ahah! There it is!

Persistent rumours about Liberal leader Jeremy Thorpe's sexuality dogged his political career. A former male model, Norman Scott, alleged a homosexual affair with Thorpe between 1961 and 1963, when homosexual acts were still illegal in Britain, and in March 1976 used a court appearance to air his claims once again, alleging that Thorpe had threatened to kill him if he made his allegations public. The scandal led to Thorpe resigning as leader of the Liberal Party on 9 May. He was replaced temporarily by Jo Grimond and then on a permanent basis by David Steel. [LES GIBBARD *Guardian* 12 May]

That Damned Elusive Israel

On 4 July, in an audacious raid, Israeli commandos rescued 100 hostages, mostly Israelis or Jews from other countries, held by pro-Palestinian hijackers at Entebbe airport in Uganda. The crisis had begun on 27 June when four militants seized an Air France flight from Israel to Paris via Athens with 250 people on board and had it diverted to Entebbe. Ugandan President Idi Amin arrived at the airport to give a speech in support of the Popular Front for the Liberation of Palestine and supplied the hijackers with extra troops and weapons. The Israeli raid took the hijackers – and Amin – completely by surprise. The French Revolution metaphors in this cartoon blend two novels: Amin appears as the wicked Madame Defarge from Dickens's *A Tale of Two Cities*, while the caption is a reference to *The Scarlet Pimpernel*. [LES GIBBARD *Guardian* 5 July]

Ah, Abdul!

'The trouble with poor, backward underdeveloped British natives is that they never plan ahead, can't look further than their noses, have never heard of irrigation, salination plants etc.' The British tendency to be patronising about other countries is neatly turned on its head here in a cartoon that shows the new Prime Minister, James Callaghan, and his Chancellor of the Exchequer, Denis Healey, inactive in the face of the hottest – and dryest – summer the UK had experienced since records began. Water was rationed in some places, and a Minister for Drought was appointed. [MICHAEL CUMMINGS *Daily Express* 15 August]

Carter in the White House

Jimmy Carter defeated Gerald Ford to become president of the United States after a closely fought contest that gave Carter 51% of the popular vote. It was the first time since 1932 that a sitting president had been dismissed from office. Carter, who emerged from the relative obscurity of a peanut farm in his native Georgia, had appealed to voters with his big smile and his slogan 'Trust me'. Ford and the Republicans suffered from the damage caused by the Watergate scandal and Ford's decision to pardon Richard Nixon. [NICK GARLAND *Daily Telegraph* 4 November]

The Sex Pistols Interview

'I think it's the *Today* programme, looking for another fascinating and stimulating interview …' On 1 December punk rock band the Sex Pistols created a storm of publicity by swearing during an early-evening live broadcast of Thames Television's *Today* programme. The presenter, Bill Grundy, had rashly suggested that the band 'say something outrageous', and their consequent use of the f-word occupied the tabloid press for days. One headline in the *Daily Mirror* famously read 'The Filth and the Fury'. [STAN MCMURTRY 'MAC' *Daily Mail* 3 December]

1977

Victory at Entebbe

Israel's daring 1976 raid to free hostages at Entebbe airport in Uganda is juxtaposed here with France's decision to release the founder of the Black September terrorist group, Abu Daoud, accused of organising the 1972 Munich Olympics terror attack, and expel him to Algiers. In response, Israel withdrew its ambassador to Paris, and the Israeli foreign minister Yigal Allon described the release as 'a shameful capitulation'. [STAN MCMURTRY 'MAC' *Daily Mail* 13 January]

Are You Really Sure that Frog Can Get Them to Vote for Us on Wednesday?

In March, following by-election losses and the defection of two Labour backbenchers to form a new Scottish Labour party, James Callaghan's Labour government became a minority administration and turned to Liberal leader David Steel to negotiate a Lib–Lab pact, an informal agreement whereby the Liberals would support the Government in the House of Commons and would be consulted about policy in return. The arrangement kept Labour in power and lasted until the following year. Jim Henson's *The Muppet Show* had gone on air for the first time the previous year. [RAYMOND JACKSON 'JAK' *Evening Standard* 22 March]

You are Supposed to Hold Your Street Party in Your Street, not Hers

Queen Elizabeth II celebrated her Silver Jubilee in June. Street parties were organised throughout the UK, over 4,000 of them in London alone. [KEITH WAITE *Daily Mirror* 5 June]

I Said, Thank Heavens I'll be Back on Duty outside Grunwicks Again Tomorrow

The Grunwick dispute over trade union recognition at the Grunwick Film Processing Laboratories began in the summer of 1976 when the largely female, Asian workforce, unhappy about their wages and working conditions, joined the union APEX, only to be sacked by their employer. Students, members of the Socialist Workers party and trade unionists joined the picket line, and often-violent confrontations between pickets and police were widely televised. Here the violence has been transferred to the floor of the House of Commons, where Eric Heffer (on his knees) along with James Callaghan are among the few recognisable figures on the government benches. [STAN MCMURTRY 'MAC' *Daily Mail* 22 June].

I was the One

Elvis Presley, 'The King of Rock 'n' Roll', died on 16 August. What is interesting about this cartoon is that it is among the first to mark the death of a famous individual less than reverently. Note the pills scatted below the throne – a reference to Elvis's addiction to prescription drugs. [KEITH WAITE *Daily Mirror* 18 August]

Israel and Egypt

Egyptian President Anwar Sadat accepted an invitation from Israeli Prime Minister Menachem Begin to visit Israel, becoming the first leader from the Arab world to do so and embarking on a political process that would lead to a peace treaty between Egypt and Israel in 1979. As this cartoon makes clear, Sadat's actions were roundly condemned by most Arab states, who felt that he had broken ranks. He was to be gunned down in Cairo by Islamist radicals in 1981. [LES GIBBARD *Guardian* 22 November]

1978

The Lib–Lab Pact

The Lib–Lab pact came under increasing tension in the early part of 1978. Many of David Steel's Liberals disliked it, Labour MPs opposed the Liberals' call for proportional representation, and Liberal finance spokesman John Pardoe and Chancellor of the Exchequer Denis Healey did not get on. As a result, on 25 April Steel announced that the Lib–Lab pact would end at the close of the parliamentary session. [LES GIBBARD *Guardian* 26 April]

I must confess, I'm starting to wonder if this is my real role in life . . .

They're Still Quite Useful about the House, Though

The technique of *in vitro* fertilisation was developed for humans in the United Kingdom by Patrick Steptoe and Robert Edwards, and the first 'test-tube baby', Louise Brown, was born in Oldham on 25 July, amid intense controversy over the safety and morality of the procedure. The Abortion Act of 1967, referred to here, gave no rights to a father to be consulted in respect of a termination of a pregnancy. [LES GIBBARD *Guardian* 26 April]

The World Cup

Angolan independence in 1975 was immediately followed by civil war in which international involvement split along predictable lines, the Soviet Union and Cuba backing the Marxist regime in Angola, the West and anti-Marxist regimes backing the nationalist movement. Here Brezhnev holds aloft the globe (Castro can be seen in Africa), while other leaders attempt to stay on top of the world: Jimmy Carter (US), James Callaghan (UK), Helmut Schmidt (West Germany), Giscard d'Estaing (France) and Hua Guofeng (China). At the time this cartoon was drawn, the football World Cup was taking place in Argentina. [MICHAEL CUMMINGS *Daily Express* 1 June]

There was I Waiting at the Church

As the British economy improved, most opinion polls showed Labour ahead, and many expected Callaghan to call a General Election. The fact that he decided not to has often been described as the biggest mistake of his premiership. In a speech at that month's Trades Union Congress he famously sang the song immortalised by music hall star Marie Lloyd, 'There Was I Waiting at the Church', intending to convey the message that an election was not on the cards. Many, however, thought that he actually meant the opposite – that the election would be called and that Margaret Thatcher's Conservatives would be unprepared.
[STAN MCMURTRY 'MAC' *Daily Mail* 8 September)

The End of Pay Restraint

'He's usually a socialist, but when it comes to pay he's a firm believer in free enterprise.' For four years Callaghan had sought – quite successfully – to keep public sector pay claims under 5% in order to safeguard the economy. However, the policy came under increasing pressure from trade unions, and when the Government agreed to tanker driver demands for a 14% raise, the floodgates opened.
[KEITH WAITE *Sunday Mirror* 24 September]

Look Out, Mr Brezhnev!

'That tough new Polish pope is about to issue a pastoral message!' Pope Paul VI died on 6 August and his successor, John Paul I, survived him only a few weeks. On 16 October the vigorously anti-communist Cardinal Karol Wojtyla of Poland became the first non-Italian pope in over 400 years.
[MICHAEL CUMMINGS *Daily Express* 18 October]

The Yuppies

'If you want to stay living round here you're going to need LOADSAMONEY!' Between 1960 and 1980 all of London's docks closed, to be replaced by residential, commercial and light industrial buildings. Many people who had lived in the area for years felt edged out by incoming young, wealthy professionals who were prepared to pay high prices for apartments, hence Margaret Thatcher's Harry Enfield-inspired taunt here. [CHARLES GRIFFIN *Daily Mirror* 12 May 1988]

Margaret Thatcher dominated 1980s Britain, but she got off to a shaky start. Her monetarist policies, which not only damaged British manufacturing but led to a rise in inflation and a doubling in unemployment levels, proved hugely unpopular, and defeat at the next election seemed a very real possibility. In the event, however, her determination not to change course – 'U-turn if you want to. The lady's not for turning,' she declared at the 1980 Conservative party conference – gained her a core of dedicated followers, while the indomitable spirit she displayed during the Falklands campaign of 1982 brought in its wake a burst of popular enthusiasm that helped sweep her back to power in 1983. Thereafter she continued to polarise opinion, loathed by those on the left, adored by those on the right. Few remained indifferent to her.

Surprisingly, perhaps, given the strong feelings she evoked, she proved quite a challenge to cartoonists. Steve Bell, for one, found little in Thatcher to go on at first. He described her simply as a 'blonde with a highish voice and a hectoring lecturing manner'. Michael Cummings probably got closer to the reality than most, but even his rendition remained quite fixed, not really changing over the

1979–90

years as its subject did. As for Les Gibbard at the *Guardian*, he initially felt that it was 'too tough and ungentlemanly to attack a lady at the start of her honeymoon'.

Bit by bit, though, cartoonists started to latch on to particular aspects of Thatcher. Steve Bell decided that there was something rather manic in her eyes and began depicting her as a psychotic, swivel-eyed woman in his 'Maggie's Farm' strip for the *Guardian* (a strip that was condemned in the House of Lords as 'an almost obscene series of caricatures'). MAC, JAK and Cummings initially concentrated on the hats she wore. Later her handbag became her 'tag of identity' (as David Low would have described it). Whatever they came up with, however, cartoonists found it almost impossible to ruffle their prey. 'I think that's sweet,' she is reported to have said during the hat period. 'I only wore that hat once; the cartoonists have never forgotten it. It looks like a bullseye.' Just as she delighted in being called the 'Iron Lady' by the Russians, who had wanted to demonise her, so she seemed to remain untouched and undaunted by the attentions of the cartoonists. Richard Wilson, who drew for *The Times* during the 1980s, believed that 'one's tiny satirical barbs just bounced off her armour-plated certainties'.

Cartoonists gunned for Labour politicians, too. Michael Foot, for example, who replaced James Callaghan as Labour leader in 1980, was presented as an absurdly bedraggled figure, with wild, out-of-control hair, heavy dark glasses and a walking stick. The infamous 'donkey jacket' that he wore for a Remembrance Day service in Whitehall (it was not, in fact, a donkey jacket but, as Foot described it, 'a perfectly good' dark green coat that had won favourable comment from the Queen Mother) and his inability to pull together a hopelessly divided Labour party proved to be godsends to cartoonists on the right and sources of profound frustration to those on the left. Tony Benn, who challenged Denis Healey for the Labour deputy leadership in 1981, was also harshly treated, his staring eyes being used to good effect by cartoonists such as Cummings, who gave them a manic aspect to imply that Benn was mad (Benn complained that Cummings 'puts a hammer and sickle on anyone he doesn't agree with').

When Foot resigned in 1983 after Labour's dismal showing at the General Election, Neil Kinnock was elected Labour leader. Like Foot, the 'Welsh Windbag', as his critics called him, provided good material for the cartoonists, with his freckles, craggy nose, bull neck and Bobby Charlton-style hair. His deputy, Roy Hattersley, was not treated charitably either. But although Kinnock went on to lose two elections for Labour, he did much to make the party more electable in the future, ditching unpopular policies and driving out dissident elements.

Labour divisions may have helped Mrs Thatcher to stay in power, but after three election victories things finally turned sour for her. In the same month the Berlin Wall came down, symbolising the end of the Eastern bloc, her leadership was challenged by a Conservative MP who was antagonised by her sceptical attitude to the European Union. The following year there was widespread opposition to the poll tax to fund local government, and by the end of November 1990 she was out of office.

The Thatcher Years

1979

I Don't Like it

'That's the third boatload of desperate, half-starved British people we've seen escaping the country.' A wry comment on Britain's economic miseries in early 1979, with a topical reference to the Vietnamese boat people who were landing in Hong Kong in increasing numbers to escape the repressive communist regime that had taken over in South Vietnam. In the course of the next seven years more than half a million people fled South East Asia, to be scattered around the Western world. [STAN MCMURTRY 'MAC' *Daily Mail* 19 January]

What Do You Think of it So Far?

By the end of January the Government's policy of keeping to a 5% limit on pay rises was in tatters as public sector workers, including ambulance drivers, sewerage staff and dustmen, went on strike. Dustbins overflowed, rubbish piled up in streets and city squares, and some cemetery workers even refused to dig graves in what became known as the 'winter of discontent'. James Callaghan's ineffectuality is graphically shown in JAK's cartoon, which portrays him as one half of the Morecambe and Wise comedy duo, complete with skew-whiff glasses. It is no coincidence that the answer to the duo's often-asked question 'What do you think of it so far?' was 'Rubbish'. [RAYMOND JACKSON 'JAK' *Evening Standard* 5 February]

It's Quite Simple

'All we have to do is remake the eggs out of this omelette the socialists cooked!' Labour's failure to manage the economy or control the unions was heavily punished by the voters at the May General Election, and Margaret Thatcher duly became Britain's first woman Prime Minister. She is shown with fellow chefs William Whitelaw and Geoffrey Howe, preparing to unbreak a few policy eggs. [MICHAEL CUMMINGS *Daily Express* 23 May]

I Only Want to Punish the Shah

The Shah of Iran had been driven from power in January, and on 1 February the Ayatollah Khomeini returned from exile to assume control of the country and declare it an Islamic republic. As relations with the West deteriorated, the price of oil sky-rocketed. Shown directly above the Ayatollah here are Helmut Schmidt, Jimmy Carter, Margaret Thatcher and Giscard d'Estaing. [MICHAEL CUMMINGS *Daily Express* 7 November]

A Heath Robinson Contraption

Former Labour cabinet minister Roy Jenkins in his Dimbleby lecture advocated the need for a new centre party that would promote radical social and constitutional reform and appeal to those people who felt alienated by the antagonistic two-party system. Increasingly disturbed at the way the Labour party was lurching towards the left, Jenkins was to be one of four senior Labour party members who would secede to form the Social Democratic Party in 1981. [JOHN JENSEN *Now Magazine* 30 November]

With Friends Like These, Who Needs Enemies

The National Executive Committee of the Labour party plot their leader James Callaghan's downfall after the loss of the 1979 election. The left-wingers shown include Michael Foot, Eric Heffer, Tony Benn and Ian Mikardo. [WILLIAM JONES 'Jon' *Daily Mail* 6 July]

1980

This is a Frightfully Rough Sea, Mrs Thatcher!

'Wouldn't it be safer to return to the *Titanic*?'
The new Conservative government's cuts in public spending led to unemployment soaring from an inherited 1 million (when the Conservatives proclaimed 'Britain isn't working') to 2 million. Far from enjoying an industrial or entrepreneurial miracle, Britain experienced its worst recession since the war. Margaret Thatcher became the most unpopular Prime Minister in the history of polling, and many so-called 'wets' in her cabinet begged her to make a U-turn in policy. [MICHAEL CUMMINGS *Daily Express* 16 March]

Zimbabwe ♟

On 4 March Marxist revolutionary Robert Mugabe became Prime Minister of the new state of Zimbabwe (formerly known as Southern Rhodesia). Despite evidence of brutal intimidation of voters by Mugabe supporters during the election, Mrs Thatcher and her Foreign Secretary Lord Carrington did not argue against the result, stating that all sides had been guilty of electoral abuses. [NICK GARLAND *Daily Telegraph* 5 March]

The Hostage

The final year of President Carter's term in office was dominated by the Iran hostage crisis, during which the United States struggled to rescue 53 diplomats and American citizens seized in the American embassy in Tehran by Iranian militants. Unsuccessful negotiations – and a disastrous military attempt to free the hostages – contributed to Carter's defeat, and Republican nominee Ronald Reagan's victory, in the 1980 presidential election. [JOHN JENSEN *Now Magazine* 2 May]

Rodney Never Uses the Front Door Since He Joined the SAS!

On 30 April a group of Iranian-born terrorists seized the Iranian embassy in Knightsbridge, London, taking 26 people hostage. After a six-day stand-off the SAS stormed the building, freeing the hostages, killing five of the gunmen – and winning enormous prestige in the process. [RAYMOND JACKSON 'JAK' *Evening Standard* 6 May]

Ah, the Starting Pistol

In protest at the Soviet invasion of Aghanistan in December 1979, Margaret Thatcher sought – unsuccessfully – to persuade British athletes not to compete at the Moscow Olympics. Sixty-two countries joined the US in boycotting the Games, while 81 took part. The Soviet Union then proceeded to boycott the 1984 Olympics in Los Angeles. [MICHAEL CUMMINGS *Daily Express* 27 June]

But Michael, Aren't We All in Greater Danger from Non-nuclear Weapons?

In November Michael Foot was elected Labour leader. His belief in unilateral nuclear disarmament was anathema to many in the Labour shadow cabinet, including Bill Rodgers who, in January 1981, defected from the Labour party, along with Roy Jenkins, David Owen and Shirley Williams, to form the centre-left Social Democratic Party. Here Cummings includes references to the continuing unrest in Northern Ireland, the massive military offensive launched on 22 September by Iraq's Saddam Hussein against Iran and the death on 8 December of former Beatle John Lennon, shot dead outside his Manhattan apartment. [MICHAEL CUMMINGS *Daily Express* 10 December]

1981

Hostage Deal

Although the Carter administration had successfully negotiated with the Iranians for the release of the American embassy hostages taken captive in 1979, they were actually set free just minutes after Ronald Reagan was officially sworn in as president – Ayatollah Khomeini being determined to humiliate Carter right to the end. [NICK GARLAND *Daily Telegraph* 8 January]

I Specially Reminded You to Put the Clock ON

On the day this cartoon was published the first ever London Marathon took place. The brainchild of Chris Brasher, former Olympic steeplechaser, it attracted 6,700 participants, who turned out in drizzle to complete the 26.2 mile (42 km) run. The goodwill of the occasion was encapsulated in the decision of American Dick Beardsley (24) and Norwegian Inge Simonsen (25) to share first place: they crossed the finishing line hand in hand after two hours, 11 minutes, 48 seconds. [KEITH WAITE *Sunday Mirror* 29 March]

They May Know Nothing about Tennis, but at Least They Speak McEnroe's Language

Wimbledon number two seed John McEnroe was fined £1,000 and came close to being thrown out of the championship when, during his second round victory over Tom Gullikson, he called umpire Ted James 'the pits of the world' and then swore at tournament referee Fred Hoyles. His phrase 'you cannot be serious', aimed at umpires on several occasions, entered the national psyche. [RAYMOND JACKSON 'JAK' *Evening Standard* 24 June]

They Went a Bit Far in Liverpool, Setting Fire to Toxteth

On 29 July Prince Charles and Lady Diana Spencer were married in St Paul's Cathedral before an invited congregation of 3,500 and an estimated global TV audience of 750 million. To celebrate the occasion bonfires were lit and hundreds of thousands of spectators gathered in and around Hyde Park to watch a spectacular pyrotechnic display. This cartoon, though, contains a reminder that earlier in the month there had been civil disturbances in Toxteth, an inner-city area of Liverpool, which had arisen in part from long-standing tensions between the local police and the black community. And in April riots had broken out in Brixton in south London, leading to widespread damage and the arrest of hundreds. [KEITH WAITE *Daily Mirror* 30 July]

Come on, Tony!

Tony Benn's challenge to incumbent Denis Healey for the deputy leadership of the Labour party proved both divisive and a distraction for the party at a time when it was hoping to capitalise on the unpopularity of Margaret Thatcher's government. Labour leader Michael Foot had appealed to Benn not to stand, but Benn had defended his decision by arguing that it was 'not about personalities but about policies'. In the event Healey emerged victorious by a margin of barely 1%. Here the fight is cheered on by Margaret Thatcher, Roy Jenkins and Shirley Williams (of the newly formed SDP) and Liberal leader David Steel. [WALLY FAWKES 'Trog' *Observer* 25 September]

Solidarity

On 13 December Poland's military ruler and prime minister General Wojciech Jaruzelski (shown in the middle), in an attempt to put a stop to the growing power and influence of the Solidarity trade union led by Lech Walesa (shown on the left), declared a state of emergency and placed leaders of Solidarity under arrest. Angry crowds formed in Warsaw, jeering and shouting 'Gestapo' at soldiers. 'Trog' is under no illusion as to whose finger is ultimately on the trigger in this confrontation – that of Soviet leader Leonid Brezhnev. [WALLY FAWKES 'Trog' *Observer* 18 December]

1982

Monetarism is Working

On 26 January the number of people out of work in Britain rose above 3 million for the first time since the 1930s. Here 'Trog' lampoons the successful Saatchi 'Labour isn't Working' poster campaign that preceded the 1979 General Election, showing it being transformed by Employment Secretary Norman Tebbit to fit in with Conservative economic policy. The bicycle is a reference to a comment made by Tebbit when it was suggested to him that the urban riots of 1981 were caused by unemployment: 'I grew up in the 1930s with an unemployed father. He did not riot. He got on his bike and looked for work, and he went on looking until he found it.' The last part of the remark was widely repeated out of context, leading many to think that Tebbit was simply telling the unemployed, 'Get on your bike and look for work'. [WALLY FAWKES 'Trog' *Observer* 31 January]

Southern Front

On 2 April Argentina, which had long claimed sovereignty over the British-held Falkland Islands in the South Atlantic, launched a successful military invasion. The following day Margaret Thatcher announced during an emergency debate in Parliament that a task force would be formed to 'restore British administration' to the Islands. It duly set sail on 5 April. In the cartoon Margaret Thatcher appears in the guise of Nelson, leading her Minister of Defence John Nott and Foreign Secretary Francis Pym. [LES GIBBARD *Guardian* 4 April]

Shucks!

At the start of the Falkland Islands crisis the US under President Reagan had tried to broker a deal between its two allies, Britain and Argentina. It was not until 30 April, after Argentina had rejected Secretary of State Alexander Haig's peace proposals, that President Reagan finally declared his full support for Britain. Argentinian forces in the Falklands eventually surrendered in June after a conflict in which 258 Britons and 649 Argentinians died. [STAN MCMURTRY 'MAC' *Daily Mail* 19 April]

I See Mr Whitelaw is Personally Supervising the Queen's Security

On 9 July Michael Fagan (31) broke into Buckingham Palace and spent ten minutes talking to the queen in her bedroom before she was able to raise the alarm. This was the sixth breach of security at the palace that year. Home Secretary William Whitelaw's concession that the incident represented a serious lapse was described by the Labour opposition as 'the understatement of the year'. [CLIVE COLLINS 'Collie' *Evening Standard* 13 July]

De Lorean

'Cocaine? Hell, no! You just shove £81 million of British taxpayers' money up your nose – and ZOWEEEE!' US car manufacturer John De Lorean had persuaded the British government to invest many tens of millions of pounds in his company in return for a commitment to build a factory in Northern Ireland, then one of the most economically depressed areas of Europe. On 20 October, however, De Lorean was arrested by the FBI for drug smuggling, and his company collapsed. His De Lorean DMC-1 had a stainless steel body and gull-wing doors. [STAN MCMURTRY 'MAC' *Daily Mail* 22 October]

West/East

In 1980 the British government announced that Tomahawk Cruise nuclear missiles would be deployed at the Greenham Common air base. Preparatory work began in 1981, prompting a protest march from Cardiff to Greenham, organised by a peace group called Women for Life on Earth. When the women arrived at Greenham a number chained themselves to the perimeter fence and within a few days they had established a peace camp. In December 1982 around 30,000 women gathered to join hands around the air base. Garland takes a critical view, juxtaposing the Greenham women's freedom to protest with the lack of civil liberties in the Eastern bloc. [NICK GARLAND *Daily Telegraph* 11 December]

1983

Bermondsey

Michael Foot's hold on the leadership of the Labour party took a severe battering over the Bermondsey by-election debacle. Labour's candidate, Peter Tatchell, was denounced by the party leader himself for supporting extra-parliamentary action, savaged by the tabloid press for his homosexuality and then trounced at the polls by the Liberal candidate Simon Hughes. Labour had held Bermondsey since 1946. [WALLY FAWKES 'Trog' *Observer* 27 February]

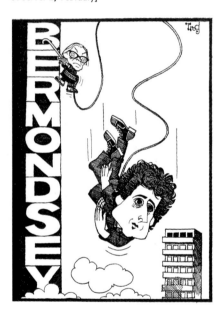

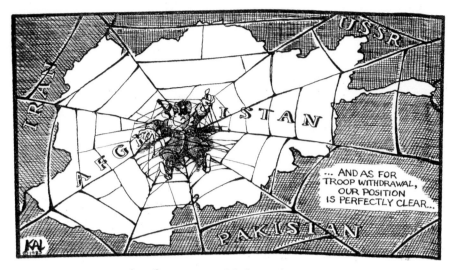

And as for Troop Withdrawal, Our Position is Perfectly Clear

The Soviet news agency TASS declared that Soviet troops would remain in Afghanistan until long-standing Soviet conditions for their withdrawal had been met. By 1983, however, despite a three-year military offensive, there was little sign that Soviet troops would be able to defeat the Afghan guerrillas. [KEVIN KALLAUGHER 'KAL' *Observer* 2 January]

Can I Help You, Madam?

Margaret Thatcher's determination to see both the closure of unprofitable coalmines and the curbing of the power of the National Union of Mineworkers (NUM) led her to appoint former head of British Steel, Ian McGregor, to run the National Coal Board. McGregor had a reputation for toughness, and at British Steel his cost-cutting programme had involved the loss of thousands of jobs. 'MAC' shows Thatcher and McGregor preparing to carve up NUM president Arthur Scargill. The miners' strike that ensued in 1984 dominated Thatcher's second term in office. [STAN MCMURTRY 'MAC' *Daily Mail* 7 March]

Stop! Do Not Attempt to Move It!

On 9 May Margaret Thatcher, buoyed by victory in the Falklands War of 1982, called a General Election for 9 June. Michael Foot's Labour opposition duly drew up a manifesto that included traditional left-wing pledges on unilateral nuclear disarmament, withdrawal from the European Community and the abolition of the House of Lords. Described by Gerald Kaufman of the shadow cabinet as the 'longest suicide note in history', it was deplored by such Labour stalwarts as Denis Healey (shown here) and played badly with the electorate. The Conservatives went on to win a landslide victory, capitalising on a split vote between Labour and the SDP–Liberal Alliance despite actually gaining fewer votes than in 1979. [PETER BROOKES *The Times* 18 May]

Here's to Three More Years of Pointless Bloodshed

Saddam Hussein and the Ayatollah Khomeini are shown toasting the third anniversary of the beginning of the Iran–Iraq War. Losses on both sides were appallingly high: by the end of the year an estimated 120,000 Iranians and 60,000 Iraqis had been killed. [KEVIN KALLAUGHER 'KAL' *Observer* 25 September]

He's Treating Us Like a Banana-skin Republic!

US President Ronald Reagan's decision to invade the former British colony of Grenada in the wake of a Cuban-inspired coup infuriated his ally Margaret Thatcher. 'You have invaded the Queen's territory and you didn't even say a word to me,' she complained in a phone call. According to her memoirs: 'At the time I felt dismayed and let down by what happened. At best the British government had been made to look impotent, at worst we looked deceitful.' Seen here with Foreign Secretary Geoffrey Howe, her discomfiture was not helped by the fact that Parliament was just about to vote on whether to allow the US to station Cruise missiles in Britain. [WALLY FAWKES 'Trog' *Observer* 30 October]

1984

The Libyan Embassy Siege

During a demonstration in London against the Libyan leader Colonel Gaddafi, a gunman, believed to have been stationed inside the Libyan embassy, opened fire, killing WPC Yvonne Fletcher. A tense stand-off between police and Libyan embassy staff ensued but ended on 27 April when the staff, claiming diplomatic immunity, were allowed to fly back to Tripoli. No one was arrested. [BERNARD COOKSON *Sun* 28 April]

The Olympic Games

In February Yuri Andropov, who had replaced Brezhnev as Soviet leader in 1982, died and was succeeded by an ailing Konstantin Chernenko. On 8 May the Soviet Union, in revenge for the boycott of the Moscow Games four years earlier, announced that it would not be attending the 1984 Summer Olympics in Los Angeles. Fourteen other Eastern bloc countries and allies, including Cuba and East Germany, joined the boycott and organised a rival event, the Friendship Games, in July and August. [PETER BROOKES *The Times* 10 May]

It Makes You Ashamed to be British, Doesn't it?

Tensions between the Coal Board and the National Union of Mineworkers (NUM) spilt over in March into a bitter strike that lasted a year. There were violent clashes between miners and police outside collieries that continued to work and at steel and power plants. Forceful policing limited secondary action, and the fact that there were large stockpiles of coal meant that the miners were unable to exert the same paralysing effect they had had on the economy in 1972. This cartoon appeared after a Spurs supporter had been shot dead and 200 fans held by police in Brussels following a riot before the UEFA Cup final against Anderlecht. [STAN MCMURTRY 'MAC' *Daily Mail* 11 May]

Star Wars

The Strategic Defense Initiative (SDI), commonly called Star Wars after the science fiction film by George Lucas, was proposed by President Reagan on 23 March when he announced: 'I call upon the scientific community who gave us nuclear weapons to turn their great talents to the cause of mankind and world peace: to give us the means of rendering these nuclear weapons impotent and obsolete.' The idea that lasers could be used to destroy incoming Soviet intercontinental ballistic missiles armed with nuclear warheads was greeted with acute scepticism by many. Here Reagan's own wife adds her voice to the debate. [KEVIN KALLAUGHER 'KAL' *Observer* 17 June]

The Brighton Bombing

On 12 October the Provisional IRA exploded two bombs in the Grand Hotel in Brighton where members of the cabinet were staying for the Conservative party conference. Five people were killed, including Conservative MP Sir Anthony Berry and John Wakeham's wife, Roberta. Several others, including Margaret Tebbit, the wife of Norman Tebbit, who was then Trade and Industry Secretary, were left permanently disabled. The Prime Minister and her husband, Denis, narrowly escaped injury. On the day this cartoon was published Margaret Thatcher said that she was not in favour of any 'sudden new initiative' on Northern Ireland. However, a month later she met the Irish Prime Minister Garret FitzGerald for an Anglo-Irish summit meeting at Chequers. [PETER BROOKES *The Times* 16 October]

Quiet, Please, While I Get through to My Broker

As part of a massive programme to reverse the nationalisation of key industries that had taken place in previous decades, British Telecom was returned to private ownership in 1984, and more than 50% of shares in the company were offered for sale to the public. The share offer was taken up by around 2.1 million people, and when dealing began on 3 December BT shares traded at an unexpectedly high level. [KEITH WAITE *Daily Mirror* 29 November]

1985

SDP and Labour

According to opinion polls, Neil Kinnock, who had taken over from Michael Foot after Labour's 1983 General Election defeat, was proving to be less of an asset to his party than David Owen, leader of the SDP, was to his. Kinnock also trailed Margaret Thatcher and David Steel in popularity. Here, while Kinnock and his team tinker with their car, David Owen whizzes past in his Sinclair C5 – an electric tricycle, capable of a top speed of 15 mph (24 kph), launched on 10 January by the computer million-aire Sir Clive Sinclair. In the event, David Owen and the C5 shared a similar fate. [NICK GARLAND *Daily Telegraph* 13 January]

The Great Betrayal

By January the miners' strike was beginning to disintegrate as miners, who were facing increasing financial hardship, started to return to work in ever-greater numbers. The NUM had failed to gain support from other key industrial trade unions, and Nottinghamshire miners were threatening to form a breakaway union. NUM president Arthur Scargill complained that the British trade union movement had left the NUM isolated, but on 3 March, a year after the start of the strike, the NUM's National Executive voted 98–91 in favour of an organised return to work. [RAYMOND JACKSON 'JAK' *Evening Standard* 29 January]

Live Aid

'If they didn't hear THAT the politicians need a DEAF-aid.' On 13 July the Live Aid concert for the starving in Africa took place at Wembley Stadium. Initiated by Bob Geldof, who had been appalled by news coverage of the 1984 famine in Ethiopia, it featured 16 hours of live music and was watched by over 1.5 billion people worldwide. Live Aid eventually raised £40 million. Half the money was spent on food and half on long-term development. [NOEL FORD *Daily Star* 15 July]

Liverpool Militants

Labour leader Neil Kinnock (shown with his deputy Roy Hattersley) took on the revolutionary socialist group Militant Tendency in the wake of accusations that it was using local Labour party organisations to spread its Trotskyite views and that it was effectively running Liverpool City Council. In the ensuing confrontation many leading Militant Tendency members were expelled from the Labour party. Bolsover MP Dennis Skinner, however, complained that Labour was in danger of losing sight of its real enemy – the Conservatives. 'They're going to spend a lot of time examining their own navel,' he argued. [NICK GARLAND *Daily Telegraph* 5 November]

The Westland Affair

'Now, Michael. There's no need to fly into a tizzy over this helicopter thing.' The Westland affair had its roots in a cabinet dispute over whether the struggling British helicopter manufacturer Westland should look to US or European companies to safeguard its future. Defence Secretary Michael Heseltine (shown complete with his trademark mane of hair) championed a European solution, and when Margaret Thatcher (who favoured the US company Sikorsky) sought to contain what had become a public row by insisting that all future statements should be cleared with the cabinet office, he abruptly collected his papers and left a cabinet meeting. Cabinet colleagues only learned subsequently that he had resigned. [RAYMOND JACKSON 'JAK' *Evening Standard* 17 December]

Hostages

'I wouldn't even dream of handing you over – I'm waiting for the price to go up.' Civil war erupted in Lebanon in 1975, only coming to an end in 1990. In the mid-1980s a number of non-Lebanese citizens temporarily resident in Beirut were taken hostage by militias, and in June 39 Americans were held by gunmen who had hijacked a TWA airliner to Beirut. [KEITH WAITE *Daily Mirror* 5 July]

1986

I Believe that We Can Eliminate All Nuclear Weapons in Three Easy Steps

As arms control talks resumed between the US and the Soviet Union in Geneva, Soviet leader Mikhail Gorbachev offered to abolish all Russian nuclear weapons within 15 years if President Reagan agreed to scrap his Strategic Defense Initiative. Gorbachev's ambition was not realised. [KEVIN KALLAUGHER 'KAL' *Observer* 19 January]

Star Wars Project

On 28 January the American space shuttle *Challenger* exploded within minutes of take-off, killing all seven astronauts on board. The disaster was a severe blow to the US space programme and also cast doubt on whether the Strategic Defense Initiative (SDI), commonly called Star Wars, was feasible. There were no further manned flights until September 1988. [WALLY FAWKES 'Trog' *Observer* 2 February]

Wow!

On 15 April US jets bombed Tripoli and Benghazi, killing 101 people, including Colonel Gaddafi's adopted daughter. Launched in response to alleged Libyan involvement in the bombing of a Berlin disco frequented by US military personnel, the attack was in part made possible by Margaret Thatcher's agreement to allow the participation of US planes based at the Upper Heyford air base. Her decision divided British opinion, as is suggested by this cartoon, which appeared shortly after the release of the all-action, gung-ho film *First Blood Part Two*, starring Sylvester Stallone as John 'Rambo'. [WALLY FAWKES 'Trog' *Observer* 18 April]

Here, Want a Taste?

On 26 April the world's worst ever civil nuclear disaster took place when a reactor at the nuclear power plant at Chernobyl, near Kiev, in the Soviet Union exploded, releasing a cloud of radioactive fall-out that drifted over parts of western and eastern Europe. The World Health Organisation estimated that 56 people died as a direct result of the explosion, but many thousands received a potentially lethal dose of radioactivity, and large areas of Ukraine, Belarus and Russia were badly contaminated. 'Operator error' was the official explanation for what happened, but design flaws and poor standards of maintenance were also major factors. [LES GIBBARD *Guardian* 30 April]

Have a Good Day in the City, Dear?

The London Stock Exchange's 'Big Bang' got off to a shaky start when its new computerised dealing system failed for an hour shortly after trading opened. Heralding a new era of deregulation and greater foreign competition, the Big Bang facilitated the aggressive, high-profile takeover bids that seemed a hallmark of the later 1980s and that were to be satirised in the 1987 film *Wall Street*, starring Michael Douglas. [CHARLES GRIFFIN *Daily Mirror* 25 October]

This AIDS Thing Must be a Lot More Serious than We Thought, Bishop

In March the Government launched its first public information campaign about AIDS and in November set up a cabinet committee to report on it. A total of £20 million was earmarked for a publicity campaign, including television and cinema commercials, under the banner 'Don't die of ignorance', and it was decided to countermand the Independent Broadcasting Authority's restriction on commercials recommending the use of condoms. [RAYMOND JACKSON 'JAK' *Evening Standard* 19 November]

1987

The General Election

Margaret Thatcher won her third term in office the day before this cartoon appeared, securing a 102-seat Conservative majority. Despite initial optimism and a professional campaign run by Neil Kinnock, Labour gained only 20 seats more than they had in 1983, while the Owen/Steel Liberal/SDP Alliance failed to make any significant headway. The Liberals and SDP merged the following year, forming the Liberal Democrats. [KEVIN KALLAUGHER 'KAL' *Today* 12 June]

Yes, That'll Do Nicely

On 19 August a 27-year-old man, Michael Ryan, armed with several weapons including an AK-47, went on the rampage in the Berkshire town of Hungerford and killed 14 people before finally turning one of his guns on himself. All his weapons were legally owned. A year later the Government banned the private ownership of semi-automatic weapons. [DAVE GASKILL *Today* 21 August]

Spycatcher

Former MI5 officer Peter Wright's book *Spycatcher*, which, among other things, alleged that in the 1960s MI5 had conspired to discredit Labour Prime Minister Harold Wilson, was banned by the Government. However, attempts to stop copies printed in America and Australia entering the country failed, and the Government was eventually forced to climb down. The notoriety surrounding the attempted ban turned the book into a best-seller. [MICHAEL CUMMINGS *Daily Express* 12 August]

The October Hurricane

An anxious Chancellor of the Exchequer, Nigel Lawson, considers what will happen to the Government's £7.2 billion sell-off of BP only a day after the Black Monday stock exchange crash, when billions of pounds were wiped off the value of shares. Garland's cartoon contains another topical allusion: on 16 October the southeast of England was hit by the worst storms in over 250 years. Sixteen people were killed, thousands of buildings severely damaged, and some 15 million trees toppled. [NICK GARLAND *Independent* 20 October]

Lest We Forget – What Heartless, Murdering Scum the IRA Are

During a Remembrance Day service in Enniskillen in Northern Ireland on 8 November the IRA detonated a bomb that killed 11 and injured 63. Margaret Thatcher described the bombing as 'utterly barbaric'. 'It desecrated the dead and was a blot on mankind.' [STAN MCMURTRY 'MAC' *Daily Mail* 9 November]

It's a Knockout

In June Prince Edward persuaded various members of the royal family to take part in a televised *It's a Royal Knockout* to raise money for charity. The slapstick event turned out to be something of a public relations disaster for the monarchy. [MICHAEL CUMMINGS *Daily Express* 27 November]

1988

Dr Waldheim

'Dr Waldheim's busy rehearsing his address to the nation, but you could say he's in defiant mood.' Former UN Secretary-General Kurt Waldheim became president of Austria in 1986, at which point accusations about his activities during the Nazi era began to surface. On 8 February a six-man international commission concluded that Waldheim had been aware of Nazi atrocities and had done nothing to stop them but that he had not personally participated in them. Insisting that he was innocent, Waldheim rejected calls for his resignation, but he was shunned by most of the international community and did not run for the presidency again in 1992. [DAVE GASKILL *Today* 15 February]

This is Terrifying – The Serfs Believe What I Say!

By 1988 Mikhail Gorbachev's policies of *perestroika* (restructuring) and *glasnost* (openness), the one intended to overhaul the economy of the Soviet Union, the other designed to introduce a degree of freedom of expression, were beginning to run away with him. Various parts of the Soviet Union started to push for greater independence from Moscow's rule, notably the Baltic states of Estonia, Lithuania and Latvia, and the Soviet republics of Ukraine, Georgia and Armenia. [MICHAEL CUMMINGS *Daily Express* 28 February]

Irresistible Force …
Immovable Object

Margaret Thatcher's cabinet became increasingly split over attitudes to Europe, her Chancellor Nigel Lawson and Foreign Secretary Geoffrey Howe favouring closer economic cooperation and Britain's entry into the Exchange Rate Mechanism, the Prime Minister herself resisting the move. Shortly after this cartoon appeared, Thatcher made a speech in Bruges in which she upheld 'willing and active cooperation between independent states' but deplored any move towards a more centralised Europe. European issues were to tear the cabinet apart in the coming months. [NICK GARLAND *Independent* 18 September]

Can't You Read? Curry's Off!

Junior Health Minister Edwina Currie was forced to resign following her claim that 'most of the egg production in this country, sadly, is now affected with salmonella'. Not surprisingly, given that sales of eggs then plummeted, her remark did not go down well with farmers. [CHARLES GRIFFIN *Daily Mirror* 19 December]

Lockerbie

On 21 December a bomb exploded on board a Pan Am 747 jumbo jet, causing it to crash on to the town of Lockerbie in the Scottish borders. All 259 passengers were killed, as were eleven people on the ground. Two men linked with Libyan intelligence were eventually charged with planting the bomb. [BERNARD COOKSON *Sun* 23 December]

All-day Drinking

'For 14 years I've endured his varicose veins, his marital problems and his only joke … but that was lunchtimes and evenings only!' The Government relaxed licensing laws, allowing pubs to stay open all day. [STAN MCMURTY 'MAC' *Daily Mail* 23 August]

1989

At Least Our Other Daughter-in-law is the World's Best Undresser, Dear

1989 was not a good year for the royal family. [DAVE GASKILL *Today* 13 January]

I Told You to Stick to Barbara Cartland!

Salman Rushdie's novel *The Satanic Verses* was accused of blasphemy by many Muslims when it was published in 1988. On 14 February the Iranian religious leader Ayatollah Khomeini issued a fatwa, calling for the death of Rushdie and forcing him into hiding. [STAN MCMURTRY 'MAC' *Daily Mail* 16 February]

Don't Talk Daft! We Could Buy Half a Striker for That!

On 15 April 96 football supporters were crushed to death at Hillsborough during the FA Cup semi-final between Nottingham Forest and Liverpool. The disaster resulted from too many Liverpool fans being allowed in to the back of an already full stand at the Leppings Lane end of the ground and then being prevented by high steel fencing from being able to spill out on to the pitch. After a public inquiry, new safety measures were introduced at football grounds around Britain. [DAVE GASKILL *Today* 17 April]

Chinese Checkers

Following seven weeks of student demonstrations in Beijing's Tiananmen Square, the Chinese army moved in on 4 June, firing randomly on unarmed protestors and killing several hundred (estimates of the number of dead vary considerably). Some of the demonstrators had been calling for democracy in China; others had been voicing criticism of the ruling Communist party. [DAVE BROWN Sunday Times 11 June]

The Fall of the Berlin Wall

As border restrictions between Warsaw Pact countries were relaxed in 1989, the Eastern bloc began to unravel. On 9 November East Germany's new leader Egon Krenz, who had replaced the hardline communist Erich Honecker, gave permission for gates along the Berlin Wall to be opened after hundreds of people converged on crossing points. As they surged through, they were met by jubilant West Berliners. Ecstatic crowds began to clamber on top of the wall and hack large chunks out of the 28 mile (45 km) barrier. [DAVE GASKILL Today 10 November]

Thatcher vs Heseltine

The unashamedly pro-European Sir Anthony Meyer became the first to challenge Margaret Thatcher's leadership, hoping to stimulate a challenge from a higher profile figure. While the majority of Conservative MPs backed the Prime Minister, 33 voted for Meyer and a number abstained – a sign of ebbing support for Thatcher. Cole prophetically has John Major running behind Michael Heseltine (seen at the time as Thatcher's most likely challenger and successor), with Chris Patten coming in last. Sir Anthony Meyer is trying to trip her up, while Tory party chairman Kenneth Baker attempts to stop him. Willie Whitelaw and Geoffrey Howe look on. [RICHARD COLE Guardian 26 November]

1990

Oh, Look! They're Going to Do Another Estimate

The French and British governments had agreed to a fixed rail link between Britain and France in 1986, but by 1990 the project was running hugely over budget. By the time it was opened in 1994 the Channel Tunnel had cost nearly six times more than originally estimated. [RAYMOND JACKSON 'JAK' *Evening Standard* 10 January]

The Release of Nelson Mandela

'I can't get the hang of this South African cricket. How come he's out?' On 11 February South African President F W de Klerk (seen here as the umpire) released Nelson Mandela after 27 years' imprisonment. At the time Mike Gatting was leading a highly controversial cricket tour of South Africa, opposed by the ANC and the mainly black National Sports Congress. Following demonstrations and protests, the rebel tour was eventually abandoned. [CHARLES GRIFFIN *Daily Mirror* 5 February]

No to the Poll Tax

Margaret Thatcher personally championed the community charge (or 'poll tax') whereby the old system of local government funding via the rates system was to be replaced by a tax levied on each adult resident at a particular address. Felt by many to help the rich at the expense of the poor, it was hugely unpopular, provoking riots in central London at the end of March. It also helped precipitate the Prime Minister's downfall later that year. It was replaced by the council tax in 1993. [WALLY FAWKES 'Trog' *Observer* 4 March]

Warmongering Hag

In August Saddam Hussein sent Iraqi forces into Kuwait, sparking international condemnation. The UN Security Council called for the 'immediate and unconditional' withdrawal of Iraqi forces, while Margaret Thatcher, on a visit to Colorado, called in a joint press conference with President Bush for an international effort to end Iraq's 'intolerable' invasion. [STAN MCMURTRY 'MAC' *Daily Mail* 9 November]

I Am Absolutely Confident There is no Risk

Anxious to allay public worries about BSE, a disease of cattle first recognised in Britain in 1986, Agriculture Minister John Gummer not only reiterated the view of many in the scientific community that British beef was safe to eat but on 6 May publicly fed his four-year-old daughter Cordelia a hamburger at a boat show in Suffolk. Worries persisted, however, and a week after this cartoon appeared a worldwide ban was placed on British beef exports. [NICK GARLAND *Independent* 17 May]

They All Wore Grey Suits!

Antagonised by Margaret Thatcher's policies towards Europe and by her leadership style, Geoffrey Howe resigned from the cabinet on 1 November, delivering a devastating resignation speech in the House of Commons on 13 November. The following day Michael Heseltine announced that he would challenge Margaret Thatcher for the leadership. She failed to win outright in the first ballot and, after consulting her cabinet ministers individually, many of whom felt she would lose, withdrew from the second round of voting. Her Chancellor of the Exchequer, John Major, succeeded her as Prime Minister. [RAYMOND JACKSON 'JAK' *Evening Standard* 22 November]

When Margaret Thatcher resigned the premiership the majority of her colleagues followed her lead in supporting the bid by the Chancellor of the Exchequer, John Major, to succeed her. His rise to power had been swift: he had entered the cabinet only three years before as Chief Secretary to the Treasury, had been made Foreign Secretary in October 1989 and was appointed Chancellor just a few months later. He seemed genuinely surprised at the turn of events. 'Well, who would have thought it?' he is said to have told his first cabinet meeting.

So far as cartoonists were concerned, the grey-haired Major initially seemed rather unpromising material (fellow Conservative Sir Nicholas Fairbairn even remarked that to describe Major as grey 'would be an insult to porridge'). However they soon found things to focus on: his large top lip (almost duck-like, according to Steve Bell), his heavy glasses and a personality that the uncharitable felt to be somewhat 'nerdy'. Some critics compared his voice to that of the Muppets' Fozzy Bear, while the satirical TV programme *Spitting Image* came up with an all-grey puppet eating his dinner in virtual silence, with just the occasional 'Nice peas, dear' comment to his wife. Steve Bell's shorthand way of evoking this nerdiness was to depict Major with aertex Y-fronts over his trousers, so that he emerged as a sort of 'super-useless-man'. Unsurprisingly, Major, who was quite sensitive about his media image, was not overly delighted.

Ironically, given the alleged greyness of the Prime Minister, this was the decade that cartoons started to appear in colour in national newspapers. In 1986 the short-lived *Today* had been the first national colour newspaper, and, as technology improved, other papers – though not the tabloids – followed suit. For the cartoonist, colour offers both opportunities and challenges. It can aesthetically enhance a cartoon but, in the wrong hands, may distract attention from the point the cartoonist is trying to make. From a practical point of view colour also means that cartoonists now need more time to complete their work, making the challenge of dealing with rapidly changing news stories that much greater. Peter Brookes has actually reduced the format of his cartoon to accommodate colour so that he does not have to spend too much time applying it.

According to the pollsters, the Conservatives were destined to lose the General Election in April 1992 to Neil Kinnock's Labour party. In the event, however, while Major's soap box campaign style may have come in for some ridicule, Kinnock's rather presidential approach to electioneering proved even more off-putting to the electorate, and the Conservatives won with an overall majority of 21. Thereafter problems crowded in. On 16 September Britain was humiliatingly forced out of the Exchange Rate Mechanism, leaving the Government's economic credentials in tatters. A bruising battle to pass the Maastricht Treaty through Parliament in 1993 led to a visible split in the party between Eurosceptics and the leadership. And the high moral tone of Major's 'Back to Basics' campaign, launched in 1993, was undermined by a succession of Conservative scandals and accusations of sleaze. In terms of public opinion all this more than offset an improving economy and the negotiation of an IRA ceasefire, and, to no one's surprise, in 1997 the Conservatives went down to their biggest electoral defeat in almost a century.

Tony Blair now became Prime Minister. He had gained

1991–1999

the Labour leadership in July 1994 after the sudden death
of his predecessor John Smith and had spent three years
seeking to remodel the party as 'New Labour', removing
any vestiges of socialism and moving the party firmly to the
political centre ground. When he became Prime Minister
he was given an original Will Dyson cartoon by William
Mellor, the son of one of the previous editors of the *Daily
Herald*. The cartoon, published on 3 December 1913, was
entitled 'A Fantasy (Labour leaders at their devotions)', and
it criticised the then Labour leadership for toadying up
to capitalism. 'No! I don't think we want that!' was Blair's
reaction.

Because of his youth and apparent political innocence,
Blair was initially portrayed as a sort of doe-eyed Bambi by
cartoonists, who were also swift to focus on other salient
features, such as his wide, toothy smile. 'He has sticky-
out ears, receding hair, a flabby lower lip and those starry
eyes,' said Steve Bell. 'That should be enough to be going

on with.' He enjoyed a short honeymoon period, showing
a real ability to read the public mood in the aftermath of
Princess Diana's death in August. But accusations of New
Labour media 'spin' started to be voiced, and he soon, inevitably, had his share of political problems to contend with:
reform of public services, opposition from the Countryside
Alliance, the challenge of keeping Northern Ireland peace
talks going and the continuing bloodbath of the civil war in
former Yugoslavia not least among them.

Searching for Cool Britannia

1991

Stormin' Norman

Following Iraq's invasion of Kuwait the previous year, coalition forces, led by the US, launched a massive air campaign (codenamed Operation Desert Storm) on 17 January. More than 1,000 sorties a day were flown, and targets throughout Iraq were bombed. A week later Iraq was accused of dumping approximately 1 million tons of crude oil into the Gulf, causing widespread pollution. Here the commander of the coalition forces, General Norman Schwarzkopf, watches the allied aerial assault. [STEVE BELL *Guardian* 28 January]

HE WHO FIGHTS AND RUNS AWAY ...   LIVES TO FIGHT ANOTHER DAY.

He Who Fights and Runs Away ... Lives to Fight Another Day

The air offensive was followed by a land campaign that quickly achieved its objectives, and at the end of February Iraq accepted allied terms for a ceasefire. The fact that the war stopped short of removing Saddam Hussein from power was hotly debated at the time. Many felt it was right to halt the allied offensive once Kuwait had been liberated; others argued – rather as this cartoon does – that because Saddam was being left in power, the way was now open for him to suppress internal opposition and, in particular, to crush rebellions among the Shi'ites in the south and the Kurds in the north of Iraq. [NICK GARLAND *Daily Telegraph* 8 March]

The End of the Soviet Union

On 19 August a group of hardline communists, who felt that Gorbachev's reform programme had gone too far, staged a coup in Moscow. It collapsed quickly, but as well as undermining Gorbachev its failure clearly signalled the end of the old Soviet Union. [CHRIS RIDDELL *Observer* 26 August]

D'you Know of a Better Hole?

Another reworking of Bairnsfather's First World War cartoon. Prime Minister John Major and his Foreign Secretary Douglas Hurd take cover from their former leader as Margaret Thatcher attacks the Government for being 'arrogant and wrong' in its refusal to hold a referendum on the introduction of a single European currency. All the Eurosceptic bogies are here: the Maastricht Treaty, Economic and Monetary Union and the European Currency Unit. As events were to prove, Thatcher was not the only Eurosceptic in the Conservative party. [MICHAEL CUMMINGS *Daily Express* 24 November]

Are You Sure You Didn't Take it with You?

On 5 November media baron Robert Maxwell drowned while yachting off the Canary Islands. After his death investigators discovered that he had propped up his publishing empire by borrowing extensively and diverting vast sums from the Maxwell company pension funds. As the truth emerged, his empire fell apart. [BILL CALDWELL *Star* 5 December]

The Friends of John McCarthy

On 8 August journalist John McCarthy was released by Islamic Jihad in Beirut, having been kept hostage for more than five years. His fellow captives, Terry Waite and Brian Keenan, were released the same year. McCarthy's girlfriend, Jill Morrell, had spear-headed a pressure group, the Friends of John McCarthy, to keep people aware of his plight. [CHARLES GRIFFIN *People* 11 August]

1992

Relive the Glorious Past, Sir – Pre-election Polls

The 1992 General Election result proved something of a surprise. Even though Labour, under Neil Kinnock, had been marginally ahead in opinion polls, it was the incumbent Prime Minister, John Major, who actually won the election, albeit with a slender majority. Pollsters came to the conclusion that a 'Shy Tory Factor' was at work. [DAVE GASKILL *Today* 11 April]

Nothing Personal, Sir – I Was Just Expecting Someone Else

John Major's new administration had a majority of fewer than 30 seats in the House of Commons. [DAVE GASKILL *Today* 11 April]

It's Not Fair, Mummy

This cartoon appeared in the wake of the publication of Andrew Morton's bestselling *Diana: Her True Story*, a pretty devastating account of her marriage to Prince Charles. [DAVE GASKILL *Today* 8 June]

Look on the Bright Side, Old Girl, There's Only 21 Days of Annus Horribilis Left

The year was not a good one for the royal family. On 20 November Windsor Castle was badly damaged by fire, and on 9 December John Major announced to the Commons that Prince Charles and Princess Diana would be separating. As the queen said in a speech at the Guildhall: '1992 is not a year on which I shall look back with undiluted pleasure. In the words of one of my more sympathetic correspondents, it has turned out to be an Annus Horribilis.' [CHARLES GRIFFIN *Daily Mirror* 11 December]

32 Degrees in the Shade

No-fly zones were established in Iraq after the Gulf War of 1991. As this cartoon suggests, however, Saddam continued to repress civilian populations in areas hostile to him, and in August a no-fly zone was established south of the 32nd parallel to protect Shi'ite Muslims. President George Bush is shown here concentrating on domestic concerns, while John Major focuses on the escalating crisis in Bosnia, whose independence had been recognised by the US and European Community in April. [DAVE BROWN *The Times* 23 August]

Black Wednesday

The day before this cartoon appeared, the pound had come under such pressure from currency speculators that Chancellor of the Exchequer Norman Lamont first spent billions trying to prop up sterling and then announced that Britain would be withdrawing from the European Exchange Rate Mechanism (ERM). Black Wednesday shattered the reputation the Conservatives had previously enjoyed for fiscal competence, so it is not surprising that Lamont and Major appear to have lost more than their shirts (although at least Major has retained his underpants). [STEVE BELL *Guardian* 17 September]

1993

Green Shoots of Recovery

Chancellor of the Exchequer Norman Lamont's earlier optimistic claims that 'the green shoots of recovery' could be seen all around constantly came back to haunt him at a time of world recession. He left the Government in May, by which time signs of economic improvement were, in fact, starting to become apparent. [RICHARD COLE Sunday Times 11 April]

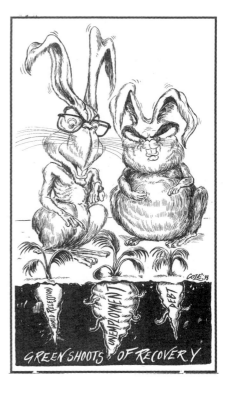

Lamont and Major

Increasingly out of favour and out of step with John Major, Norman Lamont returned to the backbenches in May, accusing the Government of being 'in office, but not in power'. Cummings's cartoon not only records the damage done to Major by Lamont's speech but also recalls a slightly embarrassing moment in Lamont's private life when he discovered that he had inadvertently let his Notting Hill home to a call girl by the name of Miss Whiplash. [MICHAEL CUMMINGS Sunday Express 10 June]

A Happy New Year?

On the day this cartoon appeared Israeli Prime Minister Yitzhak Rabin and the PLO leader Yasser Arafat shook hands on the White House lawn in Washington and signed the Oslo Accords, whereby Israel agreed to withdraw its troops from parts of the Gaza Strip and the West Bank and allow Palestinian self-government in those areas. A number of contentious issues were left for later discussion, and, even as they stood, the Accords proved unpopular with many – Rabin was to be assassinated two years later by a right-wing Israeli opposed to them. The caption is a reference to the Jewish New Year, which comes in the early autumn. [RIC BROOKES Evening Standard 13 September]

Why wasn't I Told What I was up to?

The previous year had seen the Matrix Churchill trial, when three businessmen were accused of selling arms to the Middle East that, contrary to government guidelines, had ended up in Iraq. When it became clear that the sale had been informally approved, the trial collapsed and the Scott Inquiry was set up to investigate government conduct. It quickly emerged that arms sales to Iraq had taken place not only during John Major's time in power, but during Margaret Thatcher's period of office as well, and here she is seen feeding a ravenous Saddam Hussein. When the Scott Inquiry finally reported in 1996 it was highly critical of Conservative ministers. [STEVE BELL *Guardian* 10 December]

Unfortunately I Can See a Resemblance

Allegations about Bill Clinton's private life dogged him throughout his two terms as president. Here the state of his trousers shows that Hillary Clinton is not comparing him to John F Kennedy politically, but to Kennedy's reputation as a womaniser. [DAVE BROWN *Sunday Times* 28 December]

Can You Spare a Small Donation, Sir?

Asil Nadir, a Conservative party donor and head of the Polly Peck group of companies, fled Britain for Northern Cyprus when faced with 66 charges of theft from the company. Polly Peck collapsed and the whole affair caused the Government considerable embarrassment. [RICHARD COLE *Sunday Times* 27 June]

1994

Back to Basics

The year began badly for the Conservative party. In January MP Tim Yeo resigned over reports that he had fathered a child outside marriage, while on 8 February MP Stephen Milligan was found dead, clad in stockings and suspenders and with a bin liner over his head, having taken part in a bizarre sexual ritual. The two events proved particularly embarrassing for Prime Minister John Major because only a few months before he had launched his 'Back to Basics' campaign, designed to encourage higher standards of behaviour in all walks of life. At the time this cartoon was published the Winter Olympics were taking place in Lillehammer, Norway. [MICHAEL HEATH *Mail on Sunday* 15 February]

Rwanda

Between April and June 1994 an estimated 800,000 people, mainly from Rwanda's minority Tutsi ethnic group, were murdered in a systematic campaign orchestrated by extremist elements of the country's majority Hutu population. The killings were sparked by the shooting down on 6 April of a plane carrying Rwanda's Hutu president Juvenal Habyarimana. Victims were hacked to death, burned alive and thrown dead or alive into pits or latrines. Peter Schrank not only conveys the full horror of the genocide but also comments on the UN's inability to stop it. [PETER SCHRANK *Economist* 31 May]

Piggies in the Middle

Following the sudden death in May of Labour leader John Smith, Tony Blair became favourite to take over leadership of the party. On 31 May he and the shadow Chancellor of the Exchequer Gordon Brown met at the Granita restaurant in Islington, where it is believed that they agreed that Brown would step aside and give Blair a clear run and that, in time, Blair would stand down in favour of Brown. The crown is being thrown over the heads of other leadership hopefuls Margaret Beckett, Robin Cook and John Prescott. [NICK GARLAND *Daily Telegraph* 3 June]

Cash for Questions

The Cash for Questions scandal began as a sting operation set up by the *Sunday Times* in the spring of 1994 to see if MPs could be bought. Adopting various guises to contact ten Labour and ten Conservative MPs, the newspaper offered to pay each of them £1,000 to ask a question in the House of Commons. Virtually all turned the offer down, but two Conservatives accepted, and since both were parliamentary private secretaries and thus regarded as members of the Government, the scandal did John Major's administration considerable damage. [DAVE BROWN *Sunday Times* 19 July]

Countdown to Peace Talks

Although the PLO had agreed to end the use of violence in the Oslo Accords of September 1993, attacks on Israeli settlers continued. On 25 February a disgruntled right-wing settler, Baruch Goldstein, opened fire on worshippers in the Cave of the Patriarchs in Hebron, killing 30 people before being killed himself. In retaliation, Hamas carried out several suicide attacks in Israel during April. Despite this, talks continued between the two sides on issues such as security arrangements and legal matters, and on 29 April the Israel–PLO economic agreement was signed in Paris. [DAVID SIMONDS *Guardian* 18 April]

New Labour New Britain

At his first party conference in Blackpool the new Labour leader Tony Blair relaunched the party as New Labour. At the end of his speech he declared that the party needed a new statement of aims and a 'modern' constitution. The fact that Blair was moving the party firmly to the right was not lost on Steve Bell, who has him metamorphosing into Margaret Thatcher. [STEVE BELL *Guardian* 5 October]

1995

Keep Clause IV

Clause IV of the Labour party's constitution included a distinctly socialist pledge to work for the 'common ownership of the means of production, distribution and exchange'. Anxious to move away from this, Tony Blair persuaded a special conference to replace it with a 'statement of aims and values', committing Labour to 'a dynamic economy' in which the 'enterprise of the market' is joined with the 'forces of partnership and cooperation'. Here Blair, John Prescott and Robin Cook launch a kung-fu attack on Labour diehards – an allusion to Manchester United's Eric Cantona who, two days before, had attacked a Crystal Palace fan in a similar manner. [NICK GARLAND *Daily Telegraph* 27 January]

John Major Wants to Remind You not to Forget about the Handshake when We Catch Them

A caustic comment on the decision of President Clinton not only to grant Sinn Fein leader Gerry Adams a visa to travel to the US in March but to meet him at a St Patrick's Day lunch, where the two men shook hands. The cartoon appeared two days after a huge car bomb exploded at a government building in Oklahoma City, killing 168 people and injuring more than 500. [RIC BROOKES 'Brook' *Daily Express* 21 April]

Next to a Battle Lost, the Greatest Misery is a Battle Gained

Faced with constant criticism from a right-wing and Eurosceptic faction within Conservative ranks, John Major instructed his party to 'put up or shut up' and – daringly – called a leadership contest. He convincingly beat the only other candidate, former Secretary of State for Wales John Redwood, on 4 July, but as this cartoon implies his troubles were far from over. [PETER BROOKES *The Times* 5 July]

Greater Serbia

Srebrenica in Bosnia became the scene of the worst massacre in Europe since the end of the Second World War when, in July, Bosnian Serb forces massacred over 7,000 Muslim men and boys. The town was meant to be a United Nations 'safe haven', but the UN had given the Dutch peacekeepers there an inadequate mandate, and they did not intervene to stop the slaughter. [CHRIS RIDDELL *Observer* 16 July]

Helbert and John's Naked Blue Shit Picture

Inspired by Gilbert and George's controversial 'Naked Shit Pictures', Steve Bell takes a swipe at the Conservative party leadership, showing John Major and Michael Heseltine bathing in a pair of (presumably John Major's) underpants, with Defence Secretary Michael Portillo on the left and Home Secretary Michael Howard on the right. The SAS reference is an allusion to a rather unfortunate speech made by Portillo at that year's Conservative party conference in which he declared: 'Around the world three letters send a chill down the spine of the enemy – SAS. And those letters spell out one clear message: don't mess with Britain. The SAS has a famous motto: Who Dares Wins. We will dare, we will win.' The *Guardian* did not run the cartoon. [STEVE BELL 3 October (unpublished)]

Greater Israel

On 4 November Israeli Prime Minister Yitzhak Rabin was assassinated as he left a peace rally in Tel Aviv. The assassin was Yigal Amir, one of the founders of an illegal Jewish settlement on the West Bank and a member of an extreme right-wing organisation. [MARTIN ROWSON *Guardian* 6 November]

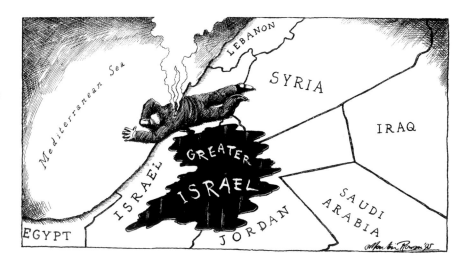

1996

Yeltsin and Chechnya

Boris Yeltsin, the first president of the Russian Federation, had ordered a military invasion of Chechnya in late 1994 in an attempt to stop the republic breaking away from the federation. Fought with increasing brutality, the war cost the lives of tens of thousands of Chechens and made nearly a quarter of a million homeless. Yeltsin's tactics were widely criticised in the West – hence the reference to Stalin in this cartoon. Yeltsin's fondness for alcohol had, by this time, become notorious. [PETER SCHRANK *Independent on Sunday* 19 January]

IRA Bomb

A 17-month IRA ceasefire was shattered by the explosion on 10 February of a truck bomb at South Quay, near Canary Wharf on the Isle of Dogs. Two people were killed and 40 others injured. Chris Riddell's figure of peace is reminiscent of ones drawn earlier in the century – for example, in Will Dyson's cartoon of 1919 marking the Treaty of Versailles. [CHRIS RIDDELL *Observer* 11 February]

Dunblane

On 13 March 43-year-old Thomas Hamilton opened fire in a primary school in Dunblane, Scotland, killing 16 children and their teacher. He then turned the gun on himself. [STEVE BELL *Guardian* 14 March]

Hitting the Heart

Steve Bell's cartoon reflects on the tit-for-tat killings in Israel, where the Israeli government responded to the indiscriminate suicide bombings of buses by bulldozing hundreds of Palestinian homes in its search for terrorists. [STEVE BELL *Guardian* 5 March]

Mad Cow

In March government ministers publicly accepted new scientific advice that there was a link between BSE in cattle and the terminal Creutzfeldt–Jakob disease (CJD) in humans. Coming in the wake of recent and equally public denials of a link, it is not surprising that Prime Minister John Major looks distinctly ill-at-ease. [NICK GARLAND *Daily Telegraph* 24 March]

New Labour, New Danger

The launch of the Conservative's 'New Labour, New Danger' poster campaign marked one of the low points in what was to become Britain's most negative General Election campaign since the war. The advertisements, showing Blair with glowing demon eyes, were censured by the Advertising Standards Authority. [NICK GARLAND *Daily Telegraph* 8 July]

1997

Hong Kong

The day after this cartoon was published Hong Kong was handed back to China, after more than 150 years of British control. The last governor, Chris Patten, made a farewell speech in which he said: 'The story of this great city is about the years before this night and the years of success that will surely follow it.' [PETER SCHRANK *Independent on Sunday* 30 June]

Time to Bring on Our Secret Weapon

The Conservative party went into the 1997 General Election campaign well behind in the polls. There was a sense of exhaustion after 18 years in power, the party was bitterly divided over Europe, and it had acquired a reputation for sleaze. Here Conservative party chairman Dr Brian Mawhinney wheels out a line of John Majors, soapboxes in hand, hoping that the tactic of getting the Prime Minister to make direct contact with the electorate will prove as successful in 1997 as it had been in 1992. It was not. [PETER SCHRANK *Independent on Sunday* 2 March]

Intimate Pictures Nobody's Going to Publish

On 10 September, after 30 years of sectarian violence, Sinn Fein formally renounced the use of force to achieve its political ends, signing up to the so-called Mitchell Principles, developed by a former US Senate leader. Suspicious Unionist politicians, however, kept away. Peter Brookes's cartoon depicts the seemingly impossible: Sinn Fein leader Gerry Adams shaking hands with the Rev. Ian Paisley, leader of Northern Ireland's militantly loyalist DUP, and Adams's colleague Martin McGuinness shaking hands with Ulster Unionist Party leader David Trimble. Nearly ten years later, on 26 March 2007, Adams and Paisley met face to face for the first time. [PETER BROOKES *The Times* 10 September]

Queen of All Our Hearts

On 31 August Diana, Princess of Wales was killed in a car crash in the Pont de l'Alma road tunnel in Paris. The caption to this cartoon recalls an interview she gave in 1995 when she said that she wanted to be remembered as the 'queen of people's hearts' and for all her charitable work. [CHARLES GRIFFIN *Daily Express* 1 September]

Diana's Funeral

After Diana's funeral in Westminster Abbey her coffin was taken by road to the Spencer family home at Althorp for private burial. This first version of Steve Bell's cartoon bears the words 'Global Interstiff' on the side of the hearse, but at the request of the *Guardian* the cartoonist changed this to 'Non-Royal Windsor's' in the published version. [STEVE BELL *Guardian* 4 September]

Every Time We Think We've Fixed it, There's Another Leak

In November 1997 the Government decided that Formula One racing would be exempt from the sponsorship ban about to be put on tobacco advertising. The press then revealed that Prime Minister Tony Blair had met representatives of Formula One before the decision was announced and that Formula One boss Bernie Ecclestone had donated £1 million to the Labour party before the General Election. Blair and Ecclestone strongly denied any connection between the donation and the exemption, and Labour returned the £1 million, but the scandal nevertheless tarnished the Government's image. Here Peter Mandelson, John Prescott and Gordon Brown try to help out their embattled leader. [PATRICK BLOWER *Evening Standard* 25 November]

233

1998

Countryside March

In its election manifesto the Labour party had promised to ban foxhunting. In response, the pro-hunting Countryside Alliance organised a massive protest rally in London. According to Conservative leader William Hague: 'This Government's inability to hear the normally quiet voice of rural Britain has created one of the biggest mass protest movements of recent years.' John Archer, from the long-running Radio 4 series *The Archers*, had recently died in a tractor accident. [MARTYN TURNER *Sunday Express* 1 March]

Hand of History

On 10 April, after two years of talks (initiated by John Major) and 30 years of conflict, the Northern Ireland Good Friday Agreement was signed. It included plans for a Northern Ireland Assembly, new cross-border institutions involving the Irish Republic and a body linking devolved assemblies across the UK with Westminster and Dublin. In the words of Tony Blair: 'I feel the hand of history on our shoulder with respect to this. I really do. I just think we need to acknowledge that and respond to it.' [PATRICK BLOWER *Evening Standard* 14 April]

Pensions

One of Gordon Brown's first acts as Chancellor of the Exchequer was to remove tax benefits to pensions and insurance funds, in the process taking £5 billion a year for the Treasury. Seen by opposition MPs at the time as a 'stealth tax', his move became even more controversial later when many pension funds ran into deficit as equity markets declined. [NICK GARLAND *Daily Telegraph* 8 July]

234

That Prayer Breakfast in Full

On 11 September President Clinton delivered a speech at the annual White House prayer breakfast apologising for his 'inappropriate' relationship with White House intern Monica Lewinsky – a relationship he had denied earlier that year. He was later impeached for perjury and obstruction of justice, but ultimately cleared. Steve Bell makes the nature of the 'inappropriate' relationship pretty clear. [STEVE BELL *Guardian* 12 September]

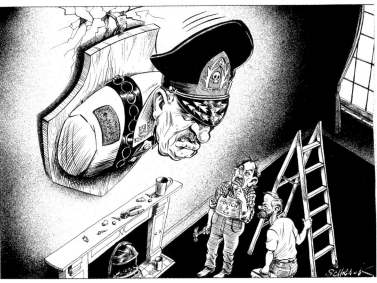

Pinochet

On 17 October, while he was visiting London for medical treatment, former Chilean dictator General Augusto Pinochet was arrested following the issuing of an extradition warrant from Spain, where he stood accused of the torture and murder of Spanish citizens while in power. He remained in Britain under house arrest for 17 months, an embarrassment to the Government but defended by Margaret Thatcher, who valued his support during the Falklands War. Eventually, Home Secretary Jack Straw released him on health grounds, and he returned to Chile. Here Tony Blair and Foreign Secretary Robin Cook ponder what to do. [PETER SCHRANK *Independent on Sunday* 25 October]

William Hague

William Hague, who succeeded John Major as leader of the Conservative party in 1997, is seen trying unsuccessfully to relight the Conservative torch. From the start, his leadership came in for criticism, and when in a public relations exercise he visited a theme park wearing a baseball cap emblazoned with the word 'HAGUE', the whole thing backfired disastrously. [CHRIS RIDDELL *Observer* 19 December]

1999

Milošević's Cupboard

When, following an intensive bombing campaign, NATO troops took over Kosovo after Serb forces had withdrawn, they found ample evidence of the atrocities committed on Kosovo's Albanian population by Slobodan Milošević's Serbian forces. According to reports, around 10,000 people had been killed in more than 100 separate massacres. [CHRIS RIDDELL *Observer* 14 June]

It is Peace in Our Time

Despite Tony Blair's protestations that a permanent peace deal in Northern Ireland was within reach, talks stalled over the issue of the decommissioning of weapons by the IRA. Blair's possible over-optimism is compared to Neville Chamberlain's falsely optimistic claim after his meeting with Hitler at Munich in 1938 that he had achieved 'peace in our time'. [WALLY FAWKES 'Trog' *Sunday Telegraph* 4 July]

Now I Really am Mad

While the European Union was prepared to start allowing imports of British beef again, the French government decided to maintain its ban, claiming that its Food Safety Agency had established that British beef was still not free from BSE. Not surprisingly, this did not go down well with the British Government. [PETER BROOKES *The Times* 19 October]

Building the Wall

The Labour government had established a Greater London Authority in 1998 and planned for a mayor to be elected in 2000. Tony Blair favoured Frank Dobson as the Labour candidate, distrusting the populist 'Red' Ken Livingstone, who had also thrown his hat into the ring (and who had led the GLC until its abolition by the Conservatives in 1986). Conservative leader William Hague taunted Blair at Prime Minister's question time: 'Why not split the job in two, with Frank Dobson as your day mayor and Ken Livingstone as your nightmare?' In the event, Livingstone ran as an independent and won. [PETER BROOKES *The Times* 9 November]

One Lump or Two, Mr President?

On 30 November a meeting of the World Trade Organisation in Seattle was disrupted by anti-globalisation protesters. President Clinton addressed the WTO as a guest speaker. [PETER BROOKES *The Times* 2 December]

We Could Have the Running Track Here and the Field Events Over There

Constructed to hold a major exhibition celebrating the beginning of the third millennium, the Millennium Dome proved both massively costly and controversial and was regarded as a white elephant even before it opened. In the light of Britain's winning of the Olympic bid for Greenwich in July 2005, Bernard Cookson's cartoon seems an inspired piece of crystal-ball gazing. [BERNARD COOKSON *Daily Express* 3 December]

Looking Ahead

At the beginning of 2001, Garland wonders what the year will have in store. Depicted (from top to bottom and left to right) are: Al Gore, George W Bush, Vladimir Putin, Ted Heath, Ken Livingstone, Robin Cook, Margaret Thatcher, Bill Clinton, Jacques Chirac, Martin McGuinness, Gerry Adams, Michael Portillo, Ann Widdecombe, Jack Straw, Tony Blair, Alastair Campbell, John Prescott, Kenneth Clarke, William Hague, Ehud Barak, Yasser Arafat, Peter Mandelson, Gordon Brown. [NICK GARLAND *Daily Telegraph* 1 January 2001]

Any optimism there may have been at the dawning of the third millennium was swiftly undermined by events. The terrorist attacks of 9/11, the ensuing 'War on Terror', the invasion of Iraq and the London bombings of July 2005 swiftly crowded in on the new century.

The controversy surrounding the Iraq War, in particular, has had a huge impact on the way in which leading figures have been depicted by cartoonists. Even before it was launched, its prime instigator, President George W Bush, was under fire from the likes of Steve Bell, who depicted him as a slack-jawed, dumb-headed, arm-swinging ape. The visual attacks then intensified after war was declared. Tony Blair, Bush's close ally, was similarly demonised by some, right up to the moment when he stepped down from the premiership. Criticised as being too ready to follow the US lead, he also attracted charges of riding roughshod over sceptics and critics. 'I detest the man and what he's done,' the *Independent*'s Dave Brown said. 'But he's great to draw. You put all that bile, hatred and angst into drawing.' 'I used to draw Blair with eyebrows up, looking eager,' Peter Brookes observed. 'Now he has one eyebrow down, showing his authoritarian tendency. There is a menace there that was not there before. His eye is not mad, just extremely authoritarian.' Steve Bell claimed to have detected a 'psychotic glint' in Blair's left eyeball and consequently depicted it as vast and deranged. According to Bell: 'In the early days I knew it was there but didn't see it in photos. Now I can see it.'

Blair, however, is not the only British political figure to have been savaged by cartoonists. The Conservatives, not to mention the Liberals and others, have also had a fairly tough time of it. Until the 1997 election debacle only one 20th-century Conservative leader – Austen Chamberlain – had not also secured the premiership. Now three leaders – William Hague, Iain Duncan Smith

Epilogue:

and Michael Howard – followed one another in fairly quick succession, none of them able to grasp the ultimate crown. Hague, despite being over six feet tall, tended to be portrayed as a schoolboy, a reference perhaps to his precocious performance at the 1977 Conservative party conference when he was only 16. Iain Duncan Smith was pilloried for his softly spoken nature, and his portrayal in cartoons was often reminiscent of Uncle Fester from the *Addams Family*. Michael Howard's Romanian roots, along with the accusation by his colleague Ann Widdecombe that he had 'something of the night' about him, inevitably suggested vampiric images to cartoonists. When Howard lost the 2005 General Election to Blair, he was replaced by old Etonian David Cameron, who came to be depicted as something of a toff or as a man a little too anxious to display his green credentials.

Few contemporary politicians, in fact, have escaped the cartoonists' censure, and this seems to have gone hand in hand with a general contemporary cynicism about the whole political sphere, which manifested itself in low turnouts at the 2001 and 2005 General Elections. Blair came to power in 1997 partly on the back of accusations of 'Tory sleaze', yet by 2006 his party was having to fight off 'cash for honours' accusations. Infighting within the Conservative party seemed to be mirrored in the Labour party, where there were constant reports of tensions between the Prime Minister and his Chancellor of the Exchequer. Reforms of public services tended to have a somewhat jaundiced reception, as did constitutional changes. All this, however, needs to be put in context. The fact is that there has not been a decade in the past 100 years when the government of the day has not eventually fallen foul of the electorate or leading politicians have not been savaged by critics. As Enoch Powell observed in *Joseph Chamberlain*: 'All political lives, unless they are cut off in midstream at a happy juncture, end in failure, because that is the nature of politics and of human affairs.'

It is always difficult to judge events close up, so the cartoons that follow have been selected simply to highlight a few of the themes that run through the early part of the 21st century. Inevitably 9/11 and its aftermath receive attention, as does the Iraq War, but there are also glimpses into other aspects of contemporary life, the Internet, global warming and *Big Brother* among them.

Into the Millennium

Fool Protest

In September 2000, in protest at high fuel prices and duties, a group of farmers and road hauliers began blockading oil refineries and distribution depots, disrupting the supply of fuel to petrol stations and causing panic buying. One consequence of the protest was that the Government abandoned the 'escalator' brought in by the Conservatives whereby fuel duties increased each year by more than the rate of inflation to discourage vehicle use and help meet environmental targets. [PETER SCHRANK *Independent* 1 November 2000]

Timmy's Just Sold Us over the Internet

British couple Alan and Judith Kilshaw paid £8,200 to adopt American twin baby girls Belinda and Kimberley over the Internet. When the affair became public, there was a media storm. The babies were eventually returned to the US. [DAVE GASKILL *Sun* 18 January 2001]

I'll be Tough on Internet Perverts …

During the 2001 General Election campaign both Labour and Conservative politicians promised to 'get tough'. Home Secretary Jack Straw committed Labour to fresh curbs on paedophile activity online. Shadow Home Secretary Ann Widdecombe undertook to introduce tougher controls on asylum seekers. Meanwhile the deputy Prime Minister, John Prescott, while campaigning in Rhyl, north Wales, hit out at a protester who had thrown an egg at him. [DAVE GASKILL *Sun* 21 May 2001]

9/11

On 11 September 2001 19 terrorists hijacked four commercial aircraft. Two of the planes, loaded with fuel and passengers, were flown into the twin towers of the World Trade Center in New York. The buildings burst into flame and then collapsed, killing thousands. A third terrorist crew smashed their plane into the Pentagon in Washington. The hijackers of the fourth airliner apparently intended to hit the White House, but passengers on the plane fought back and it crashed in a field in rural Pennsylvania. The hijackers were members of Al-Qaeda, a radical Islamic group led by Osama bin Laden. [PATRICK BLOWER *Evening Standard* 12 September 2001]

We Shall not Flag nor Fail …

President Bush, describing the 9/11 attacks as 'a national tragedy', also resolved that 'terrorism against our nation will not stand'. Tony Blair, for his part, stated: 'This is not a battle between the United States and terrorism but between the free and democratic world and terrorism. We therefore here in Britain stand shoulder to shoulder with our American friends in this hour of tragedy and we, like them, will not rest until this evil is driven from our world.' In July Blair had loaned President Bush a bust of Winston Churchill by the sculptor Jacob Epstein. [STEVE BELL *Guardian* 18 September 2001]

Your Country Needs You

The US launched an offensive against Afghanistan designed to destroy Al-Qaeda bases in the country and oust the Taliban regime that had given refuge to Osama bin Laden. Tony Blair offered the campaign his full support and committed British troops to the war effort. [PETER BROOKES *The Times* 21 December 2001]

Building up to the Iraq War

Long-standing US hostility to Saddam Hussein's regime in Iraq, along with accusations that Iraq formed part of an 'axis of evil', concern at Saddam Hussein's repeated flouting of UN resolutions on arms inspections, and the belief that he possessed weapons of mass destruction made a war against Iraq seem increasingly likely in the course of 2002. Here Bush and Blair stalk Saddam Hussein in a scene strongly reminiscent of the dust clouds that followed the attacks of 9/11. In March 2003 US forces invaded Iraq, leading a coalition that included Britain and Australia. [PETER BROOKES *The Times* 12 September 2002]

A Period of Reflection ✎

Ministry of Defence scientist David Kelly, who had worked as an arms inspector in Iraq, committed suicide on 18 July 2003 in the aftermath of a row between the BBC and Tony Blair's director of communications Alastair Campbell. It emerged that Kelly had briefed a BBC reporter who had gone on to claim that the dossier drawn up before the Iraq war, seeking to show that Saddam Hussein had weapons of mass destruction, had been 'sexed up' by Campbell. Tony Blair proposed a 'period of reflection'. An inquiry under Lord Hutton was set up to investigate the affair and proved to be sharply critical of the BBC. [ANDY DAVEY *Guardian* 22 July 2003]

Sorry

In April 2004 CBS broadcast pictures of detained Iraqis being humiliated by their US captors in the Abu Ghraib prison near Baghdad. The images caused worldwide revulsion, and George W Bush went on Arabic television to apologise for what had occurred. [CHRIS RIDDELL *Observer* 16 May 2004]

Four More Years!

George W Bush won the 2000 presidential election by the narrowest – and most controversial – of margins. On 2 September 2004 he accepted his party's nomination to run for president again, and duly won a second term in office. [PETER BROOKES *The Times* 3 September 2004]

Mind the Gap

The day after it was announced that London would host the 2012 Olympic Games, suicide bombers struck the capital's transport network, killing 52 passengers and injuring nearly 800. It soon emerged that the bombers were all young Muslims who were born and had grown up in Britain. [MORTEN MORLAND *The Times* 11 July 2005]

But More, Much More than this, We Did it Our Way

Although the military campaign against Saddam Hussein was concluded quickly, bringing peace to Iraq proved far more difficult. [Peter Schrank *Independent on Sunday* 28 May 2006]

Righty-ho, Lads!

In November 2006 Tony Blair visited Afghanistan for the first time since the US-led invasion of 2002. The year had seen a resurgence in Taliban activity and 38 British troops had been killed by the time Blair arrived in Kabul, prompting him to admit that Western leaders had underestimated how long it would take to win the 'war on terror' and to say that lessons had been learned in both Afghanistan and Iraq. [MARTIN ROWSON *Guardian* 15 November 2006]

BAA Calls for New Airport Runways

'Looks like the mayor has extended the Congestion Charge upwards.' In February 2003, in order to reduce road congestion in the capital and encourage the use of public transport, Mayor Ken Livingstone introduced a charge of £5 per vehicle to enter central London. As this cartoon shows, road congestion was not the only transport concern of the year. [PATRICK BLOWER *Evening Standard* 12 May 2003]

At Least We Get to Vote on this

2003 saw the fourth series of the hugely popular *Big Brother* on Channel 4. At the time Tony Blair was resisting calls for a referendum on a new constitution for the EU. [TIM SANDERS *Independent* 27 June 2003]

New Orleans Floods

In August 2005 Hurricane Katrina struck New Orleans, causing catastrophic flooding. The federal, state and local governments all came in for criticism over what was regarded as a tardy response to the disaster. [MORTEN MORLAND *The Times* 5 September 2005]

Whiter than White

When Lloyd George was accused in 1922 of manipulating the honours system to reward wealthy contributors to his Lloyd George Fund, Parliament's response was to pass the Honours (Prevention of Abuses) Act. Over 80 years later Labour was accused of giving peerages to a number of individuals who had made loans to the party. The charges were strenuously denied. [MORTEN MORLAND *The Times* 23 March 2006]

Bringing the Baggage on Behind

Conservative leader David Cameron's green credentials came to look a little shaky when it emerged that while he cycled to work, his baggage was carried by car. Here Andy Davey inspects some of what he regards as Cameron's political baggage: Tory fat cats, privatisers, creatures of the night, Eurosceptics and dyed-in-the-wool Thatcherites. [ANDY DAVEY Unison *Labour Link* Autumn 2006]

The Frenzy that We are not Attacking Pollution is Pure Speculation

The World Summit on Sustainable Development was held in Johannesburg from 26 August to 4 September 2002. President George W Bush came in for considerable criticism from environmental groups and others for his decision not to attend. [RICHARD COLE *Guardian* 23 August 2002]

Index

Acknowledgements

David Low cartoons © Solo Syndication and the Low Estate; Emmwood, Illingworth, JAK, Jon, Lee, Poy, Vicky cartoons © Solo Syndication; Cummings, Lancaster, Strube, Ullyett cartoons © Express Newspapers; Nick Garland cartoons © Daily Telegraph and Nick Garland; Franklin, Haselden, McLachlan, Vicky, Waite, Zec cartoons © Trinity Mirror; Butterworth cartoons © Betty Butterworth; The Leaguer of Ladysmith (1900) by Captain Clive Dixon © Private Collection/ The Bridgeman Art Library; This is the House that Man Built (1905), Mary Evans Picture Library; John Bull Concerned (1910) by Arthur Moreland, Mary Evans Picture Library; The Suffragette Silenced (1913), Mary Evans Picture Library; Regrouping (1914), Austrian postcard © Private Collection/ Archives Charmet/ The Bridgeman Art Library; John Bull Triumphant (1919) by G Ljunggren, Mary Evans Picture Library; Flapper (1928) by Andrée Sikorska, Mary Evans Picture Library; League of Nations (1931), unattributed cartoon in Kladderadatsch, Mary Evans Picture Library; Freie Bahn dem Marshallplan (1947), German poster, The Art Archive; The Capitalist Frightened by the Progress of the Soviet Economy (1967), Russian postcard, The Art Archive/Marc Charmet; Vietnam propaganda leaflet (1972) The Art Archive/National Archives Washington DC; Steve Bell cartoons © Steve Bell; Patrick Blower cartoons © Patrick Blower; Peter Brookes cartoons © Peter Brookes; Ric Brookes cartoons © Ric Brookes; Dave Brown cartoons © Dave Brown; Bill Caldwell cartoons © Bill Caldwell; Peter Clark cartoons © Peter Clark; Richard Cole cartoons © Richard Cole; Clive Collins cartoons © Clive Collins; Bernard Cookson cartoons © Bernard Cookson; Andy Davy cartoons © Andy Davy; Wally sFawkes cartoons © Wally Fawkes; Noel Ford cartoons © Noel Ford; Dave Gaskill cartoons © Dave Gaskill; Les Gibbard cartoons © Les Gibbard; Charles Griffin cartoons © Charles Griffin; Michael Heath cartoons © Michael Heath; John Jensen cartoons © John Jensen; Kevin Kallaugher cartoons © Kevin Kallaugher; Ken Mahood cartoons © Ken Mahood; Stan McMurtry cartoons © Stan McMurtry; Morten Morland cartoons © Morten Morland; Chris Riddell cartoons © Chris Riddell; Martin Rowson cartoons © Martin Rowson; Tim Sanders cartoons © Tim Sanders; Peter Schrank cartoons © Peter Schrank; Dave Simonds cartoons © Dave Simonds; Martyn Turner cartoons © Martyn Turner; Keith Waite cartoons © Keith Waite.

Every effort has been made to contact all copyright holders. The author and publishers will be happy to make good in future editions any errors or omissions brought to their attention.